EQUITY IN EDUCATION:

Issues and Strategies

Fred Rodriguez

University of Kansas

KENDALL/HUNT PUBLISHING COMPANY
2460 Kerper Boulevard   P.O. Box 539   Dubuque, Iowa 52004-0539

Printed in the United States of America
10 9 8 7 6 5 4 3 2 1

For my parents who have continually supported and believed in their children; and to my wife, Mary and our children, Nathan and Jessica.

PREFACE

We appear to be at a moment in our history in which a series of very important policy decisions will have to be made concerning American education. The two major educational policy goals we face are: creating a *quality* system of education; as well as a system of schooling that is *equitable*.

The 1990s are alive with the spirit of change in our system of education. The future of education will be affected by the recommendations of the various commissions, research studies, and task forces cited throughout this book. To what extent change takes place - remains to be seen. It would appear that the tidal wave of recommendations will produce basic changes in how teachers are trained, in how their career opportunities will be structured, and in how elementary and secondary schools will be organized.

It is all too easy when discussing *equity* in education to ignore the diversity of policies and practices within the concept and thereby to limit the scope of its development. Equity in education, as a general category, is all too often collapsed into one or the other of its constituent elements: for example, the special needs and programs for students from ethnic minority groups or the problems and possibilities of teaching in a multiracial classroom. *One of the purposes of this text is to broaden the terms of reference so that the various elements that comprise equity can be individually distinguished and yet still seen as part of a coordinated whole-school concept.*

The 'buzz words' of the '90s are: *equity and excellence.* What do these two terms mean? Are they mutually exclusive? Quite to the contrary, they reinforce one another. Equity and excellence are in conflict only if *equal outcomes* are expected. Excellence means that some students will do better than others; equity means that each student will be given an equal chance. The crucial test of the reforms urged in the various reports will be whether improvements in American education become available for ALL students.

The topics and issues presented in this text are designed to stimulate discussion, create dialogue, and provide varying perspectives about the issues at stake in the current debate over quality-with-equity in our schools.

I raise the issues in this book not only with the hope of resolving them here, but also with the belief that it is necessary to place the various issues surrounding equity in a broader perspective. *To treat equity as an administrative problem or as merely the re-shifting of curriculum priorities denies the relationships between equity and the other aspects of our educational system.* The reform for equity improvement must be accompanied by significant changes in a variety of other areas within our schools.

Chapter One - <u>Equity: An Evolving Concept</u> provides the historical development of equity; identifies the disparities between the concept of equity and the lack of implementation in our schools;

and concludes with a definition for equity and the premise that it is based upon. Chapter Two - Quality-with-Equity: Bridging the Gap examines the relationship of quality and equity; the nature of the national reports and their implications for equity; the five levels of equity and the steps for understanding the equity concept in our schools. Chapter Three - Educating All Our Children: A Call for Effective Schools is designed to examine: the effective schools movement; accreditation standards, teacher testing and certification; current trends to create more effective schools, and the continuum of equitable competence for schools. Chapter Four - The Heart of Equity: The Classroom Teacher addresses the issues of: effective teaching; the need for reform; teacher expecations, and the tracking of students.

Chapter Five - At-Risk: One-Third of the School Population. is organized in the following manner: the population of at-risk students is described in terms of composition, growth and educational performance; and the failure of current national educational reforms to consider their special needs is discussed. Chapter Six - Pluralism in America: Diversity in Our Schools is designed to focus on one dimension of equity - that is, ethnicity in the United States and the role and responsibility that our schools should take. Chapter Seven - A Host of Languages: Policies and Issues provides a variety of viewpoints on the educational needs of linguistically different students and the most popular methods used in addressing those special needs. Chapter Eight - Equity and the Courts: Selected Laws and Case Examples highlights the laws that are most central to the concept of equity and outlines the roles and rights of teachers and students. Chapter Nine - Instructional Materials: Policies and Strategies addresses the importance of instructional materials in education, identifies who selects textbooks and instructional materials, examines state adoption policies, identifies criteria for the selection of materials, and provides the opportunity to evaluate materials. Chapter Ten - Stages and Strategies for Improving Equity outlines a three-level process with specific examples on what should be considered in the equity improvement process.

This approach to equity is unique for two reasons. First, the book adds the needed conceptual clarity to what is meant by equity. Throughout the text, equity is defined, identified and incorporated as an integral part of an effective school. *Equity is not treated as a singular issue that is to be considered and implemented if the need arises, rather it is presented as an imperative for becoming an effective school.*

Second, the issues identified throughout the text are intended to: stimulate the reader; develop an interaction between the issues; and to provide the opportunity to generate written reactions and responses. The book offers no easy solutions to the problems facing education; rather it warns that what appears to be simple solutions are often only partial answers that may waste resources and frequently not adequately provide for students. What is needed is a fundamental change in the prevailing approach to educating students. No single formula for creating such educational settings is proposed here. Emphasis is on the development of the many links to equity which reflect the diversity and pluralism that characterizes our country. I have strived to articulate realistic notions of what constitutes equity and have suggested ways to do better the things that are necessary. Everything that should be known about equity has not been put into this book. No single book can address all the issues involving equity; this book intentionally covers only those issues most central to the task of improving all our schools to have a more equitable and quality system. This book does not, for example, address specific ethnic groups, the concept of culture, sex and gender, religion, age, or exceptionalities. There are numerous publications that are available for you with these specific issues and information.

In short, the book attempts to assist you develop an equity perspective to your philosophy of teaching and learning. As educators we are being held more accountable for providing ALL our students with the most meaningful and quality educational exerience we can. The personal contributions you make can only lead to an improved social and educational system and an increasingly mature perspective for you, your colleagues, and for all of your students.

I wish to acknowledge those individuals and institutions who were supportive and provided permission to include their excellent work. Shirley McCune and Gretchen Wilbur - McRel Sex Equity Center, Harriet Doss-Willis - NCREL, Charles Moody - University of Michigan, School of Education, Donna Gollnick - NCATE, Harold Hodgkinson - Institute of Educational Leadership, Oris Amos, Wright State University, AACTE - No One Model American, Association of American Publishers (AAP), and Larry Cuban and David Tyack, Stanford University. Photo by Don Jardon.

I have been a teacher for all but two years of my professional life. I have a great faith in education and I have profited much from the involvement in all its phases. My experience in teaching has contributed enormously to my growth and fulfillment, not just as a teacher, but as a person as well. I am deeply grateful to this institution called a school and believe it to be the most significant profession. As a member of the education family, however, I am also keenly aware of its shortcomings, especially its slowness to respond to the current needs of society and youth and to the new perspectives offered by our diverse population. Perhaps this book may help to speed those needed adaptations. If so, I will be happy to have made some small contribution to the profession that has given so much to me.

F.R.

Table of Contents

List of Figures...ix

Preface i

CHAPTER 1 **Equity Education: An Evolving Concept**...................................1

The Historical Development of Equity 2

Ethnic Studies..3

Multiethnic Education 4

Multicultural Education 5

No One Model American...5

Defining Equity in Education... 10

Summary... 13

Questions for Discussion 14

Worksheet 1 15

Worksheet 2 17

CHAPTER 2 **Quality with Equity: Bridging the Gap** 23

The Cycle of Excellence and Equity... 23

Quality-with-Equity: Where is the Gap? 25

Excellence in the 80s - The Nature of the Reports... 25

The Nature of the Reports and Equity 27

What is meant by Quality-with-Equity? 29

Equity in Education: A Five Level Approach. 31

Summary. 34

Worksheet 1 36

CHAPTER 3 Educating All Our Children: A Call for Effective Schools....43

Reform: A Call for School Improvement 44

Quality of the School vs. Background of the Student...................................... 44

What is an Effective School? 45

A Call for More Effective Teacher Education Programs. 47

Accreditation Standards for Teacher Education Programs 47

A Growing Shortage of Minority Teachers. 49

Accreditation of Local Schools.. 49

Teacher Testing and Certification. 52

Creating More Effective Schools: Current Trends.. 54

The Continuum of Equitable Competence for Schools 57

Summary. 61

Worksheet 1 62

CHAPTER 4 The Heart of Equity: The Classroom Teacher 71

Effective Teaching. 72

The Need for Reform 72

Teacher Expectations. 76

The Power of Tradition and Educational Reform 79

Grouping and Tracking Practices. 80

Continuous Progress Programs. 84

Cooperative Learning 84

Success for All. 85

Summary 86

Worksheet 1 95

CHAPTER 5 At-Risk: One-Third of the School Population 101

Growth of the At-Risk Population 102

At-Risk Students: Who are They?. 103

Compensatory Education. 110

Current Responses 112

Reforms as Obstacles to the At-Risk Student 112

Addressing the Needs of At-Risk Students - Indicators 115

Assessing the Needs of At-Risk Students. 117

Guidelines for Prevention Strategies 117

Guidelines for Success 119

Guidelines for Identification Strategies 120

Summary 122

Worksheet 1 123

CHAPTER 6 Pluralism in America: Diversity in Our Schools 129

What is an Ethnic Group?. 133

Ethnic Minority Group 133

The Melting Pot 134

The Anglo-Conformity Theory 137

Cultural Pluralism. 138

Summary 140

Worksheet 1 142

Worksheet 2. 143

Worksheet 3. 146

CHAPTER 7 A Host of Languages: Policies and Issues 153

Historical Overview 154

Legal Implications 158

Bilingual Education 167

English as a Second Language 169

Summary 170

Worksheet 1. 172

CHAPTER 8 Equity and the Courts: Selected Laws and Case Examples... 181

What Laws Affect Schools?...182

Constitutional Provisions for Education...184

Significant Court Cases Affecting Schools...186

Summary...200

Worksheet 1 201

Worksheet 2...204

CHAPTER 9 Instructional Materials: Policies and Strategies...................217

Impact of Textbooks and Instructional Materials.......................................218

Who Selects the Textbooks and Instructional Materials...............................218

State Textbook Adoption Policies...218

Publishers Respond..224

Textbook Evaluation...227

What Can You Do About Biased Materials?..233

Summary...235

Questions for Discussion 236

Class Activity..237

Evaluation of Textbooks..255

CHAPTER 10 Stages and Strategies for Improving Equity 261

What we want. What we believe. What we know. What we plan. 262

Three levels for Improving Equity 263

The Concept of Change 264

An Individual Equity Action Plan 265

Levels of Equity Understanding 265

Classroom Applications 271

A Workshop Model 274

A School-Wide Model 281

Summary 289

Worksheet 1 291

INDEX 295

FIGURES

1. Equity Education: An Evolving Concept...2

2. Equity Education: A Multi-Dimensional Concept...11

3. Mid '60s to '70s = E E O...24

4. Regional Accreditation...50

5. State-Required Testing for Initial Certification of
   Teachers Testing, Enacted Before 1984 and 1984...53

6. State-Required Testing for Initial Certification of Teachers Testing
   in Effect, Planned in Next 3 Years, and Under Consideration........................54

7. Change in Number of Course Units Required for High
   School Graduation, 1980 to 1984 55

8. Increased Academic Requirements..55

9. The Continuum of Equitable Competence for Schools...................................58

10. High School Graduation Rates 104

11. States Using Minimum Competency Testing..113

12. Guidelines for Success...119

13. Guidelines for Identification Strategies...120

14. The Inventory Fact Sheet...121

15. Minority Enrollment as Percent of Public
    Elementary/Secondary School Enrollment, by State 130

16. Evolutionary Pattern of Language Treatment in the U.S.............................154

17. Number of Persons with Non-English Mother Tongues by
    State 156

18. Dates and Outcomes of Court Cases Involving
    Language Diversity..163

19. Federal Spending for Bilingual Education. 164

20. Where English is Official. 165

21. Formula for Discrimination 182

22. Federal Law Summary Sheet..185

23. State Textbook Adoption Policies...219

24. State Textbook Adoption Process. 221

25. Rating the Level of Equity Input 254

26. Classroom Applications...271

27. Analyzing Your Department. 272

28. Rating the Level of Equity Input. 275

29. Workshop Model 275

30. School-Wide Model...282

31. School-Wide Applications..284

32. Adoption...285

33. Approval...285

34. Steering Committee...286

35. Staff Responsibilities...286

36. Staff Priorities. 287

37. Classroom Resources and Involvement 287

38. Community Resources. 288

39. Incentives for Professional Growth..288

40. Evaluation...289

CHAPTER ONE

Equity: An Evolving Concept

Introduction

In the Fall of 1988 3,600,000 youngsters entered school; 25 percent of these children live in poverty; 14 percent have teenage mothers; 15 percent were either physically or mentally handicapped, 15 percent spoke a language other than English, and 14 percent were children of unmarried parents.

Today, out of 80 million households in the nation, over 9 million are headed by a single female parent, 16 percent of whom are under age 25, 50 percent unemployed, 42 percent living in central cities (Mirga, 1986). In fact, every day in America, 40 teenage girls give birth to their *third* child (Hodgkinson, 1988). Between one-fourth and one-third are latchkey children; and nearly 30 percent will not finish high school.

The 1950s family is gone. The family of today is different, maybe no better or no worse, but different. These children clearly reflect the forces at work in our society. That greater numbers will bring with them financial, racial, ethnic and socio-economic stress is becoming well known to educators. Less well understood is that if current trends persist, the proportion of children *"at-risk"* for school failure will grow with each passing year for the foreseeable future.

Today it is the nation's educational system that faces the challenge. Although at-risk children represent a minority of school enrollments, their impact on the system is great. These very children, who many educators project to be 30 percent of the school population, will inherit the responsibility for sustaining and directing the social, political and economic institutions of the nation.

The purpose of this chapter will be to: (1) provide the historical development of the equity concept, (2) identify the disparities between the principle of equity and the actual implementation of equity in our schools, and (3) define the concept of equity. Chapter One concludes with discussion questions and worksheets that are designed to: (a) build a personal knowledge base, and (b) begin to focus on our role and personal response as educators to the concept of equity in education today and in the future.

The Historical Development of Equity

If the concept equity is to provide a sense of purpose and priority for American education, it must be clearly understood. The concept of equity in education has been historically plagued with ambiguity, generality and confusion.

The 1960s and 1970s brought a new and dynamic challenge to American education. Equality of educational opportunity seemed to be the theme of the reform in our schools. Members of groups whose histories and cultures had been omitted from or stereotyped within the mainstream curriculum began to request, sometimes demand, accurate, balanced and fair representation. First Blacks, then Hispanics, Native Americans and Asian Americans called for reform. Then came the new pluralism, with America's white ethnic groups appealing for educational inclusion of their roles and history. Cutting across all racial, ethnic and mainstream American groups were women, exceptional populations, religious groups, and linguistically different groups who rightfully pointed out how their perspectives and contributions had also been omitted from the curriculum of our schools.

These various approaches were attempts to either: (1) ensure equal educational opportunities, or (2) address the special educational needs of a targeted population. (See Figure 1 - Equity Education: An Evolving Concept)

Figure 1

EQUITY EDUCATION :

AN EVOLVING CONCEPT

2

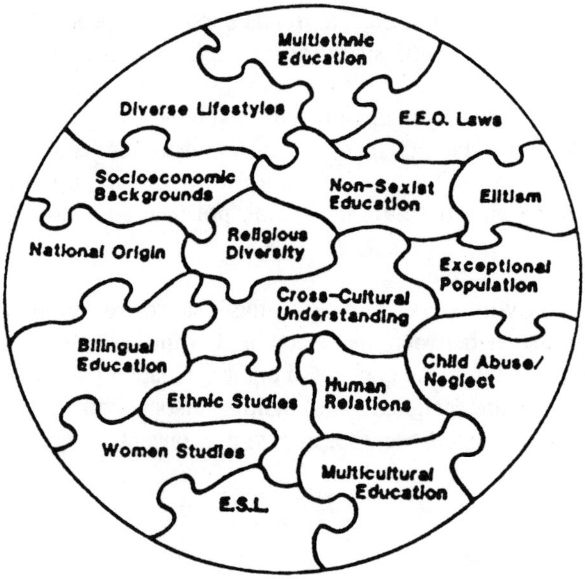

There are three approaches in particular that have been implemented for varying reasons and with varying degrees of success. They are: (1) ethnic studies, (2) multiethnic education and (3) multicultural education. By examining the rationale behind each of the three approaches; as well as the degree of success each had, we may be in a better position to understand how the concept of equity is similar and yet, different.

Ethnic Studies

When the civil rights movement began in the mid-60s Blacks - in particular - demanded that schools and other social institutions respond more adequately to their needs and aspirations. They called for more Black teachers for Black youths, community control of Black schools, and the rewriting of textbooks to make them more accurately reflect the Black history and culture within the United States. They also demanded Black studies courses. In time, other ethnic groups such as Mexican- Americans and American Indians, made similar demands on schools and colleges. Those institutions that did respond, established courses on specific ethnic groups, characterized by monoethnic courses. The assumption was that only a member of an ethnic group should teach a course on that group, and a focus on White racism and how Whites have oppressed non-white minorities. A pervasive assumption made during the ethnic studies courses was that Black studies, for example, were needed only by Black students and that Asian-American studies were needed only by Asian-American students.

Colangelo, Foxley and Dustin (1979) describe ethnic studies as the *focus of the specific richness and uniqueness of cultural groups. Ethnic studies include the historical and cultural knowledge of a particular group.* Emphasis is on the individual as an ethnic member."

Banks (1984) one of the leading scholars on minority education, defines ethnic studies as *the scientific and humanistic study of the histories, cultures, and experiences of the ethnic groups within a society. Ethnic studies refers primarily to the objectives, concepts, methods and materials that make up the courses of study within schools, colleges and universities.*

However, according to Foerester (1976), ethnic studies programs initiated in the past have begun to decline in popularity. There are a number of possible explanations for this trend. Ethnic studies programs have encountered the following stumbling blocks when implemented:(1) inadequate teacher preparation and commitment; (2) fragmented integration with other curriculum areas; (3) unresolved debate about content, grade levels, and student populations who would participate in such courses of study; and (4) lack of community support.

Still, others didn't favor the ethnic studies approach at all. Dawson (1977) explains, *it is unfortunate that some educators often promote separatism by advocating ethnic studies programs that are limited to the political power struggles of the racial or ethnic groups.* Although she believes there is a place in education for comprehensive study of a single racial or ethnic group, our educational systems must teach all children of all people to include understanding that emphasizes equal treatment of both minority and majority groups.

Multiethnic Education

In the late '60s and early '70s, the early proponents of ethnic studies were joined by a group of scholars advocating a *new ethnicity*. They claimed that not only have minority groups not been completely assimilated and acculturated into the American culture, but neither have many other ethnic groups, particularly those descendants of Southern and Eastern European immigrants. These included such *white ethnics* as Polish Americans, Jewish Americans, Italian Americans, Greek Americans and Slovak Americans. As more and more ethnic groups began to demand separate courses and the inclusion of their histories and cultures in the curriculum, schools and colleges began to offer multiethnic studies courses which focused on several ethnic cultures and which viewed the experiences of ethnic groups from comparative experiences. (Banks, 1981)

A basic assumption of multiethnic education is that ethnic groups have had both similar and different experiences in the United States and that a comparative study of ethnic cultures can result in useful concepts, generalizations and theories.

Banks (1981), defines multiethnic education as, *the process used by educational institutions to reform their environments so that students from diverse ethnic and racial groups will experience educational equity.* Before we proceed, let's understand the use of the term "educational equity" as it is used by Banks. First, it should be understood that his scholarship and research has been primarily minority education, specifically the incorporation of ethnic studies and multiethnic education. Second, "educational equity" refers to and is limited to particular racial and ethnic groups. For example, Banks (1981) outlines the basic goals of multiethnic education:

(1) Should help students view historical and contemporary events from diverse ethnic perspectives.

(2) Should also help individuals develop cross-cultural competency the ability to function within a range of cultures.

(3) Should provide students with cultural and ethnic alternatives.

(4) Should also try to reduce ethnic and cultural encapsulation and enable students to understand their own cultures better.

(5) Should also help students to expand their conceptions of what it means to be human, to accept the fact that ethnic minority cultures are functional and valid, and to realize that a culture can be evaluated only within a particular cultural context.

There is an infinite amount of factual information available about the great number of ethnic groups in American society. It would be unrealistic to assume that all levels of education can or should encompass all of it. Even if they could, the merits of this approach to "multiculturalism" are questionable. There are many reasons to suspect that the mere memorization of ethnic facts is

4

inadequate for teachers to understand the prominence of ethnicity; and the complex dynamics of cultural diversity in America; as well as their implications for education. The *programs* of ethnic studies and multiethnic education are important, but raise concerns. For example, they tended to be only *curricular* in scope; they have had little impact on school-wide policies and practices; they have usually been offered as *electives* and have been viewed upon as separate entities to the "regular curriculum" offerings of the school; and many have been supported by temporary external funding sources.

Multicultural Education

An alternative concept for managing this ever-increasing body of information on ethnicity, pluralism and overall school practices and policies lead to the concept of multicultural education.

The acknowledgment of the importance of our diversity in education by a major educational organization was reflected in a statement by the American Association of Colleges for Teacher Education (AACTE, 1973). In an action reflecting its commitment to alleviating social problems through education, the AACTE Commission on Multicultural Education, formed in the aftermath of the Kent State and Jackson State tragedies, developed a definitive statement on multicultural education. The multicultural statement, *No One Model American,* is a significant product of the Commission's work. The statement serves as an excellent introductory statement to the concept of multicultural education and our understanding of how the concept was eventually interpreted by the schools. The commission members at that time raised a concern with the term *multicultural* not being a euphemism for disadvantaged. Rather, the statement encompassed broad ethnic and cultural spheres. The statement was presented in the interest of improving the quality of society through an increased social awareness on the part of teachers and teacher educators. The official statement follows:

No One Model American

Multicultural education is education which values cultural pluralism. Multicultural education rejects the view that schools should seek to melt away cultural differences or the view that schools should merely tolerate cultural pluralism.

Instead, multicultural education affirms that schools should be oriented toward the cultural enrichment of all children and youth through programs rooted to the preservation and extension of cultural diversity as a fact of life in American society, and it affirms that this cultural diversity is a valuable resource that should be preserved and extended. It affirms that major education institutions should strive to preserve and enhance cultural pluralism.

To endorse cultural pluralism is to endorse the principle that there is no one model American. To endorse cultural pluralism is to understand and appreciate the differences that exist among the nation's citizens. It is to see these differences as a positive force in the continuing development of a society which professes a wholesome respect for the intrinsic worth of every individual. Cultural pluralism is more than a temporary accommodation to placate racial and ethnic minorities. It is a concept that aims toward a heightened sense of being and a wholeness of the entire society based on the unique strengths of each of its parts.

Cultural pluralism rejects both assimilation and separatism as ultimate goals. The positive elements of a culturally pluralistic society will be realized only if there is a healthy interaction among the diverse groups which comprise the nation's citizenry. Such interaction enables all to share in the richness of America's multicultural heritage. Such interaction provides a means of coping with intercultural tensions that are natural and cannot be avoided in a growing, dynamic society. To accept cultural pluralism is to recognize that no group lives in a vacuum - that each group exists as part of an interrelated whole.

If cultural pluralism is so basic a quality of our culture, it must become an integral part of the educational process at every level. Education for cultural pluralism includes four major thrusts: (1) the teaching of values which support cultural diversity and individual uniqueness; (2) the encouragement of the qualitative expansion of existing ethnic cultures and their incorporation into the mainstream of American socioeconomic and political life; (3) the support of explorations in alternative and emerging life styles; and (4) the encouragement of multiculturalism, multilingualism, and multidialectism. While schools must insure that all students are assisted in developing their skills to function effectively in society, such a commitment should not imply or permit the denigration of cultural differences.

Educational institutions play a major role in shaping the attitudes and beliefs of the nation's youth. These institutions bear the heavy task of preparing each generation to assume the rights and responsibilities of adult life. In helping the transition to a society that values cultural pluralism, educational institutions must provide leadership for the development of individual commitment to a social system where individual worth and dignity are fundamental tenets. This provision means that schools and colleges must assure that their total educational process and educational content reflect a commitment to cultural pluralism. In addition, special emphasis programs must be provided where all students are helped to understand that being different connotes neither superiority nor inferiority, programs where students of various social and ethnic backgrounds may learn freely from one another; programs that help different minority students understand who they are, where they are going, and how they can make their contribution to the society in which they live.

Colleges and universities engaged in the preparation of teachers have a central role in the positive development of our culturally pluralistic society. If cultural pluralism is to become an integral part of the educational process, teachers and personnel must be prepared in an environment where the commitment to multicultural education is evident. Evidence of this commitment includes such factors as a faculty and staff of multiethnic and multiracial character, a student body that is representative of the culturally diverse nature of the community being served, and a culturally pluralistic curriculum that accurately represents the diverse multicultural nature of American society.

Multicultural education programs for teachers are more than special courses or special learning experiences grafted onto the standard program. The commitment to cultural pluralism must permeate all areas of the educational experience provided for prospective teachers.

Multicultural education reaches beyond awareness and understanding of cultural differences. More important than the acceptance and support of these differences is the recognition of the right of these different cultures to exist. The goal of cultural pluralism can be achieved only if there is full recognition of cultural differences and an effective educational program that makes cultural equality real and meaningful. The attainment of this goal will bring a richness and quality of life that would be a long step toward realizing the democratic ideals so nobly proclaimed by the founding fathers of this nation. (Reprinted with Permission)

The statement has been considered the foundation of much of the discussion concerning equal educational opportunity within our schools for the past 16 years. The statement has served well for a number of years to remind us that the struggle for equity in our schools has been a long one. Yet, it seems that the eloquence of the statement has fallen on deaf ears because significant changes to reflect equity within our schools has been scattered, mixed and poorly conceptualized.

Educators such as Baker, Chinn, Garcia, Gay, Gollnick, Grant and others became interested in the educational reform movement that would not only address the issues or concerns of ethnic groups, but the educational issues of other cultural groups such as women, exceptional populations, religious groups, linguistically different groups, socioeconomic status and age. This broader, encompassing reform movement became known as *multicultural education.* It was intended to be more multi-dimensional in its conception, that is - more than a curricular issue. However, the research evidence since the mid 70s indicates that this never occurred. In fact, the concept of multicultural education has also been interpreted as one dimensional; that is, a euphemism for minority education.

Multicultural education became a popularized slogan, and the power and potential of the concept was lost to many. Progress was impeded, to a large degree, by the lack of conceptual clarity concerning its goals and content. Thus, multicultural education as a general category, was all too often collapsed into one or another of its constituent elements: the special needs of students from ethnic minority backgrounds, or the problems and possibilities of teaching in an ethnically diverse school or classroom. This is what happened to multicultural education.

The Multicultural Approach and Teacher Education

Simply attempting to define the term *multicultural education* was one of the major stumbling blocks for a clearer understanding. As educators continued to define it, the struggle failed to reap any benefits of the concept within our schools, at virtually all levels. As was mentioned earlier, the concept of multicultural education was an idea with the goal of being broader than ethnic studies or multiethnic education, but this plan never materialized. To understand the confusion over the past several years in understanding this educational concept, I offer a sample of definitions from my former students.

"Multicultural education is the concept which promotes cross-cultural understanding and acceptance and the celebration of differences."

"Multicultural education reaches beyond isolation and chauvinism recognizing the obligation of each human being to every other human being at the same time preserving the rightful self-interests of all."

"Multicultural education is education which is sensitive to the societal implications of mankind's interdependence."

"Multicultural education is a set of competencies needed to enhance an individual's effective and responsible participation in society's affairs."

7

"Multicultural education is attaining an increased awareness of the broad societal perspective essential to an understanding of our society as it is today and will be tomorrow."

"Multicultural education is an educational concept which endorses cultural pluralism as a reality."

"Multicultural education is an educational approach which involves all schools, persons and disciplines which will provide ALL students with a more meaningful and relevant educational experience."

It should be noted that many schools -at all levels- have made commitments (written or oral) to the concept of multicultural education. Although to date there is a huge gap between principle and practice for the vast majority of schools; that is, incorporating multicultural concepts as an integral part of the total educational process.

The most popular approach used to incorporate multicultural concepts within many public schools has been the *course/or special events approach*. The content of many of these courses or programs have been heavily slanted toward cultural things (food, festivals, and heroes/heroines), history, social issues, special events or ceremonies, or a combination of these.

What about teacher education programs? How have they addressed multicultural education in the preparation of future teachers?

The American Association of Colleges for Teacher Education (AACTE, 1980) collected data from 446 teacher education programs concerning the development and implementation of multicultural education with their programs. This study examined 13 specific programs. In closely analyzing each of these programs, one begins to get a clearer picture of how these particular teacher education programs have interpreted and responded to multicultural education.

Most often multicultural education was addressed as a component in foundation courses, or a component in methodology courses. Most multicultural *programs* were easily identifiable because the concepts have not been integrated throughout the total teacher education program. Thus, they are 'adjunct' programs called bilingual, multicultural or Indian studies.

Washburn (1983) completed a more comprehensive study of 3,038 postsecondary institutions to identify multicultural teacher education programs. He identified 135 schools offering multicultural teacher education programs in 33 states and the District of Columbia. Although the schools identified their programs as *multicultural* in nature, the heaviest emphasis was on the Hispanic American culture (bilingual education).

The principle problem which emerges from an analysis of these two studies is not one of content, but is one of interpretation and application of a multicultural perspective in teacher education.

The missing element in ethnic studies, multiethnic education and multicultural education is that they have been thought of as a *subject matter focus* and *not a multi-dimensional concept* that involves the whole school. As Banks (1981) notes, *concepts such as multicultural education, multiculturalism, multiethnic education, ethnic education, ethnic studies, cultural pluralism, and ethnic pluralism are often used interchangeably or to convey different but highly ambiguous meanings.*

This gap between principle and practice has occurred despite the best intentions of literally thousands of individuals, schools, publishers, state departments of education, and accreditation agencies. The primary reason for this gap has been and continues to be the absence of a holistic view of multicultural education, a view which incorporates and integrates multicultural perspectives and teaching throughout the entire education system.

Evolving From Multicultural to Equity Education.

We must understand that terms serve as ground rules for perceiving and understanding educational concepts. As we have learned, terms may have more than one meaning and thus may convey varying perceptions to different people and organizations. Ethnic studies, multiethnic education and multicultural education have been and continue to be popular approaches for addressing specific concerns for a number of educators, scholars, organizations and agencies. Because of the historical and evolutionary way in which these three approaches have developed, the reader may understandably conclude that when multiethnic education emerged, ethnic studies disappeared. However, this is not what has happened. Baker (1983) has indicated, *ethnic studies or multiethnic education can be an entity unto itself. Multicultural education requires the input of ethnic studies and multiethnic education and its foundation builds on the knowledge that is gained from the exploration of ethnic cultures.*

The rationale for incorporating an equity perspective within all schools comes from many sources. Teachers and their professional organizations, parent groups, state education agencies, colleges and universities, as well as public organizations, accreditation agencies, and foundations have all expressed the view that all Americans need to better understand, respect, appreciate and accept the diversity that exists in our society.

As a teacher educator for the past eleven years at a major university, I have had the primary role and responsibility for teaching the *multicultural education courses*. Through this personal experience, I have learned (what the research supports) that is, the term *multicultural education* is often miscommunicated, certainly misinterpreted and eventually poorly designed and implemented by schools and teachers. It is my belief that the concept will continue to be plagued with uncertainty and misguided focus.

As we have seen there may be problems with consensus definitions, but it is imperative for each of us to determine our own understanding of equity. Perhaps if we address equity from what it is NOT then maybe we can begin to gain a clearer understanding of what equity means.

Equity in Education - What It Is Not:

* *Equity in education is not a course or a subject area.*

* *Equity in education is not a unit of study on societal problems and concerns.*

* *Equity in education is not aimed at training teachers to work exclusively with ethnic minority student populations.*

* *Equity in education is not dependent upon the geographic setting of a school or the demographics of the student population.*

* *Equity in education is not a program that is added to the current school offerings.*

* *Equity in education is not limited to only the delivery of a curriculum in a school setting.*

* *Equity in education is not treating all students the same.*

Defining Equity in Education

Equity in education is defined as:

> **The fair and equal treatment of all members of our society who are entitled to participate in and enjoy the benefits of an education.**
>
> **Equity in education is based on the premise that all students - regardless of race, color, national origin, sex, native language, age, social or economic status, family structure and lifestyle, religious preference or exceptionality have the right to an education of equal quality.**

The concept of equity in education is multidimensional. (See Figure 2 - Equity Education: A Multi-Dimensional Concept). *Equity in education is at least three things: an idea or concept, an educational reform movement and a process.* The concept concerns itself with relationships between student and teacher, parent and teacher, teacher and community, and the host of interpersonal and intrapersonal relationships that are central to the educational process. It is also concerned with the overall school policies and practices, that our school systems endorse and reinforce - which may or may not be detrimental to the education some students receive. Equity is concerned with the outcomes of student achievement at all levels. Simply, it is not enough to understand these differences which may be involved in our systems of education. What is required is the positive endorsement of such differences and a system responsive to those unique qualities that students bring to our schools.

Equity in education is the structuring of educational priorities, commitments, and process to reflect the reality of our diversity as a fact of life in the United States. Educational priorities must focus on developing and maintaining an awareness of our diversity as reflected by individuals, groups and communities. It requires commitment of educators to the basic concept of diversity as it is expressed through dimensional aspects of ethnicity, sex, language backgrounds, exceptionalities, religious beliefs, socioeconomic backgrounds and lifestyles. Equity in education recognizes that the maintenance of this diversity is crucial not only to a particular group's survival, but to the basic tenets that support the democratic ideal.

Equity in Education: What are the Real Issues?

America is composed of many groups. The benefits of citizenship are distributed unevenly among these groups. Symptoms of inequity are easy to identify. For example, in or among the poor and many ethnic minority groups, as educators, we see: abnormally high drop-out rates, poor attendance at school, more at-risk youth, lower-track placements, special education placements, limited participation in the extra-curricular programs and overall a disproportionally lower representation in gifted programs. The list goes on, and almost all the national reports reinforce this uneven distribution.

EQUITY EDUCATION: A MULTI-DIMENSIONAL CONCEPT.

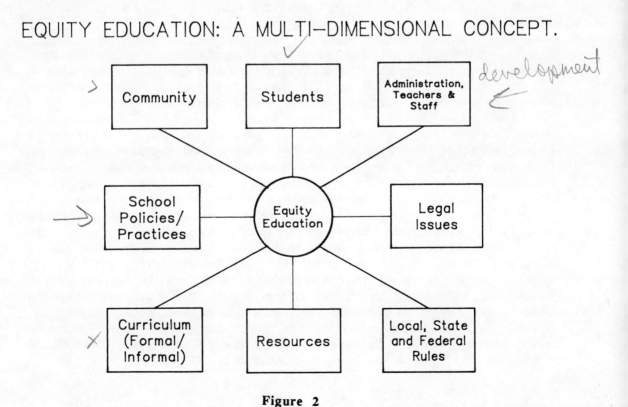

Figure 2

11

No blueprint exists for equity in education that will work for every school, nor should there be. Obviously, differences among schools would preclude the package deal from working for everyone. Schools at all levels vary in so many different ways - size, geographic location, student body, staff, grade level(s), administrative philosophies, and community support are only a few. Couple these obvious factors with the internal politics and personalities that exist - that human dimension - and one can begin to imagine the diversity that exists in our schools and communities.

One issue is how to gain a clearer sense of cultural dynamics as they affect education and how to develop effective strategies for guaranteeing real equity in education for all. For some educators, equity education is simply a matter of infusing regular school content with material which deals with different customs, dress, food, or other matters which fall under the label of cultural appreciation. This is a very limited perspective and will contribute little to the solution of the fundamental problem of inequity in our schools.

First, there is a need to view equity in education as a broader dimension than ethnic studies and multiethnic education. Second, from my teaching perspective, equity in education is synonymous with multicultural education; that is, when multicultural education is interpreted and incorporated in its intended conceptual framework. Third, there is a need to distinguish equity education from racism, sexism, elitism, ageism and exceptionalities, but simultaneously to understand the connections among those issues and equity in education. Fourth, there is a need for a working definition of what equity in education is, and what it is not.

Equity in education incorporates the idea that all students-regardless of their backgrounds- should have an equal opportunity to learn in school. Also, equity implies that some students because of their characteristics, have a better chance to learn in schools as they are currently structured than do students who do not belong to other groups or have different cultural characteristics.

Although educational leaders appear to agree that equity in education should be a part of the public schools policies and practices and an integral part of the teacher training programs, the interest has yet to become reality. Reluctance to incorporate equity appears to be four-fold: (1) many are uncertain about what equity in education means; (2) many fail to see the link between equity and quality in our schools; (3) many may understand the concept but are uncertain of how to proceed, and (4) many are staff members of homogeneous public schools and colleges that operate as if equity is not needed in their particular setting. Dawson (1984) found that many educators at such colleges and public schools viewed equity from this one-dimensional vision - ethnic minority populations. This perception is erroneous and typifies what Dawson describes as the *exemption syndrome*. Educators seem to conclude that because the school has "only a few," if any minorities, the school has no obligation to commit time and resources to equity. If this rationale is taken to a logical conclusion, one would assume that students attending these schools are being prepared for a closed society where the same economic, political, social and cultural environment found in the school will always exist. Again, these attitudes and behaviors are also a reflection of the continued misunderstanding and misinterpretation of the concept of equity.

Summary

The foundation on which this book is written is based upon three principles. It is my belief that as educators:

We must believe that all students should be treated fairly.

We must believe that all students can learn.

We must believe that it is a right of all students to receive an equitable and quality education.

One may wonder, how can any educator argue with these three basic principles? Certainly, we would like to see all our current and future educators express and practice these philosophies. However, as we will witness throughout this book, the research evidence, the national studies and the numerous books that have been written, clearly indicate that these beliefs are not held by all educators. Repeatedly, we will see that the evidence is quite clear; either: 1) many educators don't believe in these basic principles, or 2) many educators do not understand the inequities they may be creating in their classrooms through their policies and practices.

Individual differences are a reality, and as we increase opportunities for personalizing learning within an institution called the school, we have to provide a structure which will respond to human diversity. As history has indicated, the present structure has been geared to uniformity rather than diversity. During a period when excellence in education is being emphasized, the institution must be updated to gear itself more effectively to individual learners and more personalized approaches to growth and development. Therefore, the focus of the concept - equity in education - will be on school reform, and on updating the school to make it fully responsive to human variability. This, in essence, is equity in education.

QUESTIONS FOR DISCUSSION

1.   What demographic information surprised you the most? Why?
     What significance does it have for education?

2.   Why is the "No One Model American" statement important for understanding the concept of equity in education?

3.   What is ethnic studies?

4.   What is the connection between ethnic studies and multiethnic education?

5.   According to the author, what is the missing element in ethnic studies, multiethnic education and multicultural education?

6.   What were the two national studies in teacher education with regard to multicultural education? What were the findings?

7.   What is equity education? What isn't it?

8.   What is meant by the statement: Equity education is a multi- dimensional concept?

9.   What are the three basic principles this book is written upon? Do you agree with their importance? Why or why not?

WORKSHEET 1

Your Thoughts

As an educator, what are your thoughts, at this point, about equity in education? Your personal response to equity does not require you to agree with everything that has been stated. However, it is important that you seriously contemplate the concept and begin to formulate your own ideas.

Write down what you believe to be some of the more important statements, ideas, or thoughts that you have read so far.

I guess the most important idea is that "equal access" doesn't mean "come in and fail." If the student is the customer, then the teacher is successful if he reaches that customer, and he must reach each customer in different ways. Multicultural ed as opposed to ethnic studies and multiethnic ed is certainly more all encompassing, but more complex and harder to achieve. It certainly would seem to yield more satisfying results.

Were there statements, ideas, or thoughts that you couldn't agree with? What were they?

I have trouble with the idea of cultural pluralism (No One Model) because although it strives to reach common ground, in practice we see people valuing their own culture and rejecting that of others.

List the reasons why you don't agree with the above statements you have identified?

So often pride in one's own group can lead one to assume that, say, black urban people will live under their own system and white rural folks under their own. Separate is inherently unequal, and black separatists in particular should consider who'll get the short end of the stick if there is a Black America and a White America.

WORKSHEET 2

How would you respond to the following statements made by other educators?

1. "There just isn't the time to add all of these new ideas and curriculum content . . . besides, this is really an area for the social studies people to be concerned with."

Agree _____   Disagree _✓_

Why? They impact on the whole curriculum -- we can't shunt all this off on an elective, like ethnic and multiethnic studies were -- besides, social studies teachers have to teach their subject matter in the larger context just as other subject matter teachers do.

2. "I totally agree with equity in education, but I don't plan on teaching in a school with a large minority population, so I don't see that it involves me personally."

Agree _____   Disagree _✓_

Why? How do you know what population you'll have in the future? Shouldn't your students know who is in the world beyond their neighborhood? The more your students know, the better they'll do.

3. "I am not so concerned with my students knowing 'equity stuff,' but whether he/she can read, write and compute. Let's get back to the basics - the 3 r's and forget all of these frills and special interest group demands on education."

Agree _____ Disagree _✓_

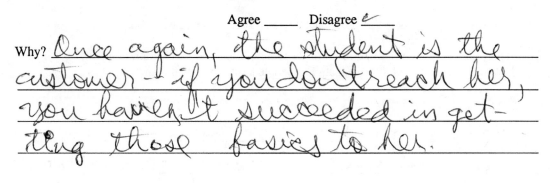

Why? _Once again, the student is the customer - if you don't reach her, you haven't succeeded in getting those basics to her._

4. "Differences, diversity, pluralism . . . why make such a big deal about it? We don't need to identify ourselves with our ethnicity, sex, or handicap. We're Americans!"

Agree _____ Disagree _✓_

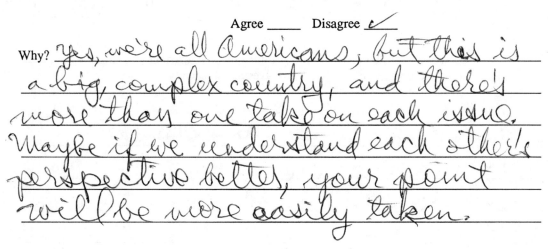

Why? _Yes, we're all Americans, but this is a big, complex country, and there's more than one take on each issue. Maybe if we understand each other's perspective better, your point will be more easily taken._

5. "America is the land of opportunity. Everyone has an equal chance to 'make it' in this coun-
    try, all you need is a little desire and initiative."

                        Agree ✓   Disagree _____

Why? Qualified agreement. The immigrant success stories are tempered by the immigrant failure stories. If we reach all
we teach, they'll have a better shot.

6. "We are currently concerned with excellence in all of our schools, and 'equity education' isn't
    a priority right now."

                        Agree _____   Disagree ✓

Why? Equity is part of excellence. Even
the external measure of test scores matters
little if you're not getting through to
everybody.

7. "This concept of equity education will promote a sense of 'separatism' in America, rather than
    uniting all of our citizens."

                        Agree _____   Disagree ✓

Why? It could, but only if we go down the
same path at ethnic studies sections or
courses. If we can keep in mind, or
allow for, difference in student background, we'll bring each other together
instead.

8. "Equity in education is something we **already** took care of in the 60s and the 70s . . . it's time to move on."

Agree _____ Disagree __✓__

Why? _Ethnic ed only reached the members_
of the group in question, and ignore
such facets as class, social group,
socioeconomic group. We need to
look at the whole institution of
schooling rather than just
tack on a class.

REFERENCES

AACTE Commission on Multicultural Education. "No One Model American." Journal of Teacher Education 24, No. 4 (Winter 1973): 264-This statement has been reprinted with permission from the Journal of Teacher Education.

American Association of Colleges for Teacher Education (AACTE). Multicultural Teacher Education: Case Studies of Thirteen Programs. Volume 2. Washington: D.C., 1980.

Anderson, James M. "Contextual Approach to Multicultural Education." In Multicultural Education - A Challenge for Teachers. Foris Publications. Dordrecht: Holland 1983.

Baker, Gwendolyn Planning and Organizing for Multicultural Education. Addison-Wesley Publishing Co., Reading, MA, 1983.

Banks, James A. Multiethnic Education - Theory and Practice. Allyn and Bacon, Inc. Boston: MA, 1981.

Banks, James A. Teaching Strategies for Ethnic Studies. Third Edition, Allyn and Bacon, Inc. Boston: MA, 1984.

Colangelo, N., Foxley, Cecilia, H. and Dustin, Dick (eds.) Multicultural Non-Sexist Education - A Human Relations Approach. Kendall/Hunt Publishing Co. Dubuque: IA, 1979.

Dawson, Martha D. "From Compensatory to Multicultural Education: The Challenge of Designing Multicultural Programs." Journal of Research and Development in Education. 11 (Fall, 1977): 84-101. Also in ERIC: ED 175 067.

Foerester, Leona Ethnic Studies -No! Multicultural Education - Yes! Eric Clearinghouse on Urban Education. New York: Columbia University, 1976. ED 189 206.

The definitions cited were from graduate and undergraduate level students enrolled in C&I 705 and C&I 210 over the past eleven years. The University of Kansas, School of Education. Lawrence, KS.

Washburn, David E. "Multicultural Education in the United States." University of Pennsylvania, 1983. Unpublished Document.

SUGGESTED READINGS

Baca, L. and Chinn, P. "Coming to Grips with Cultural Diversity" Exceptional Children Quarterly 2:4 February, 1982.

Banks, James A. and Banks, Cherry A. Multicultural Education- Issues and Perspectives. Allyn and Bacon, Boston, MA. 1989.

Banks, James A. Teaching Strategies for Ethnic Studies. 2nd Edition. Allyn and Bacon, Boston: MA, 1979.

Bennett, Christine I. Comprehensive Multicultural Education - Theory and Practice. Allyn and Bacon, Boston: MA, 1986.

Chinn, Philip C. & Gollnick, Donna M. Multicultural Education in a Pluralistic Society. 2nd Edition. Charles E. Merrill Publishing Co., Columbus: OH, 1986.

Chinn, Philip C. & Gollnick, Donna M. Multicultural Education in a Pluralistic Society. The C. V. Mosby Co. St. Louis: MO, 1983.

Garcia, Ricardo L. Teaching in a Pluralistic Society: Concepts, Models, Strategies. Harper and Row Publishers, New York: 1983.

Klassen, Frank and Gollnick, Donna (Eds). Pluralism and the American Teacher. American Association of Colleges for Teacher Education (AACTE) Washington, D.C., 1977.

CHAPTER TWO

Quality-with-Equity:
Bridging the Gap

Introduction

The challenge for America's schools is one of attaining quality outcomes; but also a system of education that is equitable for all students. One of the more common themes found in the current flood of reports advocating reform of schools has been the need for attaining the twin goals of *quality* and *equity*.

Chapter 2 - **Quality-with-Equity: Bridging the Gap** is intended to examine the current insights into the dilemma of attaining a quality-with equity education. The chapter examines: (1) the gap between quality and equity; (2) the nature of the national reports and the implications for attaining equity; and (3) a five level approach to equity. There is widespread disagreement, not only on the relationship of quality with equity, but on the acceptable meanings of these two terms. Unless these issues are confronted, a quality-with-equity education is unlikely to be understood or achieved in our schools.

The Cycle of Excellence and Equity

The '50s to '80s Cycle of Excellence and Equity outlined below provides a capsule look at the evolutionary pattern we have experienced in education over the past thirty years.

'50s to mid-'60s — *Excellence*

Mid-'60s to '70s — *Equality of Educational Opportunity*

Mid '80s to Present — *Excellence*

In the first phase *1950s to mid '60s* we experienced a reform for excellence in our schools. This movement occurred after the Russians' launching of Sputnik in the late 1950s, when the media, the Congress, and the public concluded that America had fallen behind in the race for scientific and technical superiority in space because of inadequacies in the teaching of science, mathematics, and foreign languages. The "target group" for post-Sputnik school reformers had been the gifted or the high achieving students in our schools. The second phase, *mid '60s to '70s* equality of educational opportunity (EEO) represented the greatest reform period in recent history. During this period, schools were being challenged to provide for a greater diversity of students and to offer a wider perspective within the school's curriculum and practices. Non-traditional students - ethnic minority students, handicapped, limited English speaking students, non-sexist opportunities and lower-socioeconomic perspectives were all challenged. Numerous statutes, laws, and court cases had a direct impact on the way schools were operating. (See Figure 3 - Mid '60s to '70s = EEO). Since then, one shortcoming after another briefly captured the public's interest, but it was not until 1983-84 that there was another full-blown sense of crisis. As we will see, the school reformers of the early 1980s expressed their critique in more broadly democratic terms: *Why shouldn't all children get the best education we can afford to provide?* The difference between the '50s movement for excellence and the '80s reform movement toward excellence is that the '80s focus is now upon all students in all of our schools - not just a select group of high-ability students.

Figure 3

MID–60's to 70's – E.E.O.

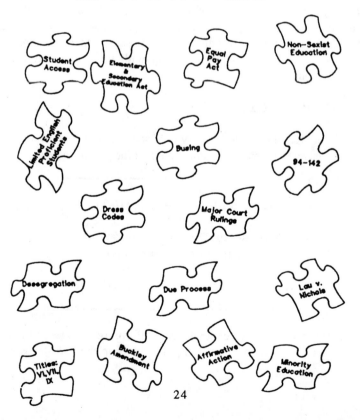

24

Quality-with-Equity: Where is the Gap?

Educational equality is an idea that has lost some of its vigor. In the '90s, some educators and schools are taking a steadfast approach to excellence. Is equity taking a backseat to this new agenda? Perhaps, in the years following <u>Brown v. Board of Education</u> (1954) - (The Supreme Court decision which determined that separate schooling was not equal),we became complacent enough to believe that just wanting schools to make things right would be enough. We became disillusioned by the extraordinary difficulties well-intentioned school people face in trying to undo past inequities and current injustices. We concerned ourselves with what education really meant. Did we want students to have merely an equal chance at an education? Did we want to guarantee equitable educational resources for all students? Or did we want to ensure equal educational outcomes? Poorly conceptualized programs, mass confusion and overall misunderstanding to whatever brand of equity we proclaimed, it eluded us. Oakes (1987) states, *Children in Head Start didn't catch up. Remedial and compensatory classes didn't seem to remediate or compensate. Children making long bus rides seemed to gain nothing but long bus rides. Millions were spent; achievement gaps between the haves and the have-nots remained.* What went wrong? Could the failure of these students to learn be attributed to a deeply rooted linguistic or cultural deficiency? Or, as unthinkable as it was, could there be an unalterable genetic difference?

We were financially generous during the 1960s and early '70s, but then the dollars got tight, and we got tired. In the attempt to correct inequality, we concluded, schools had neglected to do what they were supposed to do, teach academics. Equality moved out; academic excellence became the center of the nation's attention and commitment in the 1990s. In looking over the past two decades, there are two important points to make in regard to equity and excellence. First, in our search for the solution to the "problems" of educational inequity, our focus was almost exclusively on the *characteristics of the students themselves.* We looked for sources of their educational failures in their homes, their neighborhoods, their language, their culture and in their genes. In all of our searching, we almost entirely overlooked the real possibility that what happens *within the schools* they attend, might contribute to unequal educational opportunities and outcomes. We neglected to examine the content and processes of schooling itself for ways they might contribute to school failure. In our quest for higher standards and superior academic performance, we seem to have forgotten that schools cannot be excellent as long as there are groups of students who are not well served by them.

Excellence in the 80s - The Nature of the Reports

The education reform movement triggered in early 1983 by the report of the National Commission on Excellence in Education, <u>A Nation at Risk</u> (1983), was greeted with alarm by teachers and school administrators. Given its indictment of the quality of public education and its focus on the "rising tide of mediocrity" in the nation's schools, it was not clear whether the report was a prelude to educational improvement or the beginning of a new wave of attacks on schools and teachers. Judging from the polls, the public seemed to be in a mood to take constructive steps to improve the quality of public education, but teachers and administrators had become gun-shy over a period of three decades as a result of previous reform efforts that assigned blame recklessly, raised expectations unrealistically, and led to legislative and other initiatives that sometimes had effects on teaching exactly the opposite of what had been intended.

Each new report, Adler (1982), the Twentieth Century Fund (1983), the National Science Foundation (1983), Boyer (1983), Goodlad (1984) and the College Board (1987) captured front-page attention, editorial comments and even significant time on the television networks. Public interest in the quality of education was clearly deep. The mood for change was strong. It even began to appear that legislators were willing to appropriate more money for education if they could be convinced that additional funds would produce higher quality.

The theme of the reports, taken as a group, was that the school curriculum had become soft, particularly for children with strong academic abilities; that standards were poorly defined and low; that the quality of teachers seemed to be declining; that teacher education programs were weak; and that schools were not meeting the needs of business and industry as well as they should have been. Most of the recommendations for improving schools were couched in general terms, but the reports converged on the remedy that a common curriculum for all children should be reinstated and that clear goals and expectations for pupils in the subjects of English, history, science, and mathematics be formulated.

It became very clear in the early 1980s that the American public was becoming increasingly worried about the quality of our education, especially high school education. Educators, government agencies, the business community, and citizen groups launched research projects, commissions, and task forces to study schooling and to consider how to improve it. The following statements, drawn from a few of the studies, are presented to indicate both the nature of the problems that people were seeing in American education and the intensity of their concerns.

Public education today faces. . .a crisis in confidence in which people have lost faith in the public schools' ability to educate its students; a crisis in performance in which students from public schools are graduating without basic or marketable skills necessary to pursue further education or a job; and a crisis in the concept of democracy in which officials are willing to write off a sizable portion of the student population as being uneducable and unentitled to educational opportunities. (Love, 1985)

The nation's public schools are in trouble. By almost every measure - the commitment and competency of teachers, student test scores, truancy and dropout rates, crimes of violence - the performance of our schools falls far short of expectation. (Making the Grade, 1983)

Our Nation is at risk. Our once unchallenged preeminence in commerce, industry, science, and technological innovation is being overtaken by competitors throughout the world. . . Education is only one of the many causes and dimensions of the problem, but it is the one that undergirds American prosperity, security, and civility. We report to the American people that while we can take justifiable pride in what our schools and colleges have historically accomplished and contributed to the United States and the well - being of its people, the educational foundations of our society are presently being eroded by a rising tide of mediocrity that threatens our very future as a Nation and a people. What was unimaginable a generation ago has begun to occur - others are matching and surpassing our educational attainments. (Nation at Risk, 1983)

The Nation that dramatically and boldly led the world into the age of technology is failing to provide its own children with the intellectual tools needed for the 21st Century.

The world is changing fast. Technological know-how is spreading throughout the world - along with the knowledge that such skills and sophistication are the basic capital of tomorrow's society.

Our children could be stragglers in a world of technology. We must not provide our children a 1960s education for the 21st Century (1983) world.

The Nature of the Reports and Equity.

In the report, A Nation at Risk, the National Commission on Excellence in Education (1983) asserted:

We do not believe that a public commitment to excellence and educational reform must be made at the expense of a strong public commitment to the equitable treatment of our diverse population. The twin goals of equity and high-quality schooling have profound and practical meaning for our economy and our society, and we cannot permit one to yield to the other either in principle or practice.

In his Paideia Proposal: An Educational Manifesto, Adler (1982) argued that the revolutionary message in John Dewey's 1916 publication Democracy and Education "was that a democratic society must provide equal educational opportunity not only by giving to all its children the same quantity of public education - the same number of years in school - but also by making sure to give all of them, all with no exceptions, the same quality of education." Adler argues:

But the democratic promise of equal educational opportunity, half fulfilled, is worse than a promise broken. It is an ideal betrayed. Equality of educational opportunity is not, in fact, provided if it means no more than taking all the children into the public schools for the same number of hours, days, and years. If once there they are divided into the sheep and the goats, into those destined for economic and political leadership and for a quality of life to which all should have access, then the democratic purpose has been undermined by an inadequate system of public schooling.

In High School: A Report on Secondary Education in America , Boyer (1983) observed:

Pushed by the historic United States Supreme Court decision in Brown v. Board of Education (1954), public education was called upon to serve more equitably the historically bypassed students--the poor, the underprivileged, and the underachieving. Congress and the courts moved, belatedly, to counter years of scandalous discrimination. Racial balance and compensatory education became urgent new priorities. Schools became the battleground for social justice.

Boyer noted that in 1980, 61 percent of Black youth and 56 percent of Hispanic nineteen-year-olds held high school diplomas compared with 78 percent of White youth the same age. *"Opportunity remains unequal. And this failure to educate every person to his or her full potential threatens the nation's social and economic health."*

From Goodlad's study (1984), titled A Place Called School: Prospects for the Future, a number of recurring themes emerged, including one of equity. Goodlad sees the distribution of resources for learning, especially time, as creating inequities in opportunity to learn. He views some issues of equity as having little to do with the race or socioeconomic status of students. Others frequently do relate to socioeconomic status and race-- particularly issues of differences in content and teaching practices encountered by students depending on their enrollment in high-,middle-, or low-track classes. Goodlad argues:

The case for educational opportunity has revolved almost exclusively around the question of access to a school to be commonly attended and around discrimination based on color, race, or creed, but other considerations are now likely to expand the dimensions of controversy. Increasingly, the issue will be whether students, as a consequence of the schools they happen to attend and the classes to which they are assigned, have equality of access to knowledge.

In proposing its plan of action in Educating Americans for the 21st Century, the National Science Board Commission on Precollege Education in Mathematics, Science and Technology (1983), repeatedly stressed that its focus is on all students, not just the affluent or the gifted. Recognizing that substantial portions of our population still suffer from the consequences of racial, social and economic discrimination, compounded by watered standards, social promotion, poor guidance and token efforts, the Commission urged that the Nation should reaffirm its commitment to full opportunity and full achievement by all. In the Commission's view,

. . . equality of educational opportunity is absolutely essential to the nation's commitment to excellence. It is crucial that programs for minority and economically disadvantaged students and for students whose parents do not speak English at home continue to strive for the same level of excellence as other programs . . .Excellence and elitism are not synonymous. Too often we equate the notions of affirmative action, nontraditional student, or continuous education with mediocrity. We must open doors to create educational opportunities for a wide variety of students, and we must recognize the potential for excellence in a diverse student body. Equality and quality are not mutually exclusive.

The Education Commission of the States Task Force on Education for Economic Growth and the National Commission on Excellence in Education (1983) see the improvement of education in America as crucial to national survival. The report points out that:

Over the past generation in America, we have mounted a massive social and educational effort to deliver on that commitment. We have broadened access to education and improved the educational performance of large numbers of our citizens who for many years were put at a disadvantage by poverty, minority status or both. The civil rights reforms and social legislation of the sixties - notably the Elementary and Secondary Education Act (ESEA) - signaled a far-reaching commitment by our nation to put old wrongs right and to educate those who once were barred from access to quality education. . .Our twin goals, which we must pursue simultaneously and with equal zeal, must be ever broader access to education for all students - and access to quality as well.

Clearly, there appears to be a consensus among the reports, all of which describe the current situation as a crisis in American education--most vividly expressed in the title of the National Commission on Excellence in Education's report, <u>A Nation at Risk</u>. All call for raising the standards and enhancing the excellence of education; and all the reports speak of the twin goals of equity and excellence, of equality and quality.

What is meant by Quality-with-Equity?

Two decades ago, the popular slogan was "equality of educational opportunity" just as today's catch-word is "excellence." There is a massive body of literature concerning the issues, problems, the programs, the research efforts to provide equality of educational opportunity and quality. Yet, there appears to be no consensus on what exactly constitutes equity, just as there are differences in the meaning of quality and excellence.

Coleman's report titled, <u>Equality of Educational Opportunity</u> (1969) was instrumental in the continued debate between what is meant by equity and excellence. Section 402 of the Civil Rights Act of 1964 directed the U.S. Commissioner of Education to *conduct a survey and make a report to the President and Congress. . . concerning the lack of availability of equal educational opportunities for individuals by reason of race, color, religion, or national origin in public institutions at all levels.*

Coleman and his colleagues observed that the concept of equality of educational opportunity has had a varied past, has changed radically in recent years, and is likely to undergo further change in the future. In Coleman's view, what occurred in the 1960s was a:

. . .change in the concept of equality of educational opportunity from school resource inputs to effects of schooling. When that change occurred. . .the school's responsibility shifted from increasing and distributing equally its quality to increasing the quality of its students' achievement. This is a notable shift, and one which should have strong consequences for the practice of education in future years.

Thus the question becomes, which concept(s) of equity should guide educational policy and practice? Equality of school resources? Equality of student achievement? Equal quality in education? How is educational quality to be defined and by whom?

Equal quality education, in turn, depends on the accepted concept of excellence. And here, as with equity, varying concepts are prevalent. The National Commission on Excellence in Education (1983) defined excellence broadly to mean several related things:

At the level of the individual learner, it means performing on the boundary of individual ability in ways that test and push back personal limits, in school and in the workplace. Excellence characterizes a school or college that sets high expectations and goals for all learners, then tries in every way possible to help students reach them. Excellence characterizes a society that has adopted these policies, for it will then be prepared through the education and skill of its people to respond to the challenge of a rapidly changing world.

Like many other statements, excellence is equated with higher academic standards, tougher requirements for graduation and college admission, elimination of frills in the curriculum, limiting options for students and generally working harder in school.

Which approach to equity should guide educational planning? This issue has been raised in most of the recent reports in terms of the need to establish a common core curriculum for all. The Paideia Proposal (1982) is quite clear:

To give the same quality of schooling to all requires a program of study that is both liberal and general, and that is in several crucial, overarching respects, one and the same for every child. All sidetracks, specialized courses, or elective choices must be eliminated. Allowing them will always lead a certain number of students to voluntarily downgrade their own education.

Goodlad (1984) recommends "a common core of studies from which students cannot escape through electives, even though the proposed electives purport to be in the same domain of knowledge,". . .elimination of grouping students in separate classes on the basis of past performance, random assignment of students to heterogeneous classes - all aimed at "offering the most equity with respect to gaining access to knowledge while still preserving the more advantageous content and teaching practices of the upper tracks" through improved pedagogy, not individualized, inequitable tracks and curricula.

What makes up a general education and the common curriculum for all and how must this be differentiated to take into account individual differences? Does it mean exposing all students to the same content? If so, to what point? Does it mean common standards, or minimum standards? In what ways do we differentiate instruction and provide for diversity? Or, do we avoid it? If education is to provide for both general and specialized education, what constitutes an appropriate balance? These are the critical questions which face quality-with-equity for our schools.

As standards are raised in the movement toward achieving quality - serious questions are raised about the impact on low-achievers and so-called at-risk students. Also, this call for higher standards, more required academic courses and stiffer requirements has raised questions on the effects of the dropout problem. What will happen to students who cannot or will not meet these more rigorous standards and requirements? There are those who argue that to question whether all students can attain these new standards is being anti-academic; they say, it is only a matter of setting high expectations to be achieved. They argue that rather than frustrate students, higher standards provide an incentive and motivation for higher achievement. Doyle (1984), for example, asserts that:

Low standards are the educational equivalent of Gresham's law. Just as bad money drives out good, poor education saps academic strength. The easier it is to earn a high school diploma, the less it matters. It is a degree without distinction and, signifying little, it is not worth the effort, particularly for students with no postsecondary plans. Perhaps paradoxically, standards encourage student performance and act as a stimulus to teachers and the extended school community. No more should be asked of standards; no less should be expected.

However, as Passow (1984) suggested, those who have been involved in compensatory, remedial or dropout programs question this assertion and maybe with good reason. After all, their efforts have not always been effective and they might have done better by forgetting all about various intervention strategies and programs and simply announced higher academic standards and expectations. Nevertheless, increased academic requirements raise serious questions of quality-with-equity in terms of equal access and opportunity, and quality in terms of restricting the notion to academic excellence.

Equity in Education: A Five Level Approach

McCune and Wilbur (1986) identified five levels of integration efforts which have emerged as viable means to reduce the existing disparity in opportunity. The following is a description of their five levels of equity.

Physical Desegregation

Equal Access

Equal Treatment

Equal Outcomes

Quality Outcomes

Each differs in terms of effect; but each has been a necessary outgrowth of specific concerns over time. Heretofore integration efforts have focused on improvement primarily within the existing structures of the school system. The first three level of responses have been: physical desegregation, equal access and equal treatment. The remaining two, equal outcomes and quality outcomes, require the actual restructuring of the educational process itself. The latter are the levels which can fundamentally achieve the goals of equity by enabling the relevant preparation of all students for the information society.

Physical Desegregation

Physical desegregation was deemed necessary as a result of the 1954 Supreme Court decision of <u>Brown v. Topeka</u> which determined that separate schooling was not equal. The operating belief was that by dismantling the dual system of schooling, inequalities would be eliminated and students would be given equal opportunity regardless of race. However, it has been found through experience that even though students are placed in the same classroom, inequalities continue to remain. This is because inequities continue to exist in the expectations people hold and, thus, in their subtle treatment of students. Although desegregation is a vital step, further efforts are needed to eliminate these mental barriers.

Equal Access

When race discrimination began to be more substantively addressed as a result of the 1964 Civil Rights Act, and when sex discrimination became a legal matter through Title IX of the 1972 Educational Amendments, the question of equal access to opportunity became an issue. Disparate patterns in placement, enrollment and achievement highlighted the systematic conditions which abridged equal access. Pursuing alternative methods for providing access have been significant and deal with the more subtle characteristics of bias and stereotyping behavior. Although, once access to classrooms and programs was granted, the problems of student treatment remained.

Equal Treatment

Equal treatment issues were dealt with by attempting to treat all students alike. This contradicted the initial intent of the treatment question as it denied the different needs of each student. For example, if all students were treated alike and some did not speak English, then access to equal opportunity would still be denied to the non-English speaking students. It was during this stage that a clarification of terminology emerged. Addressing the problems of discrimination, bias, and stereotyping (more than the concept of sameness) was needed. Doing the same for everyone ignored individual differences and past histories, and in fact, perpetuated the inequalities. So the issue became more clearly defined as equity, that is striving for equal outcomes.

Equal Outcomes

Equitable practices are concerned not with treating everyone alike but with treating people in accordance with their specific needs, thus giving them perhaps different opportunities so they can have equal chances for pursuing their unique potential. This approach is guided by the goal of equitable participation in society for all people. In all areas of an equitable society - government, workforce, and education - participation would reflect the composition of the population in terms of sex, ethnicity, disability and religion. The achievement of proportional representation would signal achievement of equity.

Quality Outcomes

Educators are now asking another question - whether the schools we have had in the past will meet the needs of the future. And if they do not, then equal outcomes mean less if we are not providing a relevant education. Pursuing the fifth level, quality outcomes, becomes critical in achieving the full intent of educational equity. To achieve quality outcomes means that we must rethink the priorities of education and restructure the educational culture so that the achievement of all students reflects the skills required by the information society. An equitable educational system does not only consider equal outcomes but analyzes the worth of those outcomes in terms of ensuring a meaningful and productive life for individuals and society.

Have we achieved the mission or the concept of an equitable educational system? Have we provided opportunities for all students to pursue their interests without holding stereotypic expectations of their abilities and potential? Are we satisfied merely by providing students with an equal chance?

In the late '80s and into the early '90s, we are still dealing with desegregation issues. Schools have not successfully desegregated their faculty or student populations to accurately reflect the local population composition. In 1985, more than 30 years after the Brown decision, 63 percent of America's school children still attended predominantly minority schools (Cardenas, 1985). Equal access is not yet accomplished as course enrollment and achievement figures continually show the discrepancies between male-female, and majority-minority representation. This inadequacy is sometimes rationalized by claiming that the choice is there but schools should not promote non-traditional enrollments. However, schools do have a responsibility to break down past barriers, whether internal or external, and be proactive in identifying the benefits of each option. Although we are not striving for the same treatment for all students, we continue to find that treatment is stereotypic and that lower expectations are held for students who are poor, Black, Hispanic, or female. The treatment should differ, but should be motivated by the same goal for all students, in the pursuit of their obvious and hidden potential. Equal outcomes have not yet been attained. This is clearly evident in achievement scores, in the workforce, in educational administration, and in political positions. As for quality outcomes, the curricula driving many educational programs continue to reflect the needs of an industrial society. In analyzing the populations of unemployed and under-employed, we may also find that there are overwhelming proportions of Blacks, Hispanics and women represented. This seems to be a clear statement of the inadequacies in our present system for achieving equitable opportunities for all people.

Initial Steps for Understanding the Role of Equity in our Schools

The first step to understanding equity is to acknowledge that successful school reform efforts are contingent upon the attainment of an equitable educational system. Unless we take these issues seriously and institute proactive efforts to respond to the changing needs of students and society, we will continue to perpetuate the inadequacies. Quality cannot be realized without equity.

Quality-with-equity is a reform movement that is attempting to change the schools and other educational institutions so that students from all backgrounds will have an equal opportunity to learn. This reform movement will require changes in the total school or educational environment; it is not limited to curricular changes.

Second, the driving mission of the school must be articulated and must reflect equity goals. Consensus of the concept is necessary for commitment and authentic action by all those who are a part of the school.

Quality-with-equity is also a process whose goals will never be fully realized. Equity, like liberty and justice, are ideals toward which human beings work but never fully attain. Because the goals of equity can never be fully attained, schools must have the vision of working continually to increase the prospects of a quality-with-equity education for all students.

Third, day-to-day behaviors should be analyzed as to their consistency with the intent of the mission. This also means that colleagues hold one another accountable to the mission. The new culture committed to equity must also be supportive of individual differences and encourage the behaviors which enable the meaningful growth of all persons.

To achieve social equality is a continual process, and it requires a commitment in belief and in action to the goals of equity. Attainment is dependent upon responsiveness to on-going change and respect for diversity. To proclaim and believe that we have attained equality is only to obscure the reality and deny human rights for all people.

Summary

The crucial test of the reforms urged in these and other reports will be whether improvements in American education become available for all students. As with their emphasis on academics, the reports unanimously make reference to quality-with-equity as twin goals.

How does a school system determine if it is an excellent school? How does a school system determine if it is equitable? Certainly, these are questions that address the relationship between quality and equity. What would such a school endorse?

An excellent school is a work of art. It orchestrates the varying interests and abilities of its students, parents and community in concerted efforts toward educational quality. It enlists the creative abilities of all personnel to identify goals and to fashion programs that fit the needs of its particular clientele. It is accountable to the state for such basic outcomes as literacy in language and numbers, but it is free to innovate new materials and methods - and yet it must especially define and seek much broader dimensions of educational development. Above all, it is unique, responsive to personalities and values the needs and abilities that are never fully duplicated in any other school. Such schools would serve all of our students well. These twin goals - quality and equity - need to be re-examined and updated for the phase in which our schools are currently progressing.

As stated earlier, during the first half of this century, equity, for the most part, meant making sure that each citizen had equal access to schooling. *During the last quarter of this century and beyond, the primary interpretation of equity will be equity of educational opportunity to benefit from quality education.* That is to say, it is not enough simply for a responsive system of public education to make educational services available in established ways, to indicate, *if you cannot take advantage, it is not our problem.* Much more important today is the quality of those services and how they are delivered. As suggested, the structure of the public schools was designed in a period when, at best, equal access was the goal. However, it was discovered that equal access did not mean equal access to a quality education. This has led to the current re-examination of school arrangements and a call for educational reform - to the end that each learner may achieve his or her right to full development. In practical terms, this means, among other things, affirming that the problem is not with the learner but maybe with the school. In other words, if there are shortcomings in learning, it is not necessarily shortcomings in the student as it might be shortcomings in the school.

WORKSHEET 1

1. What is the difference between the '50s movement for excellence and the '80s excellence movement?

   The '50's response to Sputnik meant better science, math, foreign language training for our best students. The '80's movement demanded that we reach all students, as there were no "dumb" jobs left.

2. Oakes stated that research over the past two decades had almost exclusively focused on the "characteristics" of the students - in search for their school failure - what mistakes did she indicate were associated with this approach?

   We focused on the students, families, neighborhoods, what was wrong with them -- rather than what was done in the classroom.

3. Is there a common thread of concern among the various national reports and commissions cited in this chapter. What are they?

    The softness of the curriculum, the lowness of standards, the weakness of teachers and teacher ed program, the dissatisfaction of employers with students

4. What does the term "excellence" mean? Does it mean higher standards? Why or why not?

    It does mean higher standards because what we've had in the past isn't sufficient. But it must be possible for students to meet those goals.

5. How would you determine if a school is "excellent"? Explain.

    The excellent school not only sets high standards but does all in its power for students to succeed.

6. How would you determine if a school is "equitable"? Explain.

An equitable school gives all students access--in terms of physical space, teachers and staff help -- to all the learning that can be had there.

7. Is is possible to have an educational system that is both excellent and equitable? Explain.

We must not treat each student exactly the same, but we must treat each student in a way that the outcome is the same: a successful learner.

8. How do you respond to the statement, "If there are shortcomings in learning, it is not necessarily shortcomings in the student as it might be shortcomings in the school." Explain your position.

It is true that we can't lead a horse to water and necessarily expect him to drink. Nevertheless, a student can become discouraged after many years of not achieving despite her best efforts. In that case, there's a good argument that the school hasn't done its job.

REFERENCES

Adler, Mortimer J. The Paideia Proposal: An Educational Manifesto. MacMillian Publishing Co., 1982.

Boyer, Ernest L. High School: A Report on Secondary Education in America. Harper and Row, 1983.

Coleman, James S. The Concept of Equality of Educational Opportunity. Harvard Educational Review, Board of Editors, Equal Educational Opportunity. Cambridge: MA, 1969.

College Board On Further Examination: A Report on the Advisory Panel on the Scholastic Aptitude Test Score Decline. College Board Publications, New York: NY, 1977.

Doyle, Denis Issue. Association for Supervision and Curriculum Development (ASCD), Sept., 1984, p. 5.

Education Commission of the States Task Force on Education for Economic Growth. Action for Excellence. Education Commission for the States. Denver: CO., 1983. ERIC - ED 235 588.

Goodlad, John I. A Place Called School: Prospects for the Future. McGraw Hill Book Co., 1984.

Love, Ruth B. "Proceedings of the Second Conference of the University/Urban Schools National Task Force. Washington, D.C., 1985.

McCune, Shirley and Wilbur, Gretchen Equity: Have We Arrived? Heartland - McRel Sex Equity Center Newsletter Kansas City, MO., October-November, 1986. (Reprinted with Permission).

National Commission on Excellence in Education. A Nation at Risk: The Imperative for Educational Reform. U.S. Government Printing Office, Washington, D.C., 1983. Also in ERIC - ED 226 006.

National Science Board Commission on Pre-College Education in Mathematics, Science and Technology. Educating Americans for the 21st Century. U.S. Government Printing Office, 1983. ERIC - ED 233 913.

Oakes, Jeannie Keeping Track - How Schools Create Inequality Yale University Press, New Haven: CN, 1985. p. xiii.

Passow, Henry A. Equity and Excellence: Confronting the Dilemmas. ERIC Clearinghouse for Urban Education, New York: Columbia University, December 1984. ERIC - ED 251 585.

Report of the Twentieth Century Fund Task Force on Federal Elementary and Secondary Education Policy Making the Grade. The Twentieth Century Fund, New York, NY, 1983.

SUGGESTED READINGS

Adler, Mortimer J. The Paideia Proposal - An Educational Manifesto. Macmillian Publishing Company, New York: 1982.

American Association of Colleges for Teacher Education. Educating a Profession: Profiles for a Beginning Teacher. American Association of Colleges for Teacher Education, Washington, D.C., 1983.

Boyer, Ernest High School: A Report on Secondary Education in America. Harper and Row, New York: 1983.

College Board, Project Equality. Academic Preparation for College: What Students Need to Know and Be Able to Do. College Board, New York: 1983.

Education Commission of the States. Action for Excellence: A Comprehensive Plan to Improve Our Nation's Schools. Education Commission of the States, Denver, CO., 1983.

Goodlad, John I. A Place Called School: Prospects for the Future. McGraw Hill Publishing Co., New York: 1983.

National Commission on Excellence in Education. A Nation at Risk: The Imperative for Educational Reform. U.S. Government Printing Office, Washington, D.C., 1983.

National Education Association. Excellence in Our Schools, Teacher Education: An Action Plan. National Education Association, Washington, D.C., 1982.

Oakes, Jeannie Keeping Track - How Schools Structure Inequality. Yale University Press, New Haven: CN, 1985.

Powell, Arthur G., Farrar, Eleanor and Cohen, David K. The Shopping Mall High School - Winners and Losers in the Educational Marketplace. Houghton Mifflin Company, Boston: MA, 1985.

Science Board Commission on PreCollege Education in Mathematics, Science, and Technology. Educating Americans for the 21st Century: A Report to the American People and the National Science Board. National Science Board, National Science Foundation, Washington, D.C., 1983.

Sizer, Theodore Horace's Compromise - The Dilemma of the American High School. Houghton Mifflin Publishing Co., Boston: MA, 1984.

Twentieth Century Fund Task Force on Federal Elementary and Secondary Education Policy. Making the Grade. Twentieth Century Fund, New York: 1983.

CHAPTER THREE

Educating All Children: A Call for Effective Schools

Introduction

"We can, whenever and wherever we choose, successfully teach all children whose schooling is of interest to us. We already know more than we need to do that. Whether or not we do it must finally depend on how we feel about the fact that we haven't so far."

- Ron Edmonds

Equity is an encompassing concept. Consequently, developing an appropriate environment for its incorporation has implications for every facet of the educational setting. First, the future of equity depends on the ability of all who are, or will be involved, in the improvement of our schools. A coordinated effort between State and local boards of education, administrators, teacher training programs, classroom teachers and the community at large must be orchestrated. If and when this support system is in place, the likelihood of equity as in integral part of our schools is eminent; because then educators like ourselves will have the necessary support systems to ensure successful implementation.

Chapter 3, **Educating All Children: A Call for Effective Schools** is designed to: (1) examine the current call for more effective schools, (2) understand accreditation standards and their current implications for school improvement, (3) address the current movement to increase graduation requirements and the projected results of raising those standards, and (4) present a continuum for equitable competence for schools to measure their progress.

Several questions are imbedded in the outline of this chapter. For example, what is an effective school? How are teacher education programs responding to the reform movement? What agencies oversee teacher education programs? What agencies oversee pubic schools? How will the new standards being implemented across the country affect students? And finally, what does a school *look like* when they are moving along a continuum toward advanced equity competence?

Reform: A Call for School Improvement

"American schools are in trouble," is the conclusion of an eight-year study conducted by Goodlad (1984). "In fact, the problems of schooling are of such crippling proportions that many schools may not survive. Is it possible that our entire public education system is nearing collapse?"

While the crisis in education is national in scope and will require national attention, it must be dealt with, first of all, at the local and state levels. All of the recently issued studies and reports emphasized that historically, public policy decisions affecting the schools are the province of state agencies and local boards. A strategy for educational reform recognizing that fact will require collaborative efforts by governors, mayors, state legislators, chief state school officers, school board members and administrators, teachers and teacher organizations, parents, students and representatives of trade unions, businesses, industry, postsecondary institutions and other professions.

The last six years have witnessed the greatest and most concentrated surge of educational reform in the nation's history. According to the U.S. Department of Education (1984):

. . . *deep public concern about the Nation's future created a tidal wave of school reform which promised to renew American education. Citizens, perplexed about social, civic, and economic difficulties, turned to education as an anchor of hope for the future of their nation and their children. The schools survived an unprecedented firestorm of critical comment and attention from the press to emerge at the end of the year with greater public support than at any time in the recent past.*

Quality of the School vs. Background of the Student

Since the mid-'60s, educators and policy makers had believed that variations in school quality affected a child's achievement considerably less than did a child's socioeconomic background. The primary evidence supporting the earlier view was a massive study for the U.S. Office of Education by sociologist James Coleman. The report, formally called <u>Equality of Educational Opportunity</u> (popularly known as the Coleman Report, 1969), concluded that educational achievement was related more to a student's family background than to the characteristics of the school (facilities, materials, curricula, teachers and so on).

The landmark study left educators and policy makers deeply concerned. In Ravitch's (1984) words, the most important point to filter through the media was that *schools don't make a difference.* If student achievement is determined largely by family background and scarcely at all by teachers, books and facilities, the reasoning went, then improving the school is unlikely to have much effect on student achievement. The finding raised serious doubts about the likely value of compensatory education for poor children, which was beginning to build in response to the passage of federal aid to education only the year before. Other studies by Mosteller and Moynihan (1972), and Jencks (1972) and his colleagues, further supported this interpretation.

By the 1970s, however, mounting evidence indicated that school structure and organization had a powerful effect on what a child learned. Ironically, Coleman was the researcher whose work, done with his colleagues Hoffer and Kilgore, most conveyed this finding in the United States. Coleman's group concluded that the conditions of educational success were discipline (physical and intellectual), high expectations and standards (for both teachers and students), and a safe and orderly environment. According to their research, these conditions were more likely to be found in private and Catholic schools than in public schools, a conclusion that stimulated great debate and in the process actually diverted attention from the broader lessons (1984). However, they acknowledged that schools can and do make a difference in the education of all students.

What is an Effective School?

Obviously, Coleman and his colleagues have identified what conditions must exist for a school to be effective. An effective school is usually narrowly defined as one in which students score higher than expected on standardized tests of basic skills, given their socioeconomic status. A good school, however, the kind of school that Purkey and Degen discuss, goes beyond this definition. In a good school, students perform well in a number of areas. They exhibit social responsibility and ethical behavior, acquire vocational skills and good work habits, and develop higher-order thinking skills (such as problem solving, creative thinking or critical thinking). *More importantly, a good school is an equitable school, one that meets the needs of all students, whether they are at the top or at the bottom of the ability scale.*

In 1983, Purkey and Smith offered several characteristics of good schools. (They indicate that, given the state of the research these characteristics are based on, the list should not be used as a template, but as a guide).

School site management
Leadership (Principal)
Staff stability
Curriculum articulation and organization
School-wide staff development
Parental and community involvement and support
School-wide recognition of academic success
Maximized learning time
District support
Collaborative planning and collegial relationship
Sense of community
Clear goals and high expectations
Order and discipline

The *effective schools movement* is framed by three central assumptions: (1) schools can be identified that are unusually effective in teaching poor and minority children basic skills as measured by standardized tests; (2) these successful schools exhibit characteristics that are correlated with their success and that lie well within the domain of educators to manipulate; (3) the characteristics of successful schools provide a basis for improving schools not deemed to be successful. Implicit in this last assumption is a belief that the school is the appropriate place to focus educational reform efforts.

This movement is traceable to three major factors. The first is a line of research that has sought to dispel the impression left by some highly publicized studies in the 1960s (e.g., Coleman et al., 1966) that differences among schools did not make much difference in the achievement of poor and minority children. The second basis for the effective schools movement rests with the psychological climate prevalent among practitioners across the country by the mid '70s. A third factor explaining the phenomenal growth of effective schools activity is implicit in the findings of most of the national reports or studies.

Growth in school improvement activity during the past five years has been remarkable. A survey by Odden & Dougherty in 1982 pointed out that most states had a school improvement program of one form or another that reflected features of the effective schools' literature. *While lists may vary considerably in detail, features such as strong instructional leadership, an orderly school climate, high expectations, emphasis on basic skills, and frequent monitoring of instructional progress, have become something like the five steps to effective schooling.* This state-level activity is paralleled by numerous district projects designed to disseminate features found to be associated with exceptional schools.

Effective schools research tells us:

We can do better

We can control the conditions of the school

We can have good schools by design, not chance

We need to address the results of the school - not the activities of the school

The schools should not be a contributing factor to a students failure

Improvement of education is with the school as a unit of change

A Call for More Effective Teacher Education Programs

The reports all conclude that the poor quality of teachers is a major reason for the crisis in education. The National Commission on Excellence (1983), for example, found that the quality of America's teachers had slipped dramatically in recent years. The Commission concluded that *not enough of the academically able students are being attracted to teaching; that teacher preparation programs need substantial improvement; that the professional working life of teachers is on the whole unacceptable; and that a shortage of teachers exists in key fields.*

All observers agree that any efforts to reform the schools must pay careful attention to the teaching force. In Sizer's (1984) words, improving American secondary education absolutely depends on improving the conditions of work and the respect for teachers. How are teacher education programs responding to these allegations? What agency oversees the accreditation of teacher education programs, and how do those standards address equity?

Reforms in Teacher Education

A report (RATE, 1988) about the activity within teacher education programs across the country issued in the Fall of 1988 indicates a response to those allegations of the poor quality of teachers. For example, the report indicated: 73% have raised admission standards for their teacher education programs; 55% have changed exit standards for their teacher education programs; 52% have changed the liberal arts curriculum for preservice teachers; and 51% have begun using public school teachers as teacher educators.

Accreditation Standards for Teacher Education Programs

National accreditation of colleges and university programs for the preparation of all teachers and other professional school personnel at the elementary and secondary levels is the responsibility of the National Council for the Accreditation of Teacher Education (NCATE). The mission of NCATE is two-fold: (1) to require a level of quality in professional education that fosters competent practice of graduates, and (2) to encourage institutions to meet rigorous academic standards of excellence in professional education. NCATE provides a mechanism for voluntary peer regulation of the education unit that is designed to establish and uphold national standards of excellence, to strengthen the quality and integrity of professional educational units, and to ensure that requirements for accreditation are related to best professional practice. NCATE establishes standards and procedures to carry out the accreditation process, makes final determinations regarding the accreditation status of institutions, publishes an annual list of NCATE - accredited units, and provides training for those who conduct unit reviews.

NCATE has been authorized by the Council on Post-Secondary Accreditation (COPA) to adopt standards and procedures for accreditation and to determine the accreditation status of institutional units for preparing teachers and other professional school personnel. NCATE is also recognized by the U.S. Department of Education as the only authorized accrediting agency in the field of school personnel preparation.

The 1979 NCATE Standards and Equity. In the NCATE standards, effective January 1, 1979, the term *multicultural education* was explicitly addressed in the standards for the first time. In essence, the standards implied that all teacher education programs needed to meet this new focus by providing:

Provisions for multicultural education which must be evident in undergraduate and graduate programs in order to receive full accreditation.

The 1986 NCATE Standards and Equity. In October of 1986, NCATE issued new standards, procedures and policies for the Accreditation of Professional Teacher Education units. The following is a sampling of the newest standards.

Category I: Knowledge base for Professional Education - Design of Curriculum. Under Criteria for Compliance, for example, Standard I.A: states - *Each program area in the unit includes study and experiences related to culturally diverse and exceptional populations. All programs incorporate multicultural and global perspectives.*

Category II: Relationship to the World of Practice - Clinical and Field-Base Experiences. Under Criteria for Compliance, for example, Standard II. A: states - *Education students participate in field-based and/or clinical experiences with culturally diverse and exceptional populations to allow them to understand the unique contributions, needs, similarities, differences, and interdependences of students from varying racial, cultural, linguistic, religious, and socioeconomic backgrounds.*

Category III: Students - Admission. Under Criteria for Compliance, Standard III. A: states - *Incentives and affirmative procedures are used to attract quality candidates. Applicants from diverse economic, racial and cultural backgrounds are recruited.*

Category IV: Faculty Qualifications and Assignments. Under Standard IV. A: *The composition of the faculty in the education unit reflects cultural diversity.*

Category V: Governance and Resources. Standard V. A: states - *The governance system clearly identifies and defines the unit submitted for accreditation; clearly specifies the governance system under which the unit is enabled to fulfill its mission, and demonstrates that in practice the system operates as described.* (NCATE, 1986).

In comparing the two standards (1979 and 1986) - there is little doubt that the equity dimension is more evident and inclusive in the latest standards. However, one must not become overly optimistic about the impact that these newer standards will have - given the lack of overall effectiveness that the 1979 standards had on the integration of *multicultural education* concepts into training programs.

A Growing Shortage of Minority Teachers

According to the American Association of Colleges for Teacher Education (AACTE, 1988) while the current supply of teachers now approximates the demand, by 1995 more than one million teaching positions will need to be filled. At that time, the racial and ethnic composition of the teaching force will be diametrically opposed to the racial and ethnic composition of the nation's classrooms.

The AACTE study reported that 33 states have elementary and secondary minority enrollments of 20 percent or more; however, only six have higher education institutions with schools, colleges, or departments of education with minority enrollments greater than 15 percent. The study states,

The lack of highly qualified minority teachers impedes efforts to change the nature and level of achievement in our schools, both for underserved minority students and for those students who traditionally meet prevailing school standards. Coordinated action is required to attract a greater number of able minority teacher candidates, prepare them better in institutions of higher education, and demonstrate effective programs for state policy makers and administrators .

The challenge facing teacher education programs is attracting and retaining the best qualified students available. Equally as important, but a more difficult task, will be the role and responsibility of teacher training programs to recruit and retain minority students who are interested in the education profession.. There is a growing concern being expressed by teacher training programs across the country with the current and projected shortage of minority teachers. The traditional methods of recruiting students into teacher training programs will not work for the needs of the future. Teacher training programs must first be committed to attracting the non-majority student and then provide enough incentives for those students to make any real difference in the current trends we are now witnessing.

Accreditation of Local Schools: A Regional Process

Six regional accrediting agencies exist, each with its own geographic area, its own set of standards, its own accreditation policies, and its own approach to meeting its responsibilities. Regional accreditation focuses on the school's objectives, the quality of its programs, the effectiveness of its administration, its general financial stability, the strength of its faculty and library, and the quality of its student personnel program. The six regional accrediting agencies are <u>Middle States, New England, North Central, Northwest, Southern, and Western Association of Schools and Colleges.</u> (See Figure 4 - Regional Accreditation).

Regional Accreditation

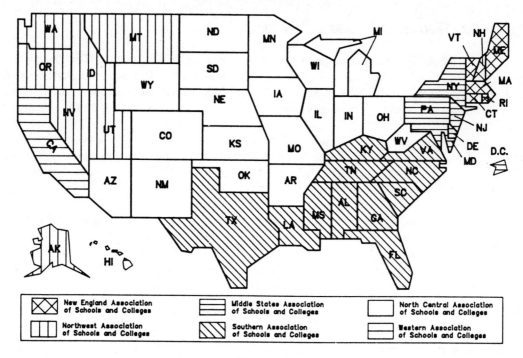

Figure 4

Outcomes Accreditation/Evaluation: The New Trend

The intent of the Outcomes Accreditation/Evaluation (OA/E) is to offer local schools two routes to accreditation. First, the more traditional process was requiring the school to meet the standards for the type of school and to undertake at least once in each seven-year cycle a comprehensive self-study of the total school program. Now, since 1986, schools have another alternative; outcomes accreditation/evaluation. An OA/E process focuses on student success, quality-with-equity programs and requires the school to document within shorter cycles the success with which the school is achieving specific learning goals it has established for itself. The school is required to meet all of the standards for the type of school plus the standards for OA/E schools. Why would a school select the OA/E process?

* Student success is at all times the focus of the school improvement/enrichment activities.

* OA/E requires the school to focus on the success of each student rather than on class averages or school averages.

* The school undertakes on-going renewal activities rather than an improvement program addressed only periodically.

* The OA/E process focuses on selected target goals which have an impact on the total school program; therefore, the attention devoted to each of the goals under study can be intense and the relationship of all components of the program to the target goals is determined.

* Improvement/enrichment activities address specific tasks the school staff wishes to accomplish; progress in accomplishing those tasks is indentifiable within the current cycle.

* In the OA/E process, the staff designs the improvement/enrichment programs for the school and monitors their implementation.

* The OA/E process encourages the school staff to use data from a variety of measures - beyond norm-referenced tests - to assess the effectiveness of the school program.

* The OA/E process helps the school document the many ways in which it is currently ensuring student success in the attainment of the goals of the school.

* The OA/E process counters the criticism that schools are afraid to be held accountable for student outcomes.

* Throughout the process, the school has available to it the expertise of resource personnel knowledgeable in various phases of assessing school effectiveness.

What is the intent of the quality-with-equity aspect of OA/E?

The accrediting agencies define quality programs as those in which student performance meets or exceeds expectations. Can a school claim to be a quality school if there are within it under-performing students - students who have not been achieving at the level of their capabilities, or students who have failed in the past and no longer respond to challenges, or minority students who believe that no one has an interest in their learning problems? _Educators who believe in quality-with-equity reject the idea that students from certain socio-economic classes do not have the ability to learn effectively or that is is acceptable for any students to perform below their capabilities, regardless of the level of those capabilities._

To make the first step toward quality-with-equity requires a critical mass of educators who believe all students can learn and who believe that it is worth the teacher's effort to provide the instruction which will make that happen. At present, not all educators believe that all students can learn effectively and not all educators who believe all students can learn are willing to expend the effort required. In the quality school, principals and teachers believe that all students can learn and that all teachers can learn to teach all kinds of students. When this is not the case, there is a clear need for a professional development program focusing on (a) beliefs about teaching and learning, and (b) strategies for teaching and learning.

Responses to the following questions will indicate the school's interest in providing a program characterized by quality-with-equity:

* Are students who come to the school with educational disadvantages being challenged?

* Are educationally advantaged students achieving at the level of their capabilities?

* Is there evidence that teachers have high expectations for every student?

* Are resources being provided to assist students in overcoming whatever educational deficits they may have brought to the school?

* What are the evidences that educationally advantaged and disadvantaged students in this school are being challenged?

The OA/E process compliments the goals of quality-with-equity and provides for educators a step-by-step approach to attaining the desired goals for a more effective school. To assist the school staff gather information needed as a basis for decision-making, a broad array of instruments are available. There are numerous surveys and questionaires pertinent to the kinds of inquiries the school staff will be making during the OA/E process. Those surveys may be used exactly as presented or may be modified in any way which would increase their pertinence to the school situation in which they are being used. As educators, who are concerned about quality-with-equity, contact your regional accreditation agency for specific information on the process and products available.

State Approval of Programs

State approval is a governmental activity that requires all professional education programs within the state to meet standards of quality in order for their graduates to be eligible for state certification. Its purpose is to ensure that those who are to be certified by the state have completed adequate higher education programs. The state education agency (SEA) or a state professional standards board usually conducts institutional reviews and develops standards and procedures for this process. The state approval system is continuously shaped by conditions and persons within the state. In those states with state approval systems, state approval is a precondition for eligibility to begin the NCATE accreditation process.

Teacher Testing and Certification.

State mandates to test teacher competence are becoming increasingly popular. According to the American Association of Colleges for Teacher Education (AACTE) in 1984, thirty states had such mandates, and twelve other states were planning such requirements. <u>See Figure 5 - State-Required Testing for Initial Certification of Teachers Testing, Enacted before 1984 and 1984</u>.

There is a widespread variation in the states' efforts. Tests may address: (1) basic skills such as English, Math, and Science; (2) professional or pedagogical skills; and (3) academic knowledge of a particular subject matter. Testing may occur before admission to the teacher education program or before certification. Some states have developed and use their own tests; others rely on nationally standardized exams. The source of the mandate for teacher testing also varies; in eleven cases it is state law, whereas in twenty-two others it is state education agency regulations (three states have both). <u>See Figure 6 - State-Required Testing for Initial Certification of Teachers Testing in Effect, Planned in Next 3 Years, and Under Consideration</u>.

State—Required Testing for Initial Certification of Teachers
Testing Enacted Before 1984 and in 1984

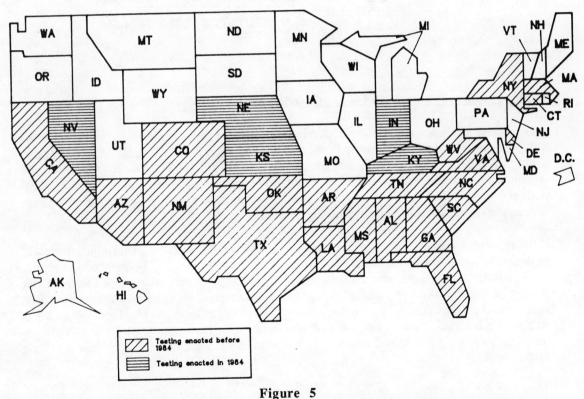

Figure 5

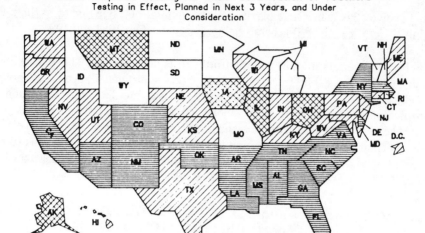

State-Required Testing for Initial Certification of Teachers
Testing in Effect, Planned in Next 3 Years, and Under Consideration

Figure 6

Creating More Effective Schools: Current Trends

What policies and practices are being implemented? First, nearly two-thirds of the states increased high school graduation requirements between 1980-84. (See Figure 7 - Change in Number of Course Units Required for High School Graduation, 1980 to 1984). Will the increased academic requirements affect all students the same way? If it is the consensus of many of the national reports and studies - that there are significant numbers of students in our schools that are not being well served - what will be the result of raising the standards?

If stricter academic requirements do what they were adopted to do, no doubt some of the effects will be desirable. On an individual basis, some students' lives may be enriched by the added exposure; other collective benefits may accrue, such as large percentages of upcoming cohorts internalizing the critical thinking skills of science because society made study in that field imperative. More students will pursue rigorous, challenging courses. Some will be better prepared for college work, will require less remediation there, and can gain more credit for advanced placement. Stronger backgrounds in academic subjects may make it possible for college students to specialize in their studies earlier.

There remains, however, the possibility that these added requirements will prove counter-productive for substantial numbers of students, and thus ultimately for society. To explore this issue, it may be useful to divide entrants of high school into four categories. (See Figure 8 - Increased Academic Requirements).

The first category corresponds roughly to the 31 percent of academically successful students who eventually enter four-year colleges. Category two reflects the fact that 18 percent of high school students enter two-year college programs after high school. The third category is the approximately 24 percent of students who are currently destined for - or typically interested in - further education; but they are likely to enter the work force immediately upon graduation. The last category of students are those most likely to fail and dropout of school prior to graduation; they now do so at a national rate of 27 percent (Brandt, 1985)

Change in Number of Course Units Required for High School Graduation, 1980 to 1984

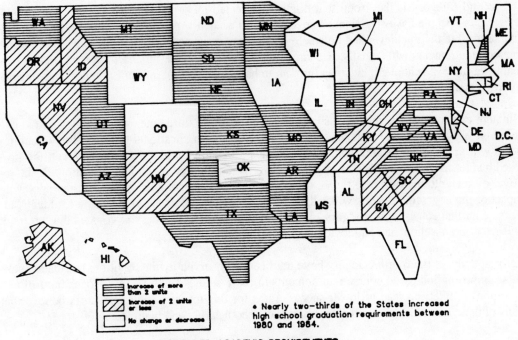

* Nearly two-thirds of the States increased high school graduation requirements between 1980 and 1984.

INCREASED ACADEMIC REQUIREMENTS

Will They Affect All Students the Same Way?
(Breakdown of High School Entrants)

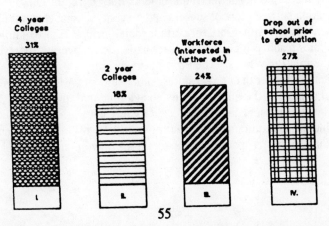

Barring the possibility that course content will be diluted to accommodate students with less academic aptitude, new requirements will probably change life very little for the first category of students. College entrance requirements and expectations have always governed programs of study for college- bound students, and college requirements generally demand as much or more than the mandates require. Moreover, since these top performers have always expended great effort in school, impressive quantitative increments in their achievement are unlikely. The greatest difference for these students will perhaps be slightly different academic distribution and fewer available electives.

The second category is the group that might be affected most positively by new requirements. These young people have sufficient perseverance and academic orientation to have postsecondary aspirations, but their achievement falls below that of the most academically talented. Whether increased requirements will actually discourage their efforts remains an unsettled issue. The intervening variable of school climate may turn out to have a significant influence on how this population responds.

Although current national averages suggest that most of the third category of students graduate from high school, large percentages of these students are in vocational tracks that new requirements will scale down or eliminate in most states. As an example of this movement, the proposed budget for fiscal year '87-88 recommends zero funding for vocational education. If the removal of such alternatives results in extensive withdrawals among this category, the aggregate impact of the new requirements will reduce rather than increase academic learning for many students. Simultaneously, this category of students will be denied access to courses that promote their retention in school and employability.

Many students in the fourth category have not been well served by the traditional academic subjects. Imposing increased course requirements in these studies (with stronger focus on drill and repetition) is likely to lead to lower success rates for this group. Some educators believe that many of these borderline students may drop out of school earlier and in greater numbers.

Increased Requirements and Equity Education.

Many believe that the increased academic requirements may hit equity broadside. The present strong negative correlation between school success and diversity among students already challenges the capacity of our schools to compensate for certain social groups. For example, current reports of Hispanic drop-out rates reach as high as 35 percent nationwide. Overall, Black drop-out rates are 21 percent - twice the rate for Whites. The drop-out rates among the lower socioeconomic students are also significantly higher than those among other students. If more third and fourth-category students respond to increased requirements by abandoning their pursuit of a diploma, society's "have-nots" will be the ones most negatively affected by the new requirements. Concern is therefore growing that if increased requirements push drop-out rates still higher, education, already unable to forestall the formation of a "permanent underclass," may unwittingly make a bad situation worse (Brandt, 1985)

The national commitment to excellence and higher standards place a serious responsibility on all of us to weigh any proposal very carefully if it seems likely to disengage more people from the functioning society. I am not suggesting that we should be anti-academic or anti-higher standards, but I am suggesting that we need to seriously examine the *logic* and possible *consequences* of such reforms. Let me provide an analogy. For a number of years the high jump bar has been set at four feet. We had some students who were able to make that height, but we also had students who were unable to meet that challenge. Now, we have raised the bar to four feet six inches. Common sense would tell us that we will more than likely have greater numbers of students who will not be able to meet this new height. To carry the analogy farther, if one does not provide additional coaching/or practice time for those particular students, the logic of raising the bar is questionable. Simply to raise the standards, and not address the needs for a growing number of students in our schools, will only enhance the likelihood of more students not being successful.

The Continuum of Equitable Competence for Schools

The word competence is used because it implies having the capacity to function effectively. An equitably competent school system -at all levels- acknowledges and incorporates the importance of the multi-dimensional aspects of equity.

Certainly this description of equitable competence seems idealistic. How can a school accomplish of these things? How can a school achieve the higher expectations, new attitudes and policies? Equity competence may be viewed as a goal towards with schools can strive. Accordingly, becoming equitably competent is a developmental process. No matter how proficient a school may become, there will always be room for growth and improvement. It is a process in which the school can measure its progress according to the school's goals and specific objectives for school improvement. As the objectives are defined the school will be guided toward a more progressively equitable system. First, it is important for a school to internally assess its level of equitable competence.

To better understand where a school is in the process of becoming more equitably competent, it is useful to think of the possible ways of responding to school improvement. Imagine a continuum which ranges from Inequality to Advanced Equitable Competence. There are a variety of possibilities between these two extremes. (See Figure: 9 - The Continuum of Equitable Competence for Schools).

Inequality. The most negative end of the continuum is represented by attitudes, policies, and practices which are destructive to certain groups of students, consequently to the individuals within that group. The most extreme example of this orientation are schools which actively participate in the systematic attempt to treat groups differently. An historical example, would be the Plessy v. Ferguson(1896) Supreme Court decision - which stated the doctrine of "separate but equal." While we currently do not see many examples of this extreme in our schools, it provides us with a reference point for understanding the various possible responses to equitable competency. A school which adheres to this extreme assumes that one race is superior and should eradicate "lesser" groups because of their perceived subhuman position. Bigotry coupled with vast power differentials allows the dominant group to disenfranchise, control, exploit or systematically destroy the targeted population.

THE CONTINUUM OF EQUITABLE COMPETENCE FOR SCHOOLS

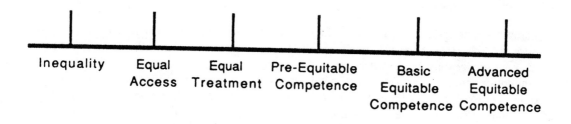

| Inequality | Equal Access | Equal Treatment | Pre-Equitable Competence | Basic Equitable Competence | Advanced Equitable Competence |

Figure 9

Equitable Access. The next position on the continuum is one at which the school does not intentionally seek to be negative, but lacks the capacity to help targeted populations. The system remains extremely biased, believes in the superiority of the dominant group and assumes a paternal posture towards "lesser" groups. These schools may disproportionately apply resources, discriminate against people of color, support segregation as a desirable policy. The schools enforce racist policies and maintain stereotypical beliefs about certain groups. Such schools are often characterized by ignorance and an unrealistic fear of people who happen to be different that the majority. The characteristics of equitable access include: discriminatory hiring practices, subtle messages to people of color that they are not valued or welcome, and generally lower expectations of diverse students.

Equal Treatment. At the midpoint of the continuum the school has an expressed philosophy of being unbiased. They function with the belief that "diversity" makes no difference and that we are all the same. Schools are characterized by the belief that approaches traditionally used by the majority are universally applicable; if the school worked as it should, all people - regardless of background - would be served with equal effectiveness. This view reflects a well intended liberal philosophy; however, the consequences of such a belief are to make the school so ethnocentric as to render them useless to all but the most assimilated.

Such schools ignore cultural strengths, encourage assimilation and blame the students for their problems. Members of diverse backgrounds are viewed from the cultural deprivation model which asserts that problems are the result of inadequate resources. Outcome is usually measured by how closely the students approximates a middle class non-minority student. These schools may participate occasionally in special projects with targeted populations when monies are specifically available or with the intent of "helping" the disadvantaged population. Unfortunately, such projects are often conducted without proper guidance and are the first casualties when funds run out. Equal treatment schools suffer from a deficit of information and often lack the avenues through which they can obtain the needed information. While these schools often view themselves as unbiased and responsive to non-majority needs, their enthocentrism is reflected in attitude, policy and practice.

Pre-Equitable Competence. As schools move toward the positive end of the scale they reach a position referred to as equitable pre-competence. This stage on the continuum implies movement. This pre-equitable school realizes its weaknesses in serving certain students and attempts to improve some aspect(s) of their programs to a specific population. Such schools try experiments, hire minority staff, explore how to reach targeted populations more effectively, initiate staff development for their staffs on cultural diversity, enter into needs assessments concerning targeted populations, and recruit diverse populations to serve on boards of directors and advisory committees.

Pre-equitable schools are characterized by the desire to deliver a quality education and a commitment to civil rights. These schools are responsive to non-majority populations, by asking, "what can we do?" One danger at this level is a false sense of accomplishment or of failure that prevents the school from moving forward along the continuum. A school may believe that the accomplishment of one goal or activity fulfills their obligation to the expressed needs of a targeted community or may undertake an activity that fails and are therefore reluctant to try again.

Another danger is tokenism. The pre-equitable school, however, has begun the process of becoming equitably competent and often only lacks information on what is possible and how to proceed.

Basic Equitable Competence. Basic equitably competent schools are characterized by acceptance and respect for difference, continuing self-assessment regarding diversity, careful attention to the dynamics of difference, continuous expansion of cultural knowledge and resources, and a variety of adaptations to models in order to better meet the needs of all students. The basic equitable school works to hire unbiased teachers and staff, seeks advice and consultation from the community and actively decides what is and is not capable of providing.

Advanced Equitable Competence. The most positive end of the scale is advanced equitable competence or an effective school. This point on the continuum is characterized by holding diversity in high esteem. The advanced equitable school seeks to add to the knowledge base of equitable competence by conducting research, establishing pilot projects, and disseminating the results of demonstration projects. The advanced equitable school hires staff who are specialists in equity issues. Such schools advocate equity throughout the school system and improved relations between cultures throughout our society.

In conclusion, the degree of equitable competence a school achieves is not dependent on any one factor. *Attitudes, policies,* and *practice* are three major arenas where development can and must occur if a school is to move toward equitable competence. Attitudes change to become less ethnocentric and biased. Policies change to become more flexible and culturally impartial. Practices become more congruent with the culture of the student from one year to the next. Positive movement along the continuum results from an aggregate of factors at various levels of a school's structure. Every level of the school (school board, policymakers, administrators, teachers and students), can and must participate in the process. At each level the principles of valuing difference, self-assessment, understanding dynamics, building cultural knowledge and adapting practices can be applied. As each level makes progress in implementing the principles, and as attitudes, policies and practices change, the school becomes more equitably competent.

Summary

The goal of educational reform today is quality. Some educators believe that the new emphasis may not mesh with equity concerns; and some observers believe it may be detrimental to those who cannot meet the latest requirements.

A recent report by a coalition of child advocacy groups warned that "at risk" children have largely been ignored in the rush for educational reform. The report entitled, Barriers to Excellence: Our Children at Risk (1982), said, "policymakers at many different levels talk of bringing excellence to schools and ignore the fact that hundreds of thousands of youngsters are not receiving even minimal educational opportunities guaranteed under law." Its recommendations included continued attention to the rights of the disadvantaged, more democratic governance of the schools, the establishment of comprehensive early childhood education and day care programs, and the enactment of more equitable and adequate systems for financing schools.

Another recent study (Finn, 1981) suggests that "the new equity agenda" (one that includes both excellence and equity concerns), raises four separate issues: the differential impact of higher standards and tougher requirements; differential access to new curricula and better teaching; differential access to master teachers; and differential access to computers. These issues are very specific to individual sites. Great variation is easily possible within the same school district. Measuring these elements, and taking steps to ensure equitable treatment is likely to prove more challenging than the equity initiatives of the 1960s and '70s.

Whether the recent national, state and local efforts to improve education will be a passing phenomenon or a genuine transformation of elementary and secondary education remains to be seen. The result will depend largely on the actions of state policymakers in the next few years. Precisely, what the states should do to maintain the impetus of reform is unclear. Defining a common set of tasks for all states is impossible. What California should do (and can do) is far different from the agenda in Mississippi. Indeed, if there were a single set of solutions equally applicable to the fifty states, the federal government would probably have pursued it.

As we have seen, some observers are concerned that today's preoccupation with quality will run counter to the nation's interest in equity. Such concern, although well motivated, is misplaced. Quality-with-equity are not mutually exclusive; to the contrary, they reinforce one another. Quality and equity and are in conflict only if "equal outcomes" are expected. Quality means that some students will do better than others; equity means that each will be given an equal chance. A school that fears quality because it means unequal outcomes may be sure of one thing: That school will be neither excellent or equal.

WORKSHEET 1

1. Purkey and Smith identified several characteristics of good schools. Select five characteristics you believe to the most important for a school to incorporate. (Rank order your five selections).

   Number 1: _Clear goals, high exp._

   Number 2: _Leadership_

   Number 3: _Staff stability_

   Number 4: _Parental / comm. involvement_

   Number 5: _Collab. planning_

Provide a brief rationale for your selection and ranking:

Number 1: _We know where we're going and why_

Number 2: _We have a principal who will stand up for her school community and upholds goals & standards_

Number 3: _We have people who have worked here, want to be here_

Number 4: _Our community believes in this school and nurtures it_

Number 5: _We work together as a team, not atomistically in our separate rooms._

How do the five characteristics you have chosen compliment or conflict with an equity perspective? Explain.

①︎ could be a problem if we don't make at least probable for each student to succeed. ③︎ could be if we value keeping veterans at the expense of new blood. ②︎ could be a problem if the principal is just a Mussolini who makes the trains run on time.

2. Do you believe that prospective classroom teachers should have to take a competency test prior to certification? Why or why not?

Yes. There is a certain minimum knowledge of the subject and of pedagogy each must have.

Do you believe that "certified" classroom teachers should have to take a competency test? Why or why not?

Yes, if it was not done before. Changing standards have brought in the less qualified teacher.

3. What is the agency that governs the accreditation of teacher education programs?

NCATE

4. What is outcomes accreditation/evaluation? Briefly explain the process.

This is where the school is measured in terms of individual student success rather than just by the accreditation board + std'ized scores, where target goals are identified, staff members design and monitor compliance.

5. Identify the six phases on the continuum for equity competence for schools.

Inequality
Equal Access
Equal Treatment → Pre-Equitable Compet-
Basic Equitable Comp.
Advanced Eq. Competence

In your opinion, where do you believe most schools are on the continuum today? Explain your opinion.

Somewhere between Equal Treatment and Pre-Basic Equitable Competence. We're reaching more students and doing better, but there is still a residual--often men of a certain age -- who think it is merely necessary to provide the same thing to everyone.

6. Nearly two-thirds of the states increased high school graduation requirements between 1980-84. Will these increased academic requirements affect all students the same way? Explain.

_____ Yes ___✓___ No

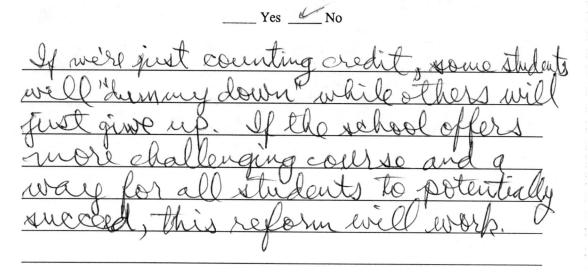

If we're just counting credit, some students will "dummy down" while others will just give up. If the school offers more challenging course and a way for all students to potentially succeed, this reform will work.

Do you agree or disagree with the concern raised by some of the educators that these new standards may be counter-productive for a significant number of students? Explain.

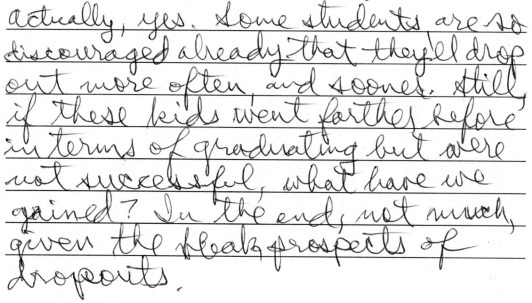

Actually, yes. Some students are so discouraged already that they'll drop out more often, and sooner. Still, if these kids went farther before in terms of graduating but were not successful, what have we gained? In the end, not much, given the bleak prospects of dropouts.

7. There is a growing shortage of minority teachers. Given that fact, how would you respond to the statement, "you don't need minority teachers to teach minority youth."

Well, you don't. Even white guys like me could do it. But we shouldn't be the only ones. Students will work with all kinds of folks someday, so their teachers too should be a variety. However, schools, like businesses, need to other incentives to get minority teachers.

8. If you were a member of a team that was asked to spend some time in a school (say a week) to determine if that school was an effective school - what would you want to know about that school or what would you look for?

I'd want to talk to a cross section of everybody: students, teachers, admin, staff, parents, community. I'd want numbers: demographic, test scores. I'd want to hear alumni, and employers and college professors. I'd want to see interaction in classrooms, hall-ways, yards, cafeteria, library.

REFERENCES

Adler, Mortimer J. The Paideia Proposal - An Educational Manifesto. Macmillian Publishing Co, New York, 1982.

Bickel, William E. "Effective Schools: Knowledge, Dissemination and Inquiry." Educational Researcher, April, 1983. p. 4.

Boyer, Ernest High School: A Report on Secondary Education in America. Harper and Row. New York, 1983.

Brandt, Ron (Ed.) With Consequences for All. The ASCD Task Force on High School Graduation Requirements, Washington, D.C., 1985.

Coleman, James S. The Concept of Equality of Educational Opportunity. Harvard University Press, Cambridge: MA, 1969.

Finn, Chester E. "A Call For Quality Education." Life Magazine, March, 1981, pp. 68-77.

Goodlad, John I. Place Called School: Prospects for the Future. McGraw Hill Book Co. New York: 1984, p. 30.

Jencks, Christopher et. al., Inequality: A Reassessment of the Effect of Family and Schooling in America. Basic Books, New York, 1972.

Mosteller, Frederick, &   Moynihan, Daniel P. (Eds.) On Equality of Educational Opportunity". Random House. New York, 1972.

National Commission on Excellence in Education. A Nation at Risk: The Imperative for Educational Reform. U.S. Government Printing Office, Washington, D.C., 1983. p. 180.

North Central Accreditation Handbook. "The NCA OA/E Guide: A Handbook for Outcomes Accreditation/Evaluation Schools. Commission on Schools - North Central Association of Colleges and Schools. Boulder, Colorado.

Odden, A., & Dougherty, U. State Programs of School Improvement: A 50-State Survey, Education Commission of the States. Denver, CO, 1982.

Purkey, S. C., & Smith, M. S. "Effective Schools - A Review." Elementary School Journal, 1983, pp. 427-452.

Ravitch, Diane The Troubled Crusade. Basic Books, Inc., New York: N.Y., 1984, p. 169.

Research About Teacher Education (RATE), Fall, 1988.

Sandefur, J. T. State Assessment Trends. American Association of Colleges for Teacher Education Briefs, Washington, D.C., 1984. p. 17.

Sizer, Theodore Horace's Compromise - The Dilemma of the American High School. Houghton Mifflin Publishing Co., Boston: MA, 1984.

U.S. Department of Education. The Nation Responds: Recent Efforts to Improve Education. U.S. Government Printing Office, Washington, D.C., 1984, p. 11.

SUGGESTED READINGS

Adler, Mortimer J. The Paideia Proposal: An Educational Manifesto. Macmillian Publishing Company, New York, 1982.

Boyer, Ernest L. High School: A Report on Secondary Education in America. Harper and Row, New York, 1983.

Goodlad, John I. A Place Called School: Prospects for the Future. McGraw Hill, New York, 1984.

Goodlad, John I. "Classroom Organization." Encyclopedia of Educational Research, 3rd Edition., ed. Chester Harris New York, 1960.

Nathan, Joe Free to Teach. Winston Press, Minneapolis, MN, 1984.

Oakes, Jeannie Keeping Track - How Schools Create Inequality. Yale University Press, New Haven, CO, 1985.

CHAPTER FOUR

The Heart of Equity: The Classroom Teacher

Introduction

The nation is experiencing a major renaissance in education. In the first three chapters, we have examined some of the flurry of educational reform that has been stimulated by actions of national commissions, governors, legislators, accreditation agencies, and state and local educational agencies. As we have seen, this educational reform movement is generating new and higher standards for students at all levels and higher expectations for educational professionals. The primary goal is to improve of the quality of teaching and learning in the schools of the United States.

As we have seen many of the recent reports view teachers as the essential ingredient of successful education. In Horace's Compromise, Sizer (1984) calls teachers "the crucial element." He writes, *an imaginative, appropriate curriculum placed in an attractive setting can be unwittingly smothered by journeyman instructors. It will be eviscerated by incompetents. On the other hand, good teachers can inspire powerful learning in adolescents, even under the most difficult circumstances.*

Chapter 4 - **The Heart of Equity: The Classroom Teacher** is intended to address the issues of: (1) What is meant by effective teaching? (2) What are the most common approaches to classroom instruction? (3) What are the expectations of the classroom teacher? and, (4) What specific policies and practices need to be addressed with regard to educational equity?

The reports all conclude that the poor quality of teachers is a major reason for the crisis in education. The National Commission on Excellence (1983), for example, found that the quality of America's teachers had slipped dramatically in recent years. The Commission concluded that "not enough of the academically able students are being attracted to teaching; that teacher preparation programs need substantial improvement; that the professional working life of teachers is on the whole unacceptable; and that a shortage of teachers exists in key fields."

All observers agree that any efforts to reform the schools must pay careful attention to the teaching force. In Sizer's words (1984), "improving American secondary education absolutely depends on improving the conditions of work and the respect for teachers."

Effective Teaching.

Effective teaching is very difficult to define because the term "effective" is so value-laden. What appears to be effective teaching to one person may be considered poor teaching by another, because each one values different outcomes or methods. One teacher may run the classroom in a very organized, highly-structured manner, emphasizing the intellectual content of the academic disciplines. Another may conduct the class in a less-structured environment, allowing the students much more freedom to choose subject matter and activities that interest them personally. Because of one's value system, an observer may identify the first teacher as an "effective" teacher, while he/she may criticize the second teacher for running "too loose a ship." Another observer may come to the opposite conclusion with respect to which teacher is better, again, because of a different set of values.

While it remains difficult to agree on what effective teaching is, effective teaching can be demonstrated. The effective teacher is one who is able to bring about intended learning outcomes. The nature of the learning is still most important, but two different teachers, as in the example above, may strive for and achieve very different outcomes and both be judged effective. *The two critical dimensions of effective teaching are intent and achievement.*

While effective teachers are defined as teachers who can demonstrate the ability to bring about intended learning outcomes, what enables them to achieve desired results with students? Have you ever stopped to think about what, if anything, makes teachers different from other well-educated adults? What should effective, professional teachers know, believe, or be able to do that distinguishes them from other people?

Some people will state the crucial dimension is the teacher's personality. Teachers, they will say, should be friendly, cheerful, sympathetic, morally virtuous, enthusiastic, and humorous. Ryan (1988) concluded that effective teachers are fair, democratic, responsive, understanding, kindly, stimulating, original, alert, attractive, responsible, steady, poised, and confident. Ineffective teachers were described as partial, autocratic, aloof, restricted, harsh, dull, stereotyped, apathetic, unimpressive, evasive, erratic, excitable, and uncertain.

It might be difficult to reach a consensus on exactly what knowledge and skills are unique to the teaching profession, but most educators would agree that special skills and knowledge are necessary and do exist. Certainly teachers must be familiar with children and their developmental stages. They must know something about events and happenings outside the classroom and school. They must possess enough command of the subject they are going to teach to be able to differentiate what is important and central from what is incidental and peripheral. They must have a philosophy of education to help guide them in their role as teachers. They must know how human beings learn and how to create environments which facilitate learning. Effective teaching, in essence, is the ability to communicate what one knows in a way others can understand them.

The Need for Reform.

Most teachers teach in much the same way they were taught - in an essentially didactic, teacher-centered mode. Often this mode is dictated by the subject matter, which is outside the students' intuitive experience; the teacher knows the material and presents it to students, whose role is to absorb it. It is important to examine the strengths and weaknesses of this practice, for it has implications for the way students experience learning and for the way they perceive school.

In most classes, it is the teacher who determines the plan, the pace, and the specific activities for the day. This is as it should be, since presumably the teacher knows the subject, knows from experience what is within the interest and ability of the class, and knows how to present material so that students can assimilate it. To encourage student learning, the easiest and most common method of developing motivation is to use grades, and the easiest format for presenting material is the lecture. In a lecture, the teacher tells the class what he/she thinks is important, although he/she may modify the telling by asking questions that call for specific answers.

This process has many benefits. In the first place, it is a very efficient method of conveying information and making sure that material is retained, at least over a short span of time. A teacher can emphasize what needs to be emphasized, make difficult concepts understandable, and present summaries of what years of experience have shown to be important. Moreover, this teacher- centered, didactic model conforms with the community's expectations about what education should be. Most parents had the same kind of experience in school and feel comfortable that this is what their children are receiving. The system provides positive reinforcement of those values between school and family.

By mastering a given body of information, students may feel that they've learned and achieved, and teachers may feel they have accomplished something tangible and measurable. There are clear expectations, narrow boundaries between what is acceptable and what is not acceptable. Beyond this, the challenge of mastery gives a sense of seriousness of purpose and accomplishment. The process teaches students to deal with pressure and stress and to live up to others' expectations of them. If the teacher is able to set challenges that go beyond what students have previously done but not beyond their reach, students can stretch their minds to learn and grow. Teacher- centered instruction sometimes has the effect of forcing students to think about topics they find fascinating but would never have approached on their own. In the best situations, a teacher's passion and enthusiasm and way of seeing the world becomes those of his/her students.

Yet, there are serious liabilities in this way of teaching and the liabilities help to account for some of the problems schools face today. Perhaps above all, the process encourages incredible passivity. In most classes one sits and listens. Some concentration is necessary, but no matter how interesting the teacher, after a number of hours of sitting and listening, boredom almost inevitably follows. Possibly, what becomes boring is not what the teacher is saying, but the very act of sitting and listening for hours in a row. It is difficult for teachers to feel how passive the student's role is, for the role of the teacher is the essence of activity. For example, the minds of classroom teachers are constantly going . . . figuring out how to best present an idea, thinking about whom to call on, whom to draw out, whom to keep quiet; how to get students involved, how to make a point more clear, how to respond; when to be funny and when to be serious. Students experience little of this, as everything is done for them. This inactivity partially explains why students sometimes fail to grasp material even after going over it several times, for in teaching ideas, one must process the ideas and work with them to really understand them. But when only listening to ideas, only a minimal degree of concentration is required.

As Adler (1984) observes, "there is little joy in most of the learning that students are now compelled to do. Too much of it is make-believe, in which neither teacher nor pupil can take a lively interest. Without some joy in learning - a joy that arises from hard work well done and from the participation of one's mind in a common task - basic schooling cannot initiate the young into the life of learning, let alone give them the skill and incentive to engage in it further."

Adler goes on to describe three teaching styles to achieve three education goals: lecturing, to transmit information; coaching, to teach a skill; and Socratic questioning, to enlarge understanding. Adler's conclusion is that "all genuine learning is active, not passive. It involves the use of the mind, not just the memory. It is a process of discovery in which the student is the main agent, not the teacher."

Goodlad (1984) found that barely 5 percent of instructional time in the schools is spent on direct questioning and less than 1 percent is devoted to open questioning that calls for higher - level student skills beyond memory. From questionnaires completed by students and from extensive classroom observations, it becomes apparent that the range of pedagogical procedures employed, particularly in the academic subjects, is very narrow. As Goodlad points out, the teaching observed in his study was characteristically telling or questioning students, reading textbooks, completing workbooks and worksheets, and giving quizzes. This pattern became increasingly dominant with the progression upward from primary to secondary classes.

There is a place in the classrooms for telling or lecturing, especially when the goal is the acquiring of organized knowledge. Teachers who can lecture well should do so. There is a place, too, for questions and answers, for structured review and drill. But there comes a time when probing questions should be asked; when the teacher should direct the student's mind from the familiar to that which is less well known but no less important. Socratic questioning is indeed the hallmark of certain great teachers. By this means, students proceed from the obvious to the subtle, from easy assumptions to supporting evidence.

Much of what the teacher must do to succeed in teaching is a matter of common sense - careful planning of each lesson, educational goals for each day's work, pacing and timing, love of the subject matter, and respect for all the students. Clarity in procedures, discipline in carrying through and the careful measurement of accomplishments are essential elements in the formula for success.

We are almost embarrassed that so much about good teaching is so familiar, but at the same time, we are encouraged by this realization. There remain some old-fashioned yet enduring qualities in human relationships that still work - command of the material to be taught, contagious enthusiasm for the work to be done, optimism about the potential of the students, and human sensitivity, that is, integrity and warmth as a human being. As Boyer (1983) expresses, "when we think of a great teacher, most often we remember a person whose technical skills were matched by the qualities we associate with a good and trusted friend."

Our class methods also promote the feeling that students have little control over or responsibility for their own education. Central to understanding this lack of responsibility is the fact that the agenda for the class is the teacher's; it is the teacher who is convinced that the subject matter is worth knowing and that the specific activities planned are the best ways of obtaining this knowledge. Students are often not convinced of this, and sometimes do not see why they have to know or do what the teacher asks. Students are products of a society which no longer automatically assumes that teacher knows best. Without the legitimacy that assumption gives, teachers face a serious motivational task wherein they must convince students that what we think is worth knowing, is worth learning.

Although we say we want to encourage responsibility, we really give little opportunity for students to make a real difference in the way a class goes, aside from doing their homework and participating. If they happen to come to class unprepared, in most cases the class goes on anyway, and students don't really feel the immediate consequences of their lack of effort. Common remarks made by students may include "it doesn't matter whether you do the work or not. The class will continue whether or not you've done your homework." In a lot of classes where students have outside reading, students claim, "The reading is either unrelated, or the teacher will lecture and explain the reading anyway, so they figure, 'why should I read it?' The teacher is just going to explain it; he/she is going to give me the summary. So why bother?"

This lack of responsibility is reinforced by the community's expectation and demand, transmitted to students, that it is the teacher's job to train the students and to maintain strict authority and control over students, to prepare them for what many envision as a rigidly-structured business world in which people must conform. At the same time, as the national reports and commissions have reported, many in the community have lost faith in the educational system and in the teachers. Some no longer believe that teachers have professional expertise and know what they're doing. So it is that while many parents (and students) want teachers to be in control, at the same time they challenge teachers' expertise and authority. As I have suggested before, there is a tendency among some students and parents to believe that poor student performance is caused by poor teaching rather than poor learning. To encourage responsibility, and to encourage students to take a more active role in their own education, teachers need more accurate, on-going information from students about their classes. With the teacher doing most of the work, there is a danger of losing students, not knowing whether they're lost, bored, tuned out, or confused.

Beyond this, our class methods often promote the idea that learning is taking down copious notes and that knowledge is passing it back on a test. We discourage students from trusting their own observations or insights and from asking questions. We also discourage students from listening to each other, for "knowledge is what the teacher tells you." Real intellectual curiosity or pursuing any subject beyond requirements tends to be discouraged because there is so much that must be mastered that there is little time for anything else. Many students don't really learn how to learn, how to follow up a question they're curious about, or why they should want to learn, except to get good grades for college and to please their parent(s). So, for many students, there are two choices: do everything that's expected, or "opt out" completely and do the very minimum. School then becomes a process of doing as little as one can and getting away with as much as one can.

If our schools are to serve the ends of education, we'd better look for ways to make them more effective. A first step toward ending this dilemma is to convince students that what we attempt to teach them is genuinely worth knowing. We can no longer assume that students act on faith in the educational process, as most of us may have done in earlier generations. When I was a teenager in school, I assumed that teachers knew what they were doing, even when I didn't always see the point myself; I trusted that it would all make sense in the end. I am not so sure that students make this assumption today.

Clearly, one direction is to continue to search for ways in which students may be more active in their own education, more responsible for what goes on in class, and more capable of giving constructive reactions and suggestions to teachers. I am certainly not suggesting that students take over the class, but rather we should strive for a better balance than what is currently the norm. Not only must we explain to students why they need to know what we're teaching them, but we must also involve them more fully with their education. We need to make sure that they come to class prepared, and must have the courage not to fill in when significant numbers are not ready for the day's lesson. And we should fail students when they deserve to fail. Our attention must be centered on the effort and responsibility students take to learn, and we must emphasize that learning is an active process on the part of the learner, not the teacher.

We need to build into our class routines some reliable means of finding out, at every step of the way, what is clear and what is not - how and what they're doing is actually getting across to students. Above all, teachers need to talk to students as much as possible. It doesn't follow that they must change their methods, but only that their methods will be more effective if they know for certain what's working and what isn't.

In all situations, it is important to reinforce learning by having students act on it, apply it, or carry it farther themselves. By the time a test comes around, it may be too late. Techniques will vary with subject matter, but the principle is the same. The more active students are in figuring out, applying, and working with information, the better they learn it.

Finally, if we give students room to grow and explore on their own, we need to watch as carefully as we can to make sure they aren't failing miserably. Certainly, they should be allowed to experience failure; the experience is an important lesson. Yet, there is a point when the failure becomes overwhelming and destructive - high risk. If our school system is to work, there must be concerned adults who can find out when students are slipping, and they must have the time and energy to do something about it.

Teacher Expectations.

What are the expectations that classroom teachers have toward students? Don't classroom teachers treat all students the same? Most educators are convinced that teacher expectations are a very critical dimension in the teaching process. Expectations have a direct effect on a teacher's behavior; they determine how teacher's view themselves and interact with others.

Consistently, the issue of high teacher expectations is repeated throughout the national reports and literature for effective schools. Most teachers occasionally harbor attitudes or feelings toward students that are detrimental to their teaching effectiveness. What does the research say?

For example, one of the more common interactions in most classrooms is the question posed by the teacher and the answer generated by the student. Is there equal opportunity to answer? No, say researchers - most teachers call more on their perceived "high" achievers to recite/perform than on those they think less able. There are several reasons for this. Teacher's don't want to embarrass a student they suspect doesn't know the answer. They want their classes to hear correct and thoughtful replies. And high quality student performances obviously reward teachers more.

Research (Antonopolis, 1972, Bloom, 1981, Rosenthal & Jacobsen, 1968, Brophy, 1974, Moran, 1981) has clearly demonstrated that positive teacher expectations improve behavior and increase achievement. When teachers are told that randomly selected students are high achievers, or that these students have been identified as "intellectual bloomers" who are expected to make high academic grades, teacher behavior varies enough to have significantly positive effects on student performance, the classroom and on I.Q. tests.

These research findings clearly demonstrate that teachers have greater expectations for, pay more attention to, and give higher grades to students who come from higher socioeconomic classes and students who are white.

Teachers are also more likely to perceive ethnic minority students and students from lower socioeconomic classes as low achievers. Teachers tend to behave differently toward students who have been labeled low achievers. The result - these students are not provided with an equal opportunity to participate in the classroom instruction and experience. Research clearly has indicated that teachers:

* Interact more with high achievers and ignore and interrupt low achievers more frequently.

* Ask more and higher-level questions of higher achievers and provide low achievers with questions that require simple recall.

* Follow up with probing questions for high achievers and call on someone else if the low achiever is unable to provide a prompt, accurate response.

* Provide a longer wait time for high achievers to respond to a question and cut off response time for low achievers who hesitate.

* Praise high achievers more often and criticize low achievers more frequently.

* Provide supportive communications for high achievers and engage in dominating behaviors with low achievers.

* Provide high achievers with detailed feedback and give less frequent, less accurate and less precise feedback to low achievers.

* Demand more work and effort from high achievers and accept less from low achievers.

* Are physically closer to high achievers than with low achievers.

* Provide more personal compliments and show greater interest in high achievers than with low achievers.

Strategies for More Positive Expectations.

The above summary of research findings may cause an uneasy feeling among classroom teachers. If research has continually been identifying these behaviors and practices about classroom teachers, then what strategies can be taken?

* All students should be held accountable to the same standards for participation in classroom discussions.

* Teachers should maintain a uniform standard of behavior for all students.

* All written and verbal evaluations should be related to academic skills and the particular abilities being assessed.

* Teachers should group students in a manner that avoids segregated instructional or classroom activities.

* Teachers should make a special effort to avoid the use of stereotypes in assessment of and reaction to pupil behavior and achievement.

* Teacher's instructional strategies should relate to the individual learning styles of the students.

* If certain students are less active in classroom discussions and activities, the classroom teacher should make special efforts to include those students.

* Teachers should provide clear and specific information about student work, indicating what is right and what is wrong, suggesting that students can improve.

TESA

Teacher Expectations and Student Achievement (TESA) is an in-service program for teachers of all subjects and across all grade levels, including college. It focuses on the need to provide both low and high performing students with equal learning opportunities. The program covers 15 classroom interactions associated with effective teaching. TESA, which was developed by the Los Angeles County Office of Education in the early 1970s, has a strong research base and was extensively field-tested and widely implemented. Phi Delta Kappa began disseminating the TESA program in 1980. Since that time, by conservative estimates, more than 10,000 coordinators and 85,000 classroom teachers have been trained to implement the program.

The program has two principle objectives:

1. To insure that following training, participating teachers will direct the positive behaviors specified in the interaction model toward students they perceive as low achievers more frequently

than prior training, and as frequently as they direct those behaviors toward students perceived as high achievers.

2. To demonstrate measurable and statistically significant gains in classroom performance for all students, both those perceived to be "low" achievers and those perceived to be "high" achievers.

Strong likes and dislikes of particular students, biases toward or against particular ethnic minority groups, low learning expectations for lower socioeconomic students and biases toward or against certain kinds of student behavior, all can reduce teaching effectiveness. Self-awareness of such attitudes toward individual pupils or classes of students is necessary if teachers are to cope with their own honest feelings and beliefs.

The Power of Tradition and Educational Reform

What policies and practices lead to these alarming differences in the opportunities students have in the schools and classrooms they attend? One such practice and policy that is contributing to this differential opportunity is that of *tracking*.

What is exactly tracking? To address this question, we need to examine the distinction between ability grouping and curriculum differentiation. Proponents of ability grouping stress flexible subject-area assignment. By this they mean that students are assigned to learning groups on the basis of their background and achievement in a subject area at any given moment, and that skills and knowledge are evaluated at relatively frequent intervals. Students showing gains can be shifted readily into another group. They might also be in different ability groups in different subjects, according to their own rate of growth in each subject. This practice suggests a common curriculum shared by all students, with only the mix of student abilities being varied. It also assumes that, within that curriculum, all groups are taught the same material.

In fact, it seems that group placement becomes self-perpetuating, that students are often grouped at the same level in all subjects, and that even a shared curriculum may be taught differently to different groups. Quite often, different ability groups are assigned to different courses of study, resulting in simultaneous grouping by curriculum and ability. Rosenbaum (1976) notes that although ability grouping and curriculum grouping may appear different to educators, in fact they share several social similarities: (1) Students are placed with those defined as similar to themselves and are segregated from those deemed different; (2) group placement is done on the basis of criteria such as ability or postgraduate plans that are unequally esteemed. Thus group membership immediately ranks students in a status hierarchy, formally stating that some students are better than others. Following Rosenbaum, the general term of tracking is applied here to both types of grouping.

Assessing Intelligence and Ability

Insufficient understanding of intelligence and unfair distinctions based on the misuse of tests result in mislabeling, misclassifying and miseducating many students. Too often, educators are overly concerned with classifying students and, as a result, rarely use high-quality, informative assessments to shape instruction at the school and to guide policy decisions.

Popular views of intelligence and ability, as well as perceptions about the distribution of talent in the general population, influence educational practice. What seems fair and reasonable at the moment - tests showing how students compare with others on global characteristics such as mathematics and verbal aptitude - turn out systematically to limit some students' access to knowledge. For the most part, tests of intelligence, ability and achievement simply rank students, separating and segregating them and sorting them for future social participation. Such tests are used to select some students for enriched educational opportunities and slate others for low-level participation. Forecasting failure for some students severely limits their subsequent opportunity in school and later life.

Once the tests identify and legitimize students' differences, students are provided with different school experiences. In contrast, current research in cognitive psychology challenges traditional forms and uses of mental measurement (Education Commission of the States, 1988). The best evidence from this work reveals an abundance of cognitive processes that go unmeasured, that children learn to be intelligent, and that it is possible for schools to nurture mental growth and produce significant gains in the intellectual development of individual learners.

A regrettable side-effect of the widespread misunderstanding of testing and its uses is the current reliance on standardized, norm-referenced tests for judging school quality. It is simplistic to think that students' scores on a set of multiple-choice test items provide very much useful information about the quality of their school experiences. Certainly these test scores reveal something about what students have learned, but because much of the variance in scores can be accounted for by individual students' family background, they say little about overall school quality. Unfortunately, not only the accomplishment of students, but also the goodness of schools, school districts, states and the nation as a whole are being judged by narrow bands of scores on standardized tests. While tests have the potential to provide useful information, they can also distract policy makers from the real business before them - supporting necessary changes in how schooling is conducted.

Grouping and Tracking Practices

Oakes (1985) defines *tracking as the process whereby students are divided into categories so that they can be assigned in groups to various kinds of classes.*

Testing individual aptitudes is the foundation for school practices that identify individual *differences* in order to determine which students get what instruction. Tracking practices begin with the assumptions that differences among students diminish instructional effectiveness, and that students can be assigned fairly and accurately to intellectually homogeneous groups for instruction. This systematic separation of students begins early in their education and forecloses opportunities for enriched coursework for many students. By the secondary level, tracking placements sort students for school opportunities and subsequent social roles.

Children assigned to low-ability classes are taught different, less socially valued knowledge and skills. Emphasis is placed on rote learning, workbooks, kits and easy material. Regardless of ability or motivation, these students' academic mobility is constrained. They stand little chance for an improved school placement because those in low-track classes are usually denied access to the knowledge necessary to participate in more rigorous and interesting work (Oakes, 1985).

Moreover, teachers in low-ability classes tend to be overly concerned with getting students to be punctual, sit quietly and follow directions. They are often seen as less concerned and more punitive. Discipline, class routines and student socializing cut into the classwork of low-ability groups, further eroding these students' opportunities for an education of value.

By contrast, teachers in high-ability classes more often encourage critical thinking and independent questioning. They are more enthusiastic, better organized and make lessons clearer. Students in these advanced groups typically spend more time on learning activities and homework. Nearly all students can indeed benefit from enriched learning opportunities and high-quality experiences in literature, languages, science and mathematics. But sorting practices regularly exclude students from classes with high-quality instruction.

Tracking the myths and misinformation that support these grouping practices constitute a severe barrier to equity in education. The quality of the curriculum and instruction for the high-ability group and the resources that support advance-track students also work well for lower-ability students. While many studies describe students' progress in mixed-ability groups, those not in the top groups or tracks suffer clear and consistent disadvantages from their academic placements. Tracking often seems to retard the educational progress of students identified as average or low. Assignment to low tracks can lower student aspiration and self-esteem and negatively affect attitudes toward school. Sadly, those children who need more time to learn appear to receive less. Those who have the most difficulty succeeding in school have fewer of the best teachers. Those who stand to benefit from classroom with rich resources nearly always get the least (Oakes & Lipton, 1988)

Virtually all studies that address the assignment of students of different academic abilities to different tracks cite severe problems with the practice. Boyer (1983) discussed the effect on students' self-image and motivation, noting that tracking has a "devastating impact on how teachers think about the students and how students think about themselves."

Goodlad (1983) identified problems more tangible than self-image. In upper tracks, he consistently found more use of effective teaching practices - more clarity, organization, and enthusiasm - and more focus on higher-level cognitive processes, such as drawing inferences, synthesizing, and making judgments. In classes that are more heterogeneous in terms of abilities, the studies agree that the teaching is more like upper-track than lower-track classes.

Another disadvantage that students in lower-track classes encounter is being in a classroom where the tone is set by a group of students who are, for the most part, unmotivated and who have low academic self-esteem. Students placed in lower tracks turn out to have higher dropout rates, more school misconduct, and higher delinquency. Track placement apparently affects students' plans for the future over and beyond their aptitudes and grades. A compounding problem is that minority and low socioeconomic students are disproportionately represented in the lower tracks. Goodlad sums up the situation with this observation:

Instead of creating circumstances that minimize and compensate for initial disadvantages in learning, teachers unwittingly create conditions that increase the difficulty of eliminating disadvantage.

Despite what we know about the effects of tracking, the practice continues. The essential question that remains is why? Why do we continue a practice that clearly runs counter to what we say we want in education? As Oakes (1985) suggests, it is in the *"power of tradition."* She also has identified four assumptions upon which the practice of tracking rests. Her research, as well as a number of others, clearly has demonstrated that these assumptions are not supported.

(1) Students learn better in groups of those who are academically similar.

(2) Slower students develop more positive attitudes about themselves and school when they are not in day-to-day classroom contact with those who are much brighter.

(3) Track placements are part of a meritocratic system with assignments earned by students and accorded through fair and accurate means.

(4) Teaching is easier when students are grouped homogeneously, and teaching is better when there are no slower students to lower the common denominator.

Oake's research in 297 classrooms suggests that these assumptions are false. If teachers accept her evidence, they should work to eliminate tracking from schools. However, emerging evidence suggest that educators have not been quick to do so. Finley (1984) found that support for the tracking system in the school came from teachers who competed with each other for high-status students.

How Did We Arrive at Tracking?

At the turn of the century, when just over ten percent of America's youth attended high schools and approximately two-thirds of these students were preparing for college, a relatively common curriculum devoid of tracking was provided. In a sense, what probably would be today's upper and perhaps middle tracks already were self-selected simply by attendance at secondary schools. A marked increase in high school attendance since then and, consequently, greater diversity in student populations changed all of this. The growth in testing not only provided measures of achievement differences among students but also a seemingly scientific basis for sorting them. Tracking became widely practiced by educators as a device for endeavoring to reduce the range of differences in a class and therefore the difficulty and complexity of the teaching task. The practice has been reinforced from outside the school by those who believe that able students are held back by slower ones when all work together in the same class.

For many people, tracking appears to be such a rationale, common-sense solution to a puzzling problem that arguments against it are often ridiculed. The concept has particular appeal for parents who believe their children to be above average in ability and therefore candidates for the more advanced classes. With advancing seniority, many teachers hope to be selected to teach the upper-track students, who are believed to be more eager to learn and less unruly.

The research findings raise some serious questions about the educational benefits claimed for tracking and suggest some negative side effects. But these findings rarely are brought forward beyond the research literature to address tracking policies and practices. If we are to seriously examine equity and establish more effective schools, the practice of sorting students must be addressed.

Methods of Selection.

For ability grouping to operate as intended, the methods of selection would need to be highly valid, objective, and reliable. The evidence is generally discouraging in this regard. When ability is controlled, disproportionate numbers of middle-class students are found in the higher tracks, with a similar disproportion of lower-class students in the lower tracks (Oakes, 1985, Boyer, 1983).

The conclusion - ability grouping is practiced in the official belief that it helps the school meet the needs of individual learners. The mass of evidence suggests that it improves the achievement of few students and lowers that of many; that it damages student's self-esteem; that selection methods tend to be inaccurate and biased; that once initial grouping decisions are made, they tend to assign a stigma that is unalterable and self-fulfilling; and that it is based on erroneous assumptions regarding the validity and stability of intelligence measures and the concept of general aptitude.

One of the goals of our society is to promote the growth of each child through schooling to his/her full academic and social potential. Students come to school with the hope that it can help them gain the academic and occupational skills that will enable them to become somebody and be successful in life. Although this hope is compatible with the espoused goal of the school, in our unequal economic system, not everyone can be equally successful. The school, by sorting, classifying, tracking and labeling students, plays a part in casting students for different occupational roles in the economic system. Questions should be raised as to whether the schools should sort young people into different kinds of roles for future employment, and if so, on what basis should the sorting be done?

The recent work of a number of educators indicates that schools perpetuate social class inequity by assigning students to different positions on the basis of family background. Schools, they say, serve as an instrument of society for allocating students to different levels of status and for making decisions about their life chances. In essence, the school classifies students as good learners, average learners, and poor learners; and these classifications influence the opportunities available to them.

Students can be grouped in two ways: in terms of their abilities and in terms of the curriculum. When ability grouping is used, students are supposedly placed into groups based upon three factors: their prior achievement in the subject area; their mastery of the skills needed to learn the subject; and their learning ability. When curriculum grouping is used, students are divided into areas on the basis of their educational and occupational aspirations so that each can receive instruction in preparation for a specific kind of future. Conant (1967) writes that the purpose of curriculum grouping is to offer "opportunities for those who wish to step from high school right into a job, on the one hand, and to also offer opportunities for those who propose to start . . . college."

Tracking may be formal or informal. For example, in some schools students are officially classified into specific tracks. In other schools there is no official classification, but counselors and teachers know which classes are more challenging and which are easier and assign students accordingly. It is the rare school that doesn't have some mechanism for sorting students. Ability grouping within a single classroom may be fixed for the year or may vary from subject to subject and from month to month. No matter how formal or informal the system may be, the essential characteristics of tracking are similar.

Are there alternatives to tracking?

Clearly, one of the most effective ways to reduce the number of students who will ultimately need remedial services is to provide the best possible classroom instruction in the first place. Therefore, an essential element of an overall strategy to serve low-achieving students is to use classroom instructional methods that have a proven ability to increase student achievement. Slavin (1988) found nearly all the successful programs for classroom change were either continuous progress models or certain forms of cooperative learning.

Continuous progress programs. *reading 4th gr., CIS*

In continuous progress models, students proceed at their own pace through a sequence of well-defined instructional objectives. However, they are taught in small groups composed of students at similar skill levels (but often from different homerooms or even different grades). For example, a teacher might teach a unit on decimals to third, fourth and fifth-graders who have all arrived at the same point in the skills sequence. Students are frequently assessed and regrouped based on these assessments.

Cooperative learning.

There is now substantial evidence that students working together in small cooperative groups can master material presented by the teacher better than can students working on their own (Slavin, 1987).

What is cooperative learning? Cooperative learning refers to a set of instructional methods, in which students work in small, mixed-ability learning groups (Slavin, 1987). The groups usually have four members - one high achiever, two average achievers, and one low-achiever. The students in each group are responsible not only for learning the material being taught in class, but also for helping their groupmates learn. Often, there is some sort of group goal.

Like continuous progress programs, cooperative learning has been found to boost the achievement of average and high achievers as well as low achievers. In addition, cooperative learning has a consistent positive influence on self-esteem and human relations. Four student team learning methods have been extensively developed and researched. Two are general cooperative learning methods adaptable to most subjects and grade levels: *Student Teams -Achievement Divisions, or STAD, and Teams-Games-Tournament, or TGT.* The remaining two are comprehensive curricula designed for use in particular subjects at particular grade levels: *Team Accelerated Instruction (TAI) for mathematics in grades 3-6, and Cooperative Integrated Reading and Composition (CIRC) for reading and writing instruction in grades 3-5.* These four methods all incorporate team rewards, individual accountability, and equal opportunities for success, but in different ways (Slavin, 1988).

A substantial body of research has established that two conditions must be fulfilled if cooperative learning is to enhance student achievement substantially. First, students must be working toward a group goal, such as earning certificates or some other recognition. Second, success at achieving this goal must depend on the individual learning of all group members (Slavin, 1983, 1984)

Success for All

Success for All (Slavin, 1988) combines the most effective programs and requires a comprehensive restructuring of the elementary school. In *Success for All*, the school takes responsibility to insure that no child falls behind in basic skills and that every child will reach the third grade on time with adequate skills. The program integrates several components from the research cited earlier. It uses a structured one-to-one tutoring program for students (especially first graders) who are falling behind in reading; preschool and extended-day kindergarten programs focusing on language skills and self-esteem; a continuous-progress program for grades 1-3 that uses many elements of cooperative learning; and a family support program to encourage parent involvement and home support of the school's goals.

The Accelerated School Model

Generally, low-achieving students are assisted with *remedial services,* which often pulls them out of regular classrooms. Unfortunately, experience has shown that this strategy will keep these students from becoming academically able because: 1) it institutionalizes them as slow learners, thus reducing expectations for their success; 2) it slows down the pace of instruction so that they get farther and farther behind their peers; 3) it emphasizes the mechanics of basic skills without giving them the substance that will keep them interested and motivated; 4) it provides no way to close the achievement gap between *disadvantaged* and *advantaged* students; and 5) it does not help teachers and parents formulate strategies to improve the learning of their students and children (Levin, 1989).

The *Stanford Accelerated Schools Project* has designed an accelerated elementary school that will help these children catch up with their non-disadvantaged peers by the end of the sixth grade. The entire school is dedicated to this objective, and this commitment is reflected in the involvement of many participants. Teachers, parents, and students have high expectations, and set deadlines for students to meet particular educational requirements. The educational staff tailors the accelerated school's dynamic, instructional programs for its own needs. And the program uses all available re-sources in the community - including parents, senior citizens, and social agencies.

The philosophy of the accelerated school is the notion that we can treat at-risk students in the same way that we treat "gifted and talented" students. In short, we must accelerate, not remediate.

Summary

Educational doctrines and practices in the United States were developed largely before 1945, following the structure of the society and the characteristics of the clientele of earlier times. When most people were employed as unskilled or semi- skilled laborers, and only 5 percent were in professional or managerial occupations, most persons could survive with little or no formal education and only a few would utilize college education in their work. Under those conditions, a major function of the schools and colleges was to sort children and youth, pushing out those who were judged least promising for further education and encouraging a few to go on. The lock-step process of instruction and the grading system were developed to sort students, rather than to help every child and youth get an education. By moving the whole class at the same rate from topic to topic, pacing the movement in terms of the performance of the average student, those with more difficulty in school learning would be certain to get further and further behind, and many would give up trying. This was reinforced by the grading system, which year by year gave low marks to those having difficulty, thus helping to discourage them from going on. At the same time, the system assigned high marks to those who learned school tasks easily and quickly, thus encouraging them to continue their formal education.

These policies and practices have existed for so long that we rarely know how sharply they differ from those of an institution devoted to effective teaching and learning. An institution concerned primarily with learning and teaching follows procedures based on the available knowledge of how people learn; whereas our schools and colleges, while only partly concerned with helping each student learn, have been preoccupied with grading, classifying and other sorting functions. This was appropriate for society in an earlier era when the positions available for the occupational, social and political elite were few in number. Then the schools and colleges were a major means for rationing educational opportunities to conform to the social structure. It seemed sensible to give everyone a chance to jump the hurdles and to record the results, reporting them in a way that would influence children, youth and their parents to seek further educational opportunities based only on earlier success.

Today we have a different situation. The critical task is no longer sorting students but rather educating a much larger proportion to meet current opportunities. An inappropriate attitude which has widespread acceptance is the practice of assessing the *deficiencies* of students, that is, the aspects in which they deviate from the norms of middle-class students. These deficiencies must be overcome, it is argued, before this student is really ready for learning what the school seeks to teach. The conception overlooks the many positive characteristics of at-risk students and thus furnishes no suggestions about strengths on which their school learning can be built.

The acceptance of the ideas that many students have limited capacity for learning and that the procedures of teaching and learning which are effective with middle-class students are the appropriate ones for all students. They lead naturally to the common practice of making small revisions in these practices in efforts to develop programs for educating at-risk students. In contrast to this, the recognition that all students can learn when effective conditions for their learning are provided stimulates an effort to construct new programs based on a systematic consideration of these conditions for effective learning.

Success has been slow and will continue to be slow as long as educators have the notion that a student's learning capacity, rather than learning experience, is the main factor in limiting a student's education.

The issue of who is educable has become a function of whom society wants to educate, rather than who is most likely to benefit from the opportunity to learn. Education has traditionally provided services to learners and has left the responsibility for learning to the student. If the learner did not learn, we questioned the quality of the learner, not the quality of the education system. If we seek to assess quality of learning we must examine much more carefully the delicate balance of interactions among learning behavior, learning environments, including the quality of teaching and learning task demands.

Teachers have long been seen as the obvious focus for intervention. After all, teachers are ultimately the ones who either teach students or fail to teach them. As Adler states, *There are no unteachable children. There are only schools and teachers and parents who fail to teach them.*

When the learning situation does not reflect the background of the student, a gap exists between the contexts of learning and the contexts of performing. This gap exists, as we have seen, most often for those students who are not a part of mainstream America. The evidence gathered throughout the past decade demonstrates that educational failure rests in the institution of schooling, and the promise of equity can only be accomplished through the transformation of schools - a restructuring of policies and practices. This growing gap between expectations and achievements of education is most serious. It affects the quality of our lives and the lives of all our students - especially those students who are not being well served by our schools.

What must concern us is the *degree* to which many schools fail to come within striking distance of being anywhere near the quality-with-equity goal. The current school reform emphasis on excellence offers an opportunity to focus on those aspects of schooling that limit learning and foreclose opportunity. Inappropriately narrow instructional activities, incomplete and unbalanced curricula and erroneous conceptions of individual differences and abilities must be corrected. For mainstream, middle-class youth, these are issues of excellence replacing mediocrity. For students at risk of school failure, they become matters of survival.

The nation needs to go beyond basic assurances of fair access to schools and school programs and expect more than equal access to mediocrity. Schools, themselves - in their organization, in curriculum and instruction and in the professional preparation and work lives of educators - limit the learning opportunities they profess to provide.

CLASS ACTIVITY

An Experience in Choice, Discrimination, Prejudice and Values

Purpose: To provide students with an experience that will sensitize them to the inter-workings of choice, discrimination, prejudice and values.

To provide students with an experience that will sensitize them to the inter-workings of grouping/or tracking of students.

To provide students with an experience that will sensitize them to the inter-workings of a classroom with a diversity of students; with a diversity of needs and problems encountered on a day-to-day basis.

Introduction

You are a member of a team of teachers who must establish a seventh-grade classroom. You are to select only 15 students from the list for the class, from the descriptions of the candidates provided. The only criteria to be used in completing this task are the following:

1. Each teacher is to independently list his/her personal choices of the 15 students to be included (by name);

2. Selections and rejections should be made thoughtfully, with the teacher prepared to provide a rationale for the choices;

3. When completed, teachers should be randomly divided into groups of 4-5. Each teacher will then share his/her choices and a brief reason for each selection. Also, each teacher will share in the group reasons why students were not selected.

4. The collective task for the team of teachers will be to establish a consensus regarding which of the 15 students will be a part of their class. A brief rationale for each choice is recommended.

Note: To save "in-class time," it is highly recommended that students do their independent selections before this class activity.

Instructors should plan to allow 30-45 minutes for small group work in class.

CONFIDENTIAL: CANDIDATES FOR CLASS ROSTER — *7th Grade*

Linda: Linda is a truly gifted student with an I.Q. of 140. She knows it and flaunts it. She is excellent in all her academic subjects and demands a lot of extra preparation time from her teachers. Her work is all above grade level. Prefers to work alone.

Accept _____   Not Accept _____

Sarah: Sarah is just a good kid. She is always polite and mannerly. Her classmates however, see her as the teacher's pet. She is always willing to assist her teachers' in daily routines. Judy has good grades overall; especially good in language arts. Single goal orientation, wants to finish assignments before taking on another.

Accept _____   Not Accept _____

Charles: Charles is the class snitch. He is the teacher's informant. He tells the teacher who was disruptive and what took place while the teacher was out of the classroom. His grades are fair. His strengths are in art and music. Charles is a poor reader. He is not a very good listener. Charles is constantly seeking adult approval. Very little parental support offered. Works well in small group acitivities.

Accept _____   Not Accept_____

Travis: Travis is generally rejected by his peers. He is noticeably financially poorer than his classmates and seems to always be untidy. His grades are about average and he is especailly good in art and physical education. He is from a single-parent family, with the father in the home. He present no behavior problem. Responds to one-to-one instruction very well. He is poor in mathematics. Likes computer work.

Accept _____   Not Accept _____

Joe: Joe is a low-achieving student. He is a hard worker, but needs a lot of one-to-one instruction. He has made excellent progress in the past two years. He seems to respond to group work best. He comes from a family that has not been successful in school; in fact his two older brothers dropped out of school. Socially, he is never seen with his classmates. He presents no classroom management problem.

Accept _____   Not Accept _____

Nancy: Nancy is best described as "out-to-lunch." She does things such as attempting math and reading seat work simultaneously, and ends up doing neither accurately nor completely. Her grades are generally poor to fair; although she is capable of doing much better work. She requires constant reminders and always needs the directions for work at least twice. She is a promising artist. Very little parental support provided. Creative, doesn't like rules - does not do well in structured activities.

Accept _____   Not Accept _____

Susan: Susan is a very mature youngster who presents no problems to her teachers. She does her work, minds her own business, is socially well-adjusted, and is a favorite with her classmates. She is a high achiever and has excellent grades. She is often used by her teachers as a very helpful peer-tutor to her lower achieving classmates. Susan enjoys reading.

Accept _____   Not Accept _____

Michael: Michael is a braggart who exaggerates most personal experiences to fantastic proportions. He is always "one up" better than anyone in class or out of class. His story telling is somewhat disruptive to the class and he demands a great deal of attention. He is from a single-parent family - with the mother in the home. He has been identified as B.D. (behavioral disorder). His grades are average; he is good in art and music. Good parental support. He seems to be a morning learner.

Accept __✓__   Not Accept _____

Grace: Grace is a very bossy and talkative young person who is constantly ordering her classmates around. Her classmates get very angered by her behavior and as a result, she has very few friends. While generally well-behaved, she often presents classroom management problems engaging in power struggles with teachers. According to school records, she has been abused and neglected by her parents. Her grades are generally good and she is especially strong in language arts. She has been caught with alcohol at a school function. Likes to evaluate solutions, doesn't like to create them.

Accept __✓__   Not Accept _____

Neil: Neil is a smart-aleck, sarcastic youngster. He can be described as a motor-mouth who is always quick with flip "put downs". There is nobody he can't and won't put down, teachers included. He has a long track record of spending a great deal of time in the principal's office. He is a high achiever (I.Q. 127), but isn't motivated most of the time. He is athletically and musically inclined. His grades are good. Good parental support. Multi-goal oriented, good sense of priorities - may not work on goal deemed important by others.

Accept __✓__   Not Accept _____

Franklin: Franklin, not "Frank", is upper-middle class, an academically good student, and the class pest. He always finishes his work quickly and accurately. Then, he proceeds to pester, tease, and generally annoy his slower-working classmates in a wide variety of imaginative ways. He cannot sit still for any length of time. Seems to enjoy group work. All of his grades are good. He is especially strong in math and science. Because of both his academic quickness and his disruptive behavior, it is a constant strain on his teacher's resources to keep him meaningfully busy. Good parental support. Opinionated, judgemental, works well in structured events.

Accept _____   Not Accept __✓__

George: George is from a very poor background. His family is large and is widely known in the community as the welfare family. He is considered a compulsive liar and a thief. He has a long record of stealing in the school system and in the community. He seems to lie about anything even in the most obvious situations. He is good in class, with no management problems, but a constant eye is always needed. He has no friends. His grades are generally good, very promising in mathematics. Works well in small group activities. Likes to read and work on the computer.

Accept __✓__   Not Accept _____

Helen: Helen is physically more mature than the other young ladies in class. Her clothes are "anti-establishment." She is from a single-parent family. Socially, she is never seen with students her own age and is very quiet in class. She has average grades in most subjects and presents no behavior management problem. It is difficult to get her involved in class discussions. She prefers to do her work independently.

Very little parental support. Single goal orientation - prefers to finish assignments before taking on another one.

Accept _____   Not Accept_____

Matt: Matt comes to school when things are going good for his family - which isn't that often. Matt lives on the "other side of the tracks". Financially, he is very poor and his family is unemployed. He has displayed average academic ability, but his number of absences are more of a problem than his ability. He is two years older than his classmates. He creates no management problem, but is always late with homework and unprepared when he does come to school. No parental support. Enjoys reading and responds better to instruction in the afternoon.

Accept _____   Not Accept _____

Elaine: Elaine is the class clown. While she is a very bright and capable student, she would rather invest her time and energy to get a laugh from her classmates. She is very capable in math, science, and social studies - yet her grades are only fair in these three subjects. She needs and, in fact, demands constant attention, supervision, and structure from her teachers. She enjoys group work, and is very popular with her classmates. She has been caught with alcohol on the school grounds. Very little parental support. Doesn't complete any goals.

Accept _____   Not Accept _____

Ryan: Ryan is of bi-racial parentage and an only child. He tends to be the class bully because of his considerable size advantage over the other students in class. He has been identified as "learning disabled". Overall, his grades are low with the exception of math. His parents have recently separated and he is living with is mother. Good parental support. Works well in small group activities. Enjoys field experiences and is a morning learner.

Accept_____   Not Accept _____

Paula: Paula is a student who is non-descript. She is that invisible student who is easy to forget and overlook. She is extremely shy and reluctant to socially interact with other students. She never volunteers nor participates in any activities other than the required class work. She is in class every day; assignments are always on time. Her grades are average; she is especially strong in reading. She could easily be overlooked if teachers didn't make a conscious effort to include her. Prefers to work independently. Does not do well in structured acitivities.

Accept _____   Not Accept_____

Carol: Carol comes from a long line of prominent and wealthy relatives. Her family is known all over the community and they have one of the finest homes in town. She tends to be verbally, socially abusive and insensitive to some of her classmates She dresses very fashionably. Her older sister and brother are currently attending an Ivy League school. Her grades are generally good; she is especially strong in language arts. She doesn't mind group work, but prefers to be with her "group." She has been caught with drugs once in school. Opinionated and judgemental.

Accept _____   Not Accept _____

91

Jonathon: Jonathon is an athlete. He has been the best at all sports for a number of years. He is athletically ahead of his classmates by at least two - three years. He lives and breathes sports. As a result, he is average in all subjects; he excels in physical education. He is an extremely capable young man, in fact, he scores very high on standardized tests. However, he is somewhat of a day-dreamer in class and has to be "pushed" to get his work done. Often comes to school without his homework completed. Has very few friends his own age. Strong parental support. Works well in small group activities. Enjoys computer work.

Accept _____   Not Accept __✓__

Margaret: Margaret is Hispanic. She is the third generation of Romeros in the community. Because of her family's strong Hispanic culture, she is limited-English proficient. She has been assigned to an ESL class that meets twice a week. As a result, she is academically one grade level below her classmates. Because of her inability to speak English, she is a poor student academically. She is well liked by her classmates and her very good looks make her a popular students in the seventh grade. She has diufficulty completeing assignments and understanding classroom discussions. She requires a lot of one-to-one instruction. She is a promising musician. Good parental support. Works well in small group activities. Doesn't complete any goals.

Accept __✓__   Not Accept _____

FOLLOW-UP QUESTIONS

1. What criteria did you base your decisions on? Your group's selections? Do you believe you were consistent?

2. There is a seating chart attached to the activity; where would you seat the students that you have selected? Does it matter?

3. Is there a common denominator for those students who were not selected to your class? What is it?

4. As we have seen, each class has a diversity of students, not only in terms of ethnicity, but of behavior, academic potential, learning styles, social backgrounds, family lifestyles, etc. Based on this activity, how do you feel about tracking or sorting students based on academic performance?

5. Which student is the most "acceptable?" Why?

6. Which student would pose the biggest challenge for you? Why?

Note: This activity has been adapted and modified from:
  Teaching in a Multicultural/Pluralistic Society
  By Amos, Jones, Williams and Brooks
  Wright State University, Summer 1980.
  (Reprinted with permission)

List Those Students Selected to Your Class

Meester Bell!
(Your name)

Neil	Margaret	Ryan
George	Michael	Paula
Helen	Travis	Elaine
Grace	Charles	Joe
Sarah	Linda	Susan

Those Students Not Selected for Your Class

Jonathan

Carol

Matt

Franklin

Nancy

WORKSHEET 1

1. How do you define effective teaching?

Teaching that keeps the needs, abilities and perspectives of students in mind when shaping lessons, explaining material -- also, teaching that works for the teacher's characteristics as well.

2. What are teacher expectations? What research evidence is most surprising to you with regard to teacher expectations?

Teachers give more to high achievers. I guess it's most surprising that they allow high achievers more time to respond to questions, in effect giving them more breaks.

Explain your response.

Given that research shows this, it's clear that if these same breaks were given to lower-achieving students, their performance would improve.

3. What is tracking? What are the assumptions that it is defended?

"The process whereby students are divided into categories so they can be assigned in groups to various kinds of classes."
• students learn better in academically similar groups • slower student develops more positive attitudes toward self + school when not in daily contact w/ brighter kids • track placement rewards students by merit
• teaching is easier in homogeneously groups, with no one bringing group up or down

4. On what basis are students placed in groups? Do you agree or disagree with the method(s)? Explain your response.

Most often standardized tests are used to determine the group. This is problematic because it misses those who do poorly on such tests, whether for cognitive or cultural reasons. That is, it disproportionately punishes minorities.

5. Identify two alternatives to tracking. Briefly explain your selections.

Continuous progress: students of similar abilities, but not nec. age groups, work through material at their own pace in small groups. Cooperative learning: students work on lessons in small groups of mixed abilities, toward a common goal.

6. Adler states, "There are no unteachable children. There are only schools and teachers and parents who fail to teach them." Do you agree or disagree with his assessment? Explain your position.

There probably are no unteachable children. The challenge is finding right methods, goals, sensibilities, or activities for any one child. Sometimes it's easy to solve: have the kid learn in the afternoon instead of the morning, use questioning instead of lecture. Other times, the answer is more elusive.

REFERENCES

Adler, Mortimer J. The Paideia Proposal - An Educational Manifesto. Macmillian Publishing Co., New York, 1982. LA/210/. A534/1982

Antonopolis, D.P. "Interactions of Teacher-Pupil Sex as Expressed by Teacher Expectations, Patterns of Reinforcement and Judgments about Pupils: A national Study." Dissertation Abstract 32 (1972): 6117-A.

Bloom, B. S. "Talent Development vs. Schooling." Educational Leadership, November, 1981. pp. 86-94. 370.5/Ed896

Boyer, Ernest High School: A Report on Secondary Education in America. Harper and Row Publishers, New York, 1983. LA/222/.B68/1983

Brophy, J.E. & Good, T. L. Teacher-Student Relationships: Causes and Consequences. Holt, Reinhart and Winston, N.Y., 1974. LB/1033/.B67

Conant, James B. The Comprehensive High School. McGraw Hill, N.Y., 1967.

Goodlad, John I. A Place Called School: Prospects for the Future. McGraw Hill Book Co. New York: 1984. LA/217/.G654/1984

Leven, H. "The Accelerating the Education of At-Risk Students." An Invitational Conference sponsored by the Stanford University School of Education with support from the Rockefeller Foundation. Conference Papers., November 17-18, 1988.

Moran, L. (Ed.) Some are More Equal than Others - What's Noteworthy on School Improvement. Mid-Continent Regional Educational Laboratory, Denver, CO, 1981.

National Commission on Excellence in Education. A Nation at Risk: The Imperative for Educational Reform. U.S. Government Printing Office, Washington, D.C., 1983.

Oakes, Jeannie Keeping Track - How Schools Create Inequality. Yale University Press, New Haven, CO.,1985. LB/3061/.O22/1985

Oakes, Jeannie "Tracking in Secondary School-A Contextual perspective." ;Educational Psychologist. 22(2), 129-154. 1987. LB/1051/.E398

Rosenthal, R., & Jacobsen, L. Pygmalion in the Classroom: Teacher Expectations and Pupils' Intellectual Development. Holt, Reinhart and Winston, N.Y. 1968. LB/1131/.R585

Sizer, Theodore. Hoarace's Compromise - The Dilemma of the American High School. Houghton, Mifflin Publishing Co., Boston: MA, 1984. LA/222/.S54/1984

Slavin, R.E., "Using Student Team Learning." 3rd Edition. Center for Research on Elementary and Middle Schools. 1986.

Slavin, Robert E."Ability Grouping and Its Alternatives: Must We Track"? American Educator, pg. 85-90, Summer 1987. L/11/.A68

The Education Commission of the States. "Access to Knowledge: Breaking Down School Barriers to Learning." By Keating, Pamela and Oakes, Jeannie. August, 1988.

SUGGESTED READINGS

L /11 /.R35 (handwritten)

Anderson, C. S."The Search for School Climate: A Review of the Research." Review of Educational Research, 1982.

LC/3731/.B37/1985 (handwritten)

Board of Inquiry, National Coalition of Advocates for Students. Barriers to Excellence: Our Children at Risk. National Coalition of Advocates for Students, Boston, MA, 1984.

other works (handwritten margin note)

Hodgkinson, Harold L. All One System: Demographics of Education - Kindergarten Through Graduate School The Institute for Educational Leadership, Washington, D.C., 1985.

Loeber, R. & Dishion, T. J. "Strategies for Identifying At-Risk Youths." Unpublished manuscript, Oregon Social Learning Center, Eugene, OR, 1982.

McNett, Ian Demograhic Imperatives For Educational Policy. American Council on Education, Washington, D.C., 1983.

Self, T. C. Dropouts: A Review of Literature, Project Talent Search. ERIC Document Reproduction Service, Arlington, VA, ED 260 307.

Slavin, R. E. Cooperative Learning. Longman, New York: NY, 1983. *LB/1032/.S54/1983* (handwritten)

Smith, R. C. & Hester, E. L. Report on the States' Excellence in Education Commissions: Who's Looking Out for At-Risk Youth? Chapel Hill, NC: MDC, Inc., 1985.

Stallings, J. A. & Hentzell, S. W. Effective Teaching and Learning in Urban Schools, CEMREL, Inc.,St. Louis,MO, 1978.

The Institute for Educational Leadership School Dropouts: Everybody's Problem. The Institute for Educational Leadership, Washington, D.C., 1986.

Tjossem, T. D. Intervention Strategies for High-Risk Infants and Young Children. University Park Press, Baltimore, MD: 1976.

U.S. General Accounting Office. School Dropouts: The Extent and the Nature of the Problem. Washington, D.C., 1986.

CHAPTER FIVE

At-Risk: One-Third of the
School Population

Introduction

The education of at-risk students has become one of the major challenges of our time. These students are heavily concentrated among minority groups, immigrants, single-parent families, and the poor. At-risk students begin school without many of the standard skills upon which the school curriculum is based. As they move through school, they drop farther and farther behind the academic mainstream; by sixth grade they are about two years behind grade level in achievement; by 12th grade, they're four years behind, and half don't graduate from high school. According to Levin (1988), about *one-third* of all students in the public schools meet the at-risk criteria, and the proportion is rising rapidly.

Concurrently, there is a growing recognition that the movement toward school reform has sparked concern that the routes to achieving excellence in our schools may bypass those students for whom traditional methods of education have often failed. There are risks for these students and their families in society at large and the risks to their educational attainment and entry into productive lives of employment are increasing.

Chapter 5, **At-Risk: One-Third of the School Population** is based on the following:

* That the series of recent national educational reforms is not likely to be successful in addressing the problems of the at-risk students because these reforms do not address the pertinent issues.

* That there are effective ways of providing appropriate educational services that must be implemented so that the rapidly increasing population of at-risk youth does not automatically grow up as a rising population of at-risk adults.

* That the benefits of such policies far exceed the costs.

* That failure to address the problems of at-risk youth will have serious consequences for the nation as a whole.

Growth of the At-Risk Population

The at-risk student population is growing at a far more rapid rate than that of the rest of the population. Although not all minorities are at risk, and many at-risk students are not members of a ethnic minority group, the minority population can be used as a proxy for assessing the size of the at-risk group in the public schools. From 1970-80, U.S. public school enrollments from pre-primary level to twelfth grade declined from about 46 million to 41 million students (National Center for Educational Statistics, 1986). At the same time, minority enrollments rose from about 9.5 million to about 11 million, or from about 21 percent to 27 percent of the total student population. Minority enrollments have been increasing at a more rapid pace than the general population because of a considerably higher birth rate and immigration - both legal and illegal - that is unprecedented in recent decades. Both factors create rapid growth, particularly among school-age populations, since immigrant families tend to be young and have children.

State figures vary widely. California is at one extreme where minority student enrollment rose from about 27 percent of the total in 1970 to about 43 percent in 1980; it is expected that minorities will become the dominant component of California's student body before 1990. While growth has not been as rapid in Texas, the proportion of minority students was about 46 percent in 1980, rising from about 37 percent in 1970. During the same period, the minority student population rose in Connecticut from 12-17 percent; in Florida from 28-32 percent; in Massachusetts from 6 to 11 percent; in New York from 25 to 32 percent; in Oregon from 5 to 9 percent and in South Carolina from 41 percent to 44 percent. According to McNett (1983), as for the major cities, by the year 2000, fifty-three major cities will have a majority minority enrollment.

An additional reason for the growth of at-risk groups in the schools is the increase among all racial groups in the number of children in poverty families. Under family structure and poverty, the proportion of children in poverty stayed about 16 percent between 1969 and 1979, but it rose precipitously to 22 percent from 1979 to 1983 (Korentz & Ventresca, 1984). This represented an increase of about 3.7 million in only four years to a total of almost 14 million children. Some 45 percent of Black school-age children and some 36 percent of Hispanic school-age children lived in poverty in 1983. Although some of the increase was associated with a rising incidence of single-parent, female-headed households, most was due to a higher poverty rate created by a changing economy, in spite of the overall economic recovery in 1983.

The evidence suggests that the proportion of at-risk students in American education is high and is increasing rapidly. While there is no precise method of estimating the total number of at-risk youth in the U.S., an estimate must include students in poverty and those whose chances of educational success are handicapped by virtue of language and cultural difference. If we assume that about three-quarters of all the minority students meet the economic and/or cultural-linguistic criteria, that accounts for almost 8 million at-risk students in 1982. In 1983, about 40 percent of minority students met the poverty criteria alone (Levin, 1985). If we augment that total by the estimated 14 percent of non-minority students who live in poverty, another 4 million students are included for a total of 12 million at-risk students out of 40 million in 1982. This suggests that at-risk students account for about 30 percent of elementary and secondary students in 1982, and the proportion is increasing. For the purposes of comparison, it should be noted that in 1982, the U.S. Department of Education estimated that 42 percent of all students between the ages of 5 and 14 had limited English proficiency in English. This estimate was based on the performance of a large national sample of students who were tested on their English proficiency. Even this total does not include the high number of at-risk dropouts who have left school but are less than 18 years old. Further, the evidence suggests that the degree of educationally disadvantaged youth is probably rising as the at-risk population is augmented by poor immigrants.

Both of these factors suggest that the challenge to American education posed by at-risk students will rise precipitously at a time when even the present needs of at-risk students have not been addressed satisfactorily. Accordingly, it is important to consider the consequences of ignoring these trends.

When the at-risk population represents a relatively small percentage of school enrollments, the failure of the schools to educate this group is tragic for its members and contrary to the principles of a democratic society. But its immediate effects were mainly confined to the at-risk population itself. For this reason, the issues could be ignored by the more advantaged majority without immediate consequences. As the at-risk groups have increased in school populations - and ultimately the overall population - the problem is no longer confined to that group. The potential consequences of inaction accrue to the larger society as well. The consequences include: (1) reduced economic competitiveness of the nation as well as states and industries that are most heavily impacted by these populations, (2) higher costs of public services associated with the impoverished and crime, (3) massive disruption in higher education, and (4) ultimately, the emergence of a dual society with a large and poorly educated underclass (National Commission on Excellence, 1983).

At-Risk Students: Who are They?

It is generally acknowledged that a growing proportion of young people are at risk of not making a successful transition to productive lives. There are a number of categories of *risk* that can be found in national, state and local reports on the topic. While a number of these categories represent social phenomenon that educators cannot address alone, it seems valuable to identify the universal conditions of youth that create the most serious at-risk circumstances.

The U.S. schools' track record in meeting the needs of special groups of students is not good, in fact, our schools are least successful with this population. U.S. schools, generally, are most successful in assisting youth from families in which: the parents have graduated from high school and have successfully completed some college coursework; the income level covers basic needs and allows some discretion in expenditure; the housing provides adequate shelter and individual privacy for reflection or study; and the language spoken in the home is a standard version of English. All of these factors contribute to the educational process by supporting the skills, values and languages that schools emphasize and by providing the additional resources in the home that reinforce schooling practices. In addition, it is important for children to be surrounded by persons who have succeeded both educationally and economically, so that the connection between education and future economic success is made. When students lack these advantages, conventional schooling tends to be much less successful in meeting their needs (Levin, 1988).

School Dropouts.

In a 1986 report to members of Congress, the United States Government Accounting Office (GAO) indicated that in October, 1985, there were approximately 4.3 million dropouts (ages 16-24) and of those, about 3.5 million were White, about 700,000 were Black, and about 100,000 were from other racial groups. Fourteen percent of youth (ages 18-19) were dropouts - 16 percent of young men and 12 percent of young women. Drop-out rates of Hispanics, Blacks and other non-white groups as well as Whites from low-socioeconomic groups are considerably higher than average for other groups. Drop-out rates for Blacks and for students in large cities with high concentrations of ethnic minorities are reported to exceed 50 percent (Kolstad & Owings, 1986) About 14 percent of sophomores in 1980 had dropped out of secondary school by the spring of their senior year in 1982. But the rates for Blacks and Hispanics are fully 50 percent higher than that of White, non-Hispanic students. Even these data understate the true disparity, since they do not account for dropouts prior to the spring of the sophomore year. Data suggests that about 40 percent of Hispanic drop-outs leave before the tenth grade (Lyke, 1986)

It's difficult to compare student dropout rates accurately because of variations in the methods of reporting student attrition. In some school districts, the "dropout" count may include students who have graduated early, had long hospitalizations, or died. But graduation rates can serve as a proxy for dropout rates. The 1984 statistics from the U.S. Department of Education are calculated by dividing the number of public high school graduates by the public school ninth grade enrollment four years earlier. They've been corrected for one variable, interstate population migration. (See Figure 10 - High School Graduation Rates).

Figure 10

High School Graduation Rates
(adjusted for migrant and unclassified students)

Minnesota	89.3%	Missouri	76.2	New Mexico	71.0
Nebraska	86.3	Wyoming	76.0	U.S. Average	70.9
North Dakota	86.3	Idaho	75.8	Tennessee	70.5
Iowa	86.0	Colorado	75.4	North Carolina	69.3
South Dakota	85.5	Arkansas	75.2	Rhode Island	68.7
Wisconsin	84.5	New Hampshire	75.2	Kentucky	68.4
Vermont	83.1	Washington	75.1	Nevada	66.5
Montana	82.1	Alaska	74.7	Arizona	64.6
Kansas	81.7	Virginia	74.7	Texas	64.6
Ohio	80.0	Illinois	74.5	South Carolina	64.5
Connecticut	79.1	Massachusetts	74.3	California	63.2
Utah	78.7	Oregon	73.9	Georgia	63.1
Maryland	77.8	Hawaii	73.2	Mississippi	62.4
New Jersey	77.7	Oklahoma	73.1	Florida	62.2
Maine	77.2	West Virginia	73.1	New York	62.2
Pennsylvania	77.2	Michigan	72.2	Alabama	62.1
Indiana	77.0	Delaware	71.1	Louisiana	56.7

Young Offenders.

According the the 1985 <u>United States Crime Statistics Report</u>, fifty percent of all arrests for serious crimes are of young people under 21 years of age. The homicide rate for non-white teens increased 16 percent and for Whites 23 percent from 1950-1978. Serious and repeat teenage criminals are placed in a variety of detention facilities, many offering limited help for continuing their education or for re-entering society. Family members and teachers are frequently victims of teenage crime. Incarcerated youth, when released from penal facilities, have increasing difficulties with school and employment and are at risk of continuing lives of crime or of being economically dependent during most of their lives.

Teen-Age Parents.

According to a special report prepared by the Select Committee on Children, Youth and Families, and the United States House of Representatives (1986), the number of births to teens under 20 was just under one-half million (499,038). This number accounts for almost 14 percent of all births in the country. Most teenage pregnancies are unintended and it is anticipated that at least one-third of teen mothers will experience a subsequent pregnancy while still in their teens. Most teen births are to women 15 to 19 years of age. Between 1960 and 1973 the number of births to girls under 15 rose from 7,500 to 13,000. Forty-nine percent of the births to the 15-17 year-old group were to unmarried teens.

The Problem Highlighted:

* *Every minute in America, two teens become pregnant.*

* *Every day in America, 40 teenage girls give birth to their third child.*

* *Only half of all teens who become parents before age 18 graduate from high school.*

* *Three out of four single mothers under 25 years of age live below the poverty line.*

* *Teen motherhood repeats itself: 82 percent of teen mothers under the age of 16 are daughters of teen mothers.*

* *A teen mother earns half the lifetime earnings of a women who waits to have children until age 20.*

* *Over $16 billion in government funds were spent in 1986 caring for teen mothers and their babies.*

* *The 385,000 first-babies born to teens in 1985 will receive more than $5 billion in welfare benefits over the next 20 years.*

* *The cost of caring for each low-birthweight baby born to teens runs from $10,000 to $15,000.*

Nearly every state reported a serious teenage pregnancy and parenthood problem and 26 states acknowledged that existing prevention and assistance services are inadequate to address the needs.

As the children of teen parents enter public schools, it is anticipated that their educational disadvantages will be severe. Parents of these children are under-educated, frequently have not had positive experiences in school, and many will not be able to provide early learning experiences for their children in preschool years.

Run Away Youth.

Over 150,000 youth run away from home each year. These youth seldom enroll in school. They frequently contribute to the dropout and teen crime statistics. There is little information or data on the extent to which the young people re-enter. School continuation and employment statistics do not clearly identify this category of youth. The risks to run-away youth are often life threatening.

Drug and Alcohol Abusers.

The National Center for Health Statistics reports that arrests of teens for drug abuse increased 600 percent between 1960-1980. Arrests for drunkenness among high school seniors rose 300 percent during the same period. Even without statistical evidence, the perspective that drug and alcohol abuse among youth represents a national crisis is currently shared by national, state and local leaders throughout the nation. The incidence of drug and alcohol use among school- age students is found in all geographic sections: urban, suburban and rural schools.

Youth Unemployment.

Educationally at-risk children tend to become at-risk adults. As adults, they have less economic opportunity, with lower personal incomes and less rewarding jobs. Society bears the related costs of their reduced productivity. Undereducation may also lead to other social burdens, among them lower levels of adult literacy, more welfare dependency, added health care costs, and more crime. According to Catterall and Robles (1988) the following statistics illuminate these statements:

* Only 25 percent of young adults (aged 21-25) who have not finished high school score well enough on a national test to indicate that they can follow directions from one place to another using a map.

* Just over 20 percent in the same population show skills that would enable them to balance a checkbook.

* The male high school dropout will earn $260,000 less over his lifetime than a graduate; a female dropout sacrifices about $200,000.

* The dropouts from a single graduating class in a large urban district were estimated to lose $200 billion in earning over a lifetime; this would cost society more than $60 billion in lost tax revenues.

* Work interruptions due to loss of job are almost twice as likely for high school dropouts than for graduates, and four times more likely for dropouts than for college graduates. Such work interruptions are almost 50 percent more likely for Hispanics than for whites, and almost 100 percent more likely for blacks than for whites.

* For young adults, each added year of secondary schooling reduces the probability of public welfare dependency by 35 percent.

* Entrance rates into the food stamp program are more than three times higher for those with only some high school than for those who simply graduate. Attaining some college beyond high school cuts the average entrance rate by more than half. Entrance rates for non-whites are 3.5 times those for whites.

Labor market opportunities are poor for high school dropouts. Low educational attainment also contributes to the failure of youth to compete in the job market. The population survey data for 1985 shows that 1 in 4 dropouts age 16-24 were unemployed, compared in 1 in 10 high school graduates who were not enrolled in school. In addition, large proportions of dropouts do not even seek work. It is estimated that approximately 3 million 14- to 16-year-olds are looking for work and another 400,000 have stopped looking. The employment prospective for Black dropouts is more bleak than for Whites. In 1972, the unemployment rate for Black teenagers was 35 percent. It rose to 43 percent in 1986 (Catterall, 1986). However, it should be recognized that the disparity in labor force participation and unemployment between all Black and White youth (dropouts and graduates) is greater now than in the past.

One can speculate that the effect of low educational attainment among those who do complete high school has significant economic and psychological effects also. These young adults are in the pool of the millions of other functionally illiterate adults.

Neglected and Abused Children.

More than 900,000 cases of child abuse and neglect were reported in 1982. This represents an increase of 45 percent over the previous five years. Children of families that live in poverty circumstances are over- represented among these cases of abuse. Neglect and abuse are coexisting conditions with other at-risk factors (National Health Statistics, 1986)

Teen Suicide.

The National Center for Health Statistics reports a steady increase in suicide rates of youth between the ages of 10 and 19. In 1984, there were 29,216 teen suicides; 20,882 White males, 6,120 White females, 1,760 Black males, 328 Black females, and 2,284 from all other groups. While these rates may not seem alarming when compared to the size of the adolescent population, Sudak and his colleagues report that these statistics represent a two to three-fold increase in suicide rates for these groups over the past 25 years (Doss, 1986). To the extent that cause can be determined, it appears that adolescent depression is a major factor. A number of state agencies and school districts are providing information and awareness sessions for counselors, teachers and parents on behaviors that may be evident in suicide-prone adolescents.

The conditions of the nation's children that are cited above represent a litany of circumstances that accompany children to school. While these are not problems that can be solved by the schools alone, they help to inform educators about at-risk conditions that affect the lives of children they are charged with educating.

To speak of children at risk is fundamentally to speak of families at risk. A focus on families directs attention to the ascribed characteristics of children that can impede their educational progress. Several of these are identified below.

Family Structure and Poverty.

A clear and disturbing trend in American society is that the poverty population is increasingly composed of children. According to Bills (1986), the financial commitment to children in poverty has actually declined over the past decade. There are more poor children now than there was a decade ago, and a high proportion of the poor are children. Part of this stems from what Bills has called the *feminization of poverty*. The increase in the number of families headed by women has been staggering. Such families are, of course, disproportionately likely to be poor. There is doubt that traditional programs of job training and placement can do much to alleviate the economic conditions of these families.

Race and Ethnicity.

To a remarkable degree, Americans seem to believe that the *race problem* has been solved, that our laws and institutions have been transformed enough so that any remaining racial achievement differentials can only be attributed to motivational shortcomings or differences in ability. Indeed, some of the long-term trends are encouraging. Black college graduates now attain jobs and incomes comparable to those of White graduates. While only 1.3 percent of Blacks had completed college in 1940, by 1982, 12.4 percent had done so.

At the same time, it is too easy to become complacent about our successes. A disproportionate number of minority students are enrolled in higher education in less prestigious junior and community colleges, and there is evidence that the rates of continuation from high school to college among minorities are actually declining. Black family income has not increased at all relative to White family income, and trends in residential and school segregation has shown, at best, inconsistent progress.

If minority access to and participation in higher education is in fact declining, this is a serious and troubling trend. It is not, however, necessarily the most important source of economic differences. Wilson and Aulletta, in their separate studies, indicate growing economic divergence within the Black population, with enormous economic disparities persisting between relative unskilled and poorly educated White and Black workers. Bills' (1986) interpretation, which seems well supported by the evidence, is that the *race* problem is increasingly a *class* problem, in that an exceptionally high proportion of Blacks are relegated to low-status jobs. He maintains that while affirmative action programs have had beneficial effects on the careers of Black professionals, they have done little to enhance the prospects of the working poor or the underclass.

Past and Current Responses

Cuban and Tyack (1988) offer a capsule examination of how schools and teachers described at-risk students, how historically educators have perpetuated misconceptions and implemented flawed solutions that hurt these students rather than helped them. Cuban and Tyack state that for almost two centuries, explanations for "low achievement" have blamed individuals, families, teachers, educational institutions, or the inequalities embedded in the political economy. Each explanation proposed a solution in keeping with the perceived cause. Over time, the blame shifted somewhat, but earlier explanations persisted alongside the new:

1. Low achievers are responsible for their own performance. This response, which had deep roots in American ways of thinking, has been the dominant way to frame the problem. In the nineteenth century, notions of "intelligence" and cultural differences were rudimentary, so educators typically explained poor academic performance in terms of flawed character: the student was lazy or immoral. In the twentieth century, when "science" informs educational decision-making, psychological interpretations prevail: low I.Q. and inadequate motivation cause academic failure. The solution has often been to educate children by separating them into categories that presumably matched their genetic make-up that is, remedial education.

2. Families from different cultural backgrounds fail to prepare and support their children's progress in the elementary and secondary grades. Moral complaints against the nineteenth-century low-achiever sometimes spilled over onto their families: parents were intemperate, undisciplined, unfamiliar with American standards of behavior. With the rise of social science in the twentieth century, finger-pointing became less moralistic. But still, parents figured largely in theories that stressed the poverty, or the supposed cultural deficits, in the families of "unteachable" children.

3. The school system cannot accommodate the range of intellectual abilities and the different destinies of its heterogeneous student body. Many reformers argued that academic failure stemmed from the rigidity of the standardized curriculum and the inflexible practices of promotion and grading. They did not frontally attack the graded school perse, for it had served the majority of students well. Rather, they argued that a single, lock-step academic course of studies produced failures because not all students were capable of studying the same subjects at the same rate.

4. Schools produce the unequal social relationships of a capitalist political economy. In this view, schools are structured to produce winners and losers. Because public education reflects in its organization and processes the unequal social relationships of production, certain children will rise to the top and others fall to the bottom because schools are dynamic instruments of the larger political economy. Although educators may be unaware of the systemic character of such class, racial, and gender discrimination, and despite resistance of students and teachers to domination, the overall results are predictable: some pupils are destined to fail because of the imperatives of the economy.

5. Children often fail academically because the school's culture differs so greatly from cultural backgrounds of their communities. In this view, the schools, not the children, should adapt to social diversity. The teachers often unconsciously served as agents of a pervasive cultural system that was geared to standardizing their pupils. Classrooms became cultural battlegrounds, in which teachers communicated lower expectations and failed to connect with their culturally diverse students. Thus, they unwittingly created student failure. (Cuban and Tyack, 1988, Reprinted with Permission)

Cuban and Tyack (1988) suggest that each of these diagnoses led to a different conclusion. Blaming the individual student or the family provided an alibi, not a solution. Blaming the rigidity of traditional education exposed institutional faults, but it led to policies that too often sequestered the "abnormal child" in an inferior and segregated corner of the system. Analyzing how the school reflected the inequalities of the larger political economy illuminated the difficulty of correcting social injustices in education and through education, but it offered no practical remedies; it made the school an ally of social injustice, not a cure for it. Spotlighting the gaps between the school's culture and the cultural backgrounds of students provided a useful corrective to the earlier ethnocentric explanations that blamed students and parents - but failed to question the basic structure and processes of schooling. Moreover, because it focused on the unconscious cultural biases of teachers, it ran the danger of personalizing the answer: more sensitive instructors were obviously needed - but where were they to come from? Adding black history to the curriculum, or bilingual strategies to the instruction, would defuse conflict, but such attempts to make schools multicultural merely added to a familiar pattern of instruction; they did not change the institution.

Almost all these diagnoses and the solutions they generated failed to alter the structure of the school. All of the labeling and its specialized programs have become part of the problem; they often reflect and reinforce stereotypes about the genetic or cultural inferiority of certain groups.

Compensatory Education

The impact of poor school performance has far reaching implications for students, and even when poor academic performance is a single factor affecting youth, it represents a very high risk factor.

The fact is that poor academic performance is typically accompanied by other risk factors. Poor grades is the most frequently reported reason for dropping out of school. Borus and Carpenter conducted a study of the correlation of dropping out of school and found that among the most important concerns was being two or more years behind grade level (Borus & Carpenter, 1984). While poor school performance is at the center of concern regarding school drop-outs, it is a serious high-risk factor for students who are currently in schools and for those who complete school with a history of low achievement. McDill (1986) and his colleagues, in an examination of the effects of higher academic standards on potential dropouts, report that the consistent failure and frustration of low academic achievement inevitably leads to increases in absenteeism, truancy and school- related behavior problems.

It has been well documented that the low achieving phenomenon often starts in the earliest grades of schooling and increases in severity as students proceed through elementary and middle schools. It was this premise that led to the development of *compensatory education* programs for *disadvantaged* children in the middle 1960s. The original intent of the Elementary and Secondary Education Act (ESEA) was to promote educational equity for poor and disadvantaged children. This act set a precedent for federal aid to education and was considered an effective way to break the cycle of poverty. Since 1965, $38 billion in federal funds has been spent on Title I (currently known as Chapter 1), the largest of the compensatory programs. Since the passage of the original Elementary and Secondary Education Act in 1965, school districts have wrestled with the problems of educating low-achieving, disadvantaged students. In addition to the difficulties of designing and implementing programs that overcome achievement deficits, schools have been constrained by regulations - to supplement, not supplant, regular programs, to serve only eligible students, to use standardized tests to determine eligibility, and to focus on reading and arithmetic.

A considerable amount of literature exists regarding the evaluation of Title I programs. Typically, they have focused on only a portion of the students at risk, and the resources that they have provided have been far short of what is required to make any substantial difference. The evidence suggests that such policies have affected small reductions in the test score gap between White and non-white students over time (Guttmacher, 1981, Catterall, 1986, and Humphrey, 1986) Even so, the educational performance of at-risk students lags considerably behind that of their more advantaged counterparts, and they are more likely to drop out before completing high school.

However, in the most recent Chapter 1 reauthorization (effective July 1, 1988), districts now have the opportunity to use complete flexibility: Chapter 1 professionals can work in regular classrooms; pull-out programs can become team-teaching situations; parent-liaison staff can work with parents of special-education students; all faculty members can participate in Chapter 1 inservice or planning activities. The prospective shift in emphasis means that rather than depending on specialists, teachers will have the opportunity to work collaboratively in addressing the educational problems of low-achieving students. Authority to conduct this *school-wide* approach is granted directly by the state educational agency upon approval of the plan. In exchange for flexibility, the legislation requires school-specific accountability and extensive parental involvement. These new regulations will challenge teachers and parents in schools across the country to provide more effective schooling for the educationally disadvantaged.

Current Responses: Improvements or Obstacles?

The current call for reform in education, spurred by the A Nation at Risk report, was not a response to the plight of the at-risk student. Rather it seemed to be premised on the concern that, in the absence of major changes in American education, the U.S. economy might lose in the competitive race for international markets in our age of high technology (Cuban, 1984).

As discussed in earlier chapters, several recommendations seek specific changes that would strengthen curriculum and standards; for example, implementing minimum competency standards for graduation, raising graduation requirements, and teacher testing and certification, are just some of the reforms recommended. For a number of reasons, these requirements are only marginally relevant to at-risk students. Some educators believe that some of the recommendations may actually be harmful, since they create additional barriers to high school completion without providing the resources and assistance necessary for the at-risk student to meet the new requirements.

The states have responded to the reform agenda by legislating some of the recommendations, discussing others, directing the attention of local education authorities to others and ignoring the remainder. Even where reform has been converted into legislation, critics have found that it often takes a rigid, mechanical approach that is unlikely to have the desired results or that provides only a large number of *questionable and idiosyncratic responses, rather than a comprehensive solution to the issues* (Toch, 1984).

Teacher Salaries and Teacher Training

Of course, if improvements in teacher salaries or professional training improve the overall quality of teaching, there will be beneficial effects for all students. But such a slow process is not an effective substitute for the reforms targeted to achieve specific educational goals for the at-risk student. Worse yet, in the absence of explicit efforts to improve education for the at-risk student, some general reforms may actually create new obstacles to improving their situation (Glazer, 1984). Notably, the setting of competency standards for a diploma, raising course requirements for graduation discussed in the previous chapter, and increasing the amount of time spent in school may all have the effect of increasing drop-out rates among the most dropout-prone populations (Levin, 1985)

Setting State Competency Standards for Receiving a Diploma.

On the surface, this may be viewed as a very attractive reform, assuring that all holders of a diploma will have certain proficiencies. But if at-risk students enter secondary schools functioning two or three years below grade level, it is likely that few of them will suddenly catch up to meet competency standards for graduation. More likely, even if they try very hard, they will not meet the stringent standards and will not receive a diploma for their efforts. The additional standards may simply discourage them from trying to remain in school. (See Figure 11 - States Using Minimum-Competency Testing).

States Using Minimum—Competency Testing

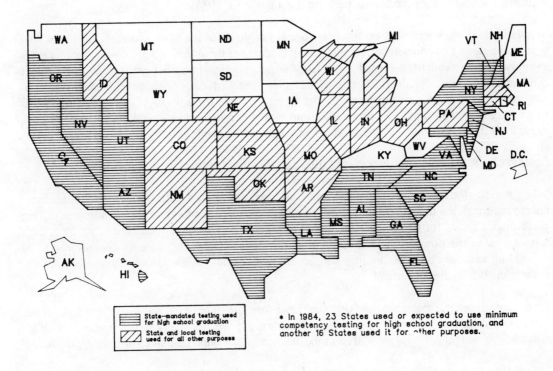

* In 1984, 23 States used or expected to use minimum competency testing for high school graduation, and another 16 States used it for other purposes.

Figure 11

There are two ways to solve this dilemma. If competencies are set at a very low level for graduation, such as at eighth- grade achievement, they will be relatively easy to satisfy, even for most of the at-risk students who do not drop out. In the past, most states have chosen low competency standards. An alternative is to choose higher standards and provide educational resources and programs for at-risk students so that they can meet the higher standards. Many of the new standards are likely to be higher than previous ones, and therefore will lead to remediation for the at-risk student. But without resources and a mandated commitment, this is unlikely to happen.

In the absence of compensatory programs, the attempt to raise standards to meet educational and job-related requirements will increase pressure on the at-risk student to drop out, even for those students who could have met the standards with appropriate educational assistance. And failure to meet standards and obtain a competency-based diploma may increase employer rejection of such students, even when they are able to perform the job (Cross, 1984).

Without a major commitment on the educational problems of the at-risk student in the earliest grades, the raising of competency standards will discourage them from completing school. This is even true when standards are used for determining promotion in earlier grades. Without major funding and programs to alleviate early deficiencies, many educators believe, too many of the at-risk students will be required to repeat grades, at great cost to the schools. Clearly, it would seem to be more effective to put those resources into remediation of achievement deficiencies at each grade level than using grade repetition as a device to meet standards.

Increases in Course Requirements for Graduation.

When at-risk students who enter ninth grade are performing at a sixth- grade level, additional course requirements in mathematics, English and science are not likely to be effective in raising performance levels for them. The additional requirements will mean that benefiting from high school level instruction will be made even more difficult. Students who are far behind need to be brought up to those norms before they can benefit from existing high school requirements, to say nothing of additional requirements.

As discussed earlier, the practice and organizational structure of tracking and sorting students in our schools will have to be seriously considered. As we can see, the many issues involved with at-risk students and other issues we will examine, are centered around the issues of tracking itself.

Increasing the Length of the School Day or School Year.

General evidence that more instructional time will improve learning outcomes is weak at best. There is virtually no evidence that the present school day or school year is the limiting factor affecting the learning of all students, or the at-risk student in particular (Pollas & Verdugo, 1986). For many of these students, the fact that they are doing poorly and see no hope of catching up reinforces the feeling of school as a oppressive environment. To require them to spend more time in such a situation without altering educational strategies to make their learning experience more successful is likely to produce greater dissatisfaction. It is imperative that the learning situation become more vital and exciting, and that the student have some sense of progress rather than feelings of failure and futility. Without these changes, forcing the at-risk student to spend more time in school is unlikely. To the contrary, it provides an additional pressure for dropping out.

As mentioned previously, most educational reforms currently sponsored by states do not address specific issues affecting at- risk students. Reforms that create more time in school or higher standards - without noticeable changes in the schooling process that will increase learning for the at-risk student - will likely increase drop-out rates among those students who can scarcely hope to meet present standards. It is clear that whatever merits the present reforms have, they are incomplete and foreshadow both a present and future tragedy unless the needs of at-risk students are addressed.

What are the Indicators for At-Risk Students?

School Attendance.

Poor attendance often begins at the earliest stages of schooling. Given the evidence of the relationship of learning time to school performance, number of days of absence from school becomes a significant predictor of low performance. When the pattern of absence is established in the primary grades, it is almost certain that it will worsen as students reach pre-adolescence. Student attendance is undoubtedly the earliest and most visible indicator of potential problems in school.

School Continuation Rates.

Dropout rates and school continuation rates are closely tied. A most salient and readily observable indicator of educational failure is the drop-out rate. While problems of conceptualizing and measuring drop-out rates are difficult for school officials, it provides a reasonable straightforward indicator of how well the educational system is doing. Clearly, given prevailing cultural and social perceptions and expectations of the meaning of a high school diploma, a decision to leave prior to graduation can only be interpreted as a failure on the part of the school or district and the student and his/her family.

Academic Performance.

School performance is another early indicator of educational risk. When students in third and fourth grades are already two years behind their age counterparts, *catching-up* becomes a difficult, if not insurmountable, obstacle. There are real differences in academic achievement that are rooted, to a great extent, in the factors discussed in the previous chapters. The cumulative effects of achievement are well documented in a number of sources. A reasonable appraisal of the magnitude and nature of achievement differences is essential for understanding and improving the educational consequences of being at-risk. While a number of successful interventions have been identified and are being tried, it seems obvious that efforts to improve instruction and learning for large numbers of students have failed to affect outcomes of significance.

Involvement in School Activities.

Studies (Pollas & Verdugo, 1986) have examined the participation of school drop-outs in school activities when they were attending. School dropouts participate in very few of the academic and social activities or recreational-related activities. The practice of isolation from the enrichment activities of schools is another indicator for educators to examine, especially as students make the transition from elementary to secondary school levels. One indicator cited by Pollas was students' participation in anti-social activities outside of school. Gang membership, numbers of hours spent on the streets, use of drugs and alcohol are likely to lead to poor school performance, early school leaving and delinquency.

Student Behavior.

Anti-social behavior in school is often accompanied by other indicators of educational risk. The manner in which schools address disruptive students can often increase the likelihood that students will increase truancy, vandalism and other unacceptable behaviors. The degree to which these patterns can be altered in the early years of schooling, the more likely students will develop healthier attitudes in later school years. The involvement of families and other community agencies is often a necessity to address the problems of disruptive students. There is also a growing body of literature that indicates the relationship of student behavior to the classroom and school climate and to the implementation of rules regarding student behavior.

Attitudes Toward School.

Closely aligned to student behavior are the attitudes toward school and toward the adults in the school. Negative attitudes that are demonstrated in the early years of school are often indicators of later school problems.

Need for Employment.

Some of the indicators cited above may be directly related to the presence of economic difficulties in families. High school students may actually be encouraged to seek employment in order to supplement family income. The awareness of the need for employment by teens may require school schedule changes, the provision of assistance and increased school-work programs.

Nature of Family Support.

Many schools have expressed the difficulty of securing the adequate assistance from families with the student experiencing problems. This is an area where premature judgments can be made. However, it is important to have supplemental services to investigate the extent of family problems that are affecting school attendance, performance, and attitudes. Such knowledge indicates the need to increase the student's support within the school.

Involvement with the Juvenile Justice System.

A number of teen crimes are committed by students who are still in school. It is likely that students who are frequently involved in crimes and are on probation to juvenile courts are at risk of failing to stay in school or are doing poorly in school.

It seems clear that the first six of these indicators of educational risk are much closer to the business of schools than the last three. They are also the indicators that are most alterable by schools (Willis, 1986).

Assessing the Needs of At-Risk Students

The unique needs of the at-risk student cannot be affectively addressed by reforms of a general nature such as increasing course requirements, raising teachers' salaries, or increasing the amount of instructional time. While these reforms may be desirable on their own merits, they should not be viewed as substitutes for direct and comprehensive strategies to solve the problems of the at-risk student. In the absence of specific academic programs, general reforms may overwhelm the abilities of an ever-growing number of at-risk students to meet the requirements for high school completion.

Approaches to change must be viewed in the context of an overall strategy for placing the challenge of the at-risk student on the national policy agenda and addressing the challenges effectively. Such an agenda should include establishing (1) guidelines for identification strategies, (2) guidelines for prevention strategies and (3) school-wide goals. The University of Michigan-School of Education-has established a set of guidelines for prevention strategies, guidelines for success, and has identified strategies for addressing the needs of at-risk students (1986).

Guidelines for Prevention Strategies.

Successful prevention strategies can take many forms and involve very different school practices. Some of the more successful strategies, for example, provide special learning experiences for preschoolers; some focus their efforts almost entirely on school improvement plans, while still others deliver services to troubled adolescents. Although successful strategies are often quite different, they tend to share certain characteristics. The University of Michigan's School of Education refers to these characteristics by the acronym ***SUCCESS***. Every prevention strategy, therefore, can be characterized by how SUCCESSful it is in its design and actual operation (1986). (See Figure 12 - Guidelines for Success).

SUCCESSful strategies will support students during times of personal crises, be unbiased about the cause(s) of student failure, consider the continuity of development, encourage individual competency and self-reliance, be empathetic towards students, address specific developmental needs and maintain a healthy sense of skepticism regarding any programs that are described as the answer to the problems that at-risk students experience. (Figure 13 - Guidelines for Identification Strategies) can be used a guideline for developing your own prevention strategies. Additionally, the following are precautionary measures for identifying individual students as at-risk:

1. *Individuals should never be identified as at risk without careful consideration of potential benefits and harm to them. The greater the possibility of harming students, either through negative labeling or denial of educational opportunities, the greater the need for protecting student rights.*

2. *Whenever possible, identification should be based on behaviors that students can control. Identification should always afford students the possibility of changing their "at risk status," by improving their grades, attendance or classroom behavior, for example. Factors should clearly reinforce desirable behavior when educational opportunities are affected.*

3. *Factors that are a matter of cultural values or beliefs, such as dress or religious preference, should never be used to identify students at risk. These factors are not appropriate criteria on which to base decisions about educational resources and opportunities.*

4. *Whenever possible, identification should be based on easily observed and interpreted behaviors, so as to assure uniformity and neutrality in how students are identified. Identification should not be based on subjective factors, unless special provisions are made for a thorough consideration of all interpretations.*

5. *Factors that are used to identify individuals should be casually related to the outcomes being prevented. Intuitive and statistical proofs of the relationship between at-risk factors and outcomes should be thoroughly considered before using them to identify individuals.*

6. *Specific individuals should not be identified as at risk if other less isolating strategies can be used to effectively deliver services to students. The need for individual identification should be carefully considered, as well as the possibility of alternative selection techniques, such as volunteering or monitoring group performance.*

7. *Individuals should never be identified as at risk of a specific outcome unless there is a reasonable chance of preventing its occurrence. School personnel should always be prepared to successfully assist individual students who are identified as at risk of failure* (Reprinted with Permission).

Figure 12

Guidelines for SUCCESS . . .

Supportive. Prevention programs need to consider how to support students when internal or external demands become personal crises. Programs that provide resources for students at these times, augmenting their own problem solving skills, prevent temporary failures from overwhelming students and disrupting their development. Prevention programs, therefore, should identify ways in which school personnel can help students during critical times in their development.

Unbiased. Successful preventions are unbiased about the causes of student failure. They neither "blame the victim" nor "blame the system" for the problems that at-risk students often experience. Successful prevention strategies consider the role of students and the school when designing and implementing programs. They encourage the development of individual students and the improvement of school practices and procedures which affect learning and growth.

Continuous. There is no special period, no single critical stage in development that determines all or most of whom a child will or can become. Cognitive and emotional development is best described as continuous and divided into many "critical" stages. Prevention strategies, therefore, must be appropriately spread across the developmental continuum. Prevention will be most successful if it aids students at numerous "critical points" in their development.

Competency-based. The most successful prevention programs tend to be those that make students more competent in a regular school setting. Many school failures are defenses against the daily frustrations and degradation that at-risk student experience at school. School-based preventions tend to fail if they do not realistically improve a student's chances of succeeding in school and life and usually that means teaching students to function better socially and cognitively.

Empathetic. Committed, empathetic adults, who understand the nature of child development and have high expectations for themselves and students, are important characteristics of successful prevention strategies. Prevention requires a particular type of understanding and sensitivity toward at-risk students, and those run by empathetic adults tend to be most successful.

Specific. Prevention programs with specific goals are more likely to succeed than those with vague objectives. Good intentions, enjoyable experiences and a reprieve from everyday stresses are often not enough to bring about personal change. School failures are always a response to specific internal and external stresses, and preventions that identify those stresses and take actions to make them manageable are more successful than others.

Skeptical. The potential benefits and dangers of early identification and prevention are far too real to proceed haphazardly. Students can be harmed, and money can be wasted on ill-conceived programs. A healthy sense of skepticism, therefore, is always warranted, especially when strategies are described as the answer to the problems that at-risk students experience. Prevention efforts will be most successful if they are carefully developed, piloted, implemented and evaluated.

Guidelines for Identification Strategies

Identification strategies can be evaluated in different ways, depending on the criteria used to assess them. We have found it useful to evaluate strategies according to their fairness, opportunities, completeness, usability and specificity. We refer to these criteria by the acronym **FOCUS**. Every identification strategy, therefore, can be evaluated in terms of how well it FOCUSes on at-risk students.

Actual strategies, however, are always a compromise between desired attributes, for many of these criteria are inversely related to each other. Attempts to be fair may, in some instances, make a strategy more time-consuming and less usable; attempts to be complete, that is, to identify all students who will eventually fail in some way may result in less specificity, the ability to identify only those who do fail.

These criteria can be used as guidelines for developing your own identification strategies. Ask yourself, "How well will our strategies FOCUS attention on at-risk students?"

Figure 13

Fairness. Identification strategies should fairly identify students as at-risk, especially when there is the possibility that identification could be harmful or used to deny opportunities. Strategies should be evaluated to determine if they protect students and recognize their rights. The fairness of an identifcation strategy should be routinely considered.

Opportunities. Identification strategies should provide timely information about students who are at-risk. Strategies should be evaluated to determine how promptly they identify at-risk students, giving the student and personnel ample opportunity to prevent school-related difficulties from occurring or getting worse. The opportunities that an identification strategy creates for prevention should be carefully considered.

Completeness. Identification strategies should attempt to identify all students who are at-risk of failing some important way. Strategies should be evaluated to determine how completely they identify students who eventually fail, given the actual occurrences of certain school-related difficulties, such as dropping out of school, substance abuse and expulsion. School personnel should consider who, if anyone, a strategy fails to identify and what the implications for that failure might be.

Usability. Identification strategies should be easy to implement and use. Strategies should be evaluated to determine whether or not they are practical, considering the time, coordination and expertise they require of school personnel. Strategies which use straightforward and easily understood techniques for identifying students are always preferable to those which require extensive data collection, record keeping, calculations and education to understand.

Specificity. Identification strategies should attempt to identify only those students who will actually fail in some way, limiting, to the extent possible, the number of students who are identified as needing special services. Ideally, that number would always be equal to the number that actually fail if school personnel do not intervene in some way. Strategies should be evaluated to determine how specifically they identify at-risk students. School personnel should consider who, if anyone, a strategy misidentifies and what the implications for that misidentification might be.

Goals for alleviating the educational disadvantages that face all students in our school - especially at-risk students - must be concrete. Just as higher standards are set for the schools, so should specific goals be set for bringing at-risk students up to the required norms. This should be done at the initial stages of schooling so that by the time students enter secondary school, they are able to benefit from regular instruction.

The establishment serves two purposes. First, it is a political statement that signals priority. Second, goals are a means for assessing progress. Therefore, specific achievement goals for at-risk students should be set at both state and local levels in the form of a measurable standard of achievement.

Inventory of Preventions.

The Inventory Fact Sheet, (See Figure 14) - has two purposes. First, to encourage you to do your own inventory of successful programs. Second, to provide an example of prevention strategies that do work. To that end, the fact sheet includes examples of internal and external programs, and it uses a form that outlines the kind of information that would be useful for you to collect (Moody, 1986)

INVENTORY FACT SHEET

Name of Program   Interpersonal Cognitive Problem Solving, "I Can Problem Solve" (ICPS)

Contact Information	Myrna Shure (215) 448-4949 Hahnemann University Broad and Vine Sts. Philadelphia, PA 19102
Target Students	The program does not require nor use any strategy for identifying students as at-risk. All students in particular grades--kindergarten through first or fifth through sixth--are targeted for services.
Description of Services	The program consists of a problem-solving curriculum and feedback strategies for teachers and parents to use when helping students evaluate their own behavior. The curriculum teaches students how to assess their feelings, consider consequences and think of their own alternatives to interactional problems with others. The feedback strategies teach adults how to help students solve their own behavioral problems, rather than merely telling students what they should do. The curriculum is infused into the normal classroom routine, and it requires approximately three forty-five minute sessions per week for a minimum of four months to implement.
Evidence of Success	Initial evaluations of the curriculum and training indicated that the program improves cognitive ability and decreases the occurrence of impulsive behavior. Inhibited children also became less withdrawn. Students who participated in the program exhibited significantly fewer behavioral problems for at least two years, even after the curriculum was discontinued. Younger children, who are in the process of developing their own cognitive style, seemed to benefit more quickly than older children from this curriculum.
Comments	This is one of several social problem-solving curricula that has been piloted and tested using school-aged children. It is particularly interesting because it doesn't require an identification strategy, for every student who participates should benefit from it in some way. Considering the Superintendent's mandate about teaching higher order thinking skills, these curricula could be widely accepted by the elementary school principals in the district. Myrna Shure, as well as George Spivack, the director of the Prevention Intervention Research Center at Hahnemann University, should have more information about this kind of prevention program.

Figure 14

121

Summary

Our nation is at risk of starting the 21st Century with one of four students failing to complete the essentials of learning. There was a time in this nation when school failure and little education did not foreclose a person's options for a self-sufficient and fulfilling life nor impede the nation's capacity in trade, defense, environmental condition, or quality of life. That time is gone. Technological advances, demographic changes, international competition, and intense pressures of providing a better life for greater numbers of people on a seemingly shrinking planet today require a citizenry educated at least through high school graduation. This is imperative for our nation.

We are not meeting that imperative. One of four youth does not graduate. The greatest proportions of those who are at-risk of not graduating are poor, minority, and of limited English proficiency. We must serve them by taking several actions now. The high school class of 2000 entered kindergarten in 1987 - one quarter of them living in poverty. Our society must commit more resources for quality and equity. We must strengthen the practice of teaching. We must provide assistance and incentives for schools to change their programs to succeed with children at-risk.

Programs abound in schools to address these students. Dropout prevention programs, sex education programs, delinquency prevention programs, vocational training programs, alternative school programs, counseling programs - each pick out a piece of the at-risk student problem. Several research centers and projects work to address these immediate problems, but they also see clearly that a common thread winds its way through each - poor academic performance in school, usually from the early years onward. Given this common thread, a scenario emerges. If schools could improve the academic performance of at-risk students beginning in the early years, this improvement would have multiple positive effects on student dropout, delinquency, pregnancy, substance abuse and other behaviors. Thus early improvement of poor academic performance could greatly alleviate multiple aspects of the overall problem.

How can we bring about a state of affairs in which schools are choosing from among proven programs, implementing those programs effectively, and producing measurable benefits for their at-risk students? Slavin (1987) offers a four pronged approach. First, each region, state and local educational agencies should establish a valid list of effective programs for at-risk students. Secondly, provide resources to help schools adopt effective practices. For one example, establish state or regional centers, staffed by personnel trained in the various effective models and in the dissemination and implementation of successful practice. Third, fund research and development of new effective models. Several groups of researchers and developers should be funded to follow a rational sequence of development, pilot-testing, small-scale evaluation, large-scale evaluation by outside independent evaluators. And Fourth, establish independent evaluation centers. These centers would oversee and assist in independent evaluations of programs conducted by state and local evaluation agencies and conduct evaluations of their own. These evaluations would be essential to insure the credibility of program effects.

WORKSHEET 1

1. Who, <u>in your opinion</u>, are the students "at risk" in our schools today? Explain.

_____

_____

_____

_____

_____

_____

2. "The U.S. schools track record in meeting the needs of special groups of students is not good." Our schools are generally most successful in assisting youth from what family characteristics?

_____

_____

_____

_____

_____

In your opinion, why have the families you described above been the most successful in our schools?

_____

_____

_____

_____

_____

In your opinion, for those *"other"* families that you didn't identify, why have they not been as successful in our schools?

_____

_____

_____

_____

_____

_____

3. What is the Chapter One program?

_____

_____

_____

_____

_____

What was it designed to accomplish?

_____

_____

_____

_____

_____

According to the research cited, have Chapter One programs accomplished their intent? Why or why not?

_____

_____

_____

_____

_____

How has Chapter One programs changed since July 1, 1988?

_____

_____

_____

_____

_____

4. What are some precautionary measures for identifying individual students as at-risk?

_____

_____

_____

_____

_____

_____

_____

5. There was a time in this nation when a high school education wasn't essential. However, today and in the future, this won't be acceptable. Explain this evolution.

_____

_____

_____

_____

_____

_____

REFERENCES

Bills, David "Students Who Are Educationally At Risk." In North Central Regional Educational Laboratory, Unpublished Report, University of Iowa, Iowa City, IA, 1986, p. 6.

Borus, Michael E. & Carpenter, Susan A. "Youth and the Labor Market: Analyses of the National Longitudinal Survey." In Michael E. Borus (Ed.), Choices in Education, Chapter 4. The W. E. Upjohn Institute for Employment Research, 1984.

Catterall, James & Robles, Eugene. "The educationally at-risk: what the numbers mean." Conference Papers, November, 1988. Stanford University.

Catterall, James S. "On the Social Costs of Dropping Out of School." University of California, Unpublished Report, 1986.

Cross, Patricia "The Rising Tide of School Reform Reports." Phi Delta Kappan Vol. 66, No. 3, November, 1984.

Cuban, Larry & Tyack, David. "Dunces, Shirkers, and forgotten children: historical descriptions and cures for low achievers." Conference Papers, November, 1988. Stanford University.

Cuban, Larry "School Reform by Remote Control: SB 813 in California." Phi Delta Kappan, Vol. 66, No. 3, November, 1984.

Doss, Harriet Willis " Students At Risk: A Review of Conditions, Circumstances, Indicators and Educational Implications." North Central Regional Educational Laboratory Elmhurst, Illinois, October, 1986. Unpublished Report. (Reprinted with permission).

Douglas County Task Force on Teen Pregnancy. "Teen Sexuality, Pregnancy and Parenting: How Can We Respond?" Conference Presentation, May 8, 1987. Lawrence, KS.

Glazer, Nathan "The Problem with Competence." American Journal of Education, Vol. 92, No. 3, 1984.

Guttmacher, Alan Teenage Pregnancy: The Problem that Hasn't Gone Away. The Alan Guttmacher Institute, Washington, D.C., 1981.

H. Hubert Humphrey Institute of Public Affairs. "Criminal and Juvenille Deliquency." Minneapolis, MN, 1986.

Kolstad, Andrew J. & Owings, Jeffery A. High School Dropouts Who Change Their Minds About School. U.S. Department of Education, Center for Statistics, Washington, D.C., April, 1986.

Korentz, Daniel & Ventresca, Marc. Poverty Among Children. Congressional Budget Office, Washington, D.C., 1984.

Levin, Henry M. "Accelerating the Education of At-Risk Students." Conference Papers, November, 1988. Stanford University.

Levin, Henry M. "The Educational Disadvantaged: A National Crisis." The State Youth Initiatives Project, Working Paper No. 6, 1985, p. 9.

Lyke, Bob High School Dropouts. Library of Congress, Congressional Research Service, Issue Brief IB 86003. Updated April 4, 1986.

McDill, Edward L.; Natriello, Gary; & Pollas, Aaron M. "A Population at Risk: Potential Consequences of Tougher School Standards for Student Dropouts." American Education Journal. Vol. 94, No. 2, February, 1986.

McNett, Ian Demographic Imperatives for Educational Policy. American Council on Education. Washington, D.C., 1983.

McPartland, James M. & McDill, Edward C. Violence in Schools: Perspectives, Programs and Positions. D.C. Heath, Lexington, MA, 1977.

Moody, Charles D. The Challenge of At-Risk Students Break Through Program for Educational Opportunity Newsletter, University of Michigan - School of Education. Volume XIV, No. 1, Summer 1986.(Reprinted With permission).

National Center for Education Statistics. The Condition of Education. U.S. Department of Education. Washington, D.C., 1984.

National Center for Health Statistics. Deaths from 72 Selected Causes by 5 Year Age Groups, Race and Sex. Vital Statistics of the United States, Vol. II, Washington, D.C., 1986.

National Commission on Excellence in Education. A Nation At Risk: The Imperative for Educational Reform. U.S. Government Printing Office, Washington, D.C., 1983.

Pollas, Aaron M. & Verdugo, Richard R. Measuring the High School Dropout Problem. U.S. Department of Education, Center for Education Statistics, Washington, D.C., 1986.

Slavin, Robert E. "Making Chapter 1 Make a Difference." Phi Delta Kappan, October, 1987, pp. 110-119.

Toch, Thomas "The Dark Side of the Excellence Movement." Phi Delta Kappan Vol. 66, No. 3, November, 1984.

SUGGESTED READINGS

Anderson, C. S."The Search for School Climate: A Review of the Research." Review of Educational Research, 1982.

Board of Inquiry, National Coalition of Advocates for Students. Barriers to Excellence: Our Children at Risk. National Coalition of Advocates for Students, Boston, MA, 1984.

Hodgkinson, Harold L. All One System: Demographics of Education - Kindergarten Through Graduate School The Institute for Educational Leadership, Washington, D.C., 1985.

Loeber, R. & Dishion, T. J. "Strategies for Identifying At-Risk Youths." Unpublished manuscript, Oregon Social Learning Center, Eugene, OR, 1982.

McNett, Ian Demograhic Imperatives For Educational Policy. American Council on Education, Washington, D.C., 1983.

Self, T. C. Dropouts: A Review of Literature, Project Talent Search. ERIC Document Reproduction Service, Arlington, VA, ED 260 307.

Slavin, R. E. Cooperative Learning. Longman, New York: NY, 1983.

Smith, R. C. & Hester, E. L. Report on the States' Excellence in Education Commissions: Who's Looking Out for At-Risk Youth? Chapel Hill, NC: MDC, Inc., 1985.

Stallings, J. A. & Hentzell, S. W. Effective Teaching and Learning in Urban Schools, CEMREL, Inc.,St. Louis,MO, 1978.

The Institute for Educational Leadership School Dropouts: Everybody's Problem. The Institute for Educational Leadership, Washington, D.C., 1986.

Tjossem, T. D. Intervention Strategies for High-Risk Infants and Young Children. University Park Press, Baltimore, MD: 1976.

U.S. General Accounting Office. School Dropouts: The Extent and the Nature of the Problem. Washington, D.C., 1986.

CHAPTER SIX

Pluralism in America:
Diversity in our Schools

Introduction

The population of the United States is changing, gradually, but profoundly. Today, we are a nation of 240 million people, about 50 million (21 percent) of whom are Black, Hispanic and Asian. Although federal and private projections vary, they all point in the same direction: Soon after the turn of the century, one out of every three Americans will be non-white (Hodgkinson, 1986).

Moreover, the average white American is 31 years old; the average Black American is only 25 and the average Hispanic American only 23. White Americans are moving out of their child- bearing years just as Black and Hispanic Americans are moving into them.

In 1980, 27 percent of public-school students were non-white, a 6 percent increase from a decade earlier. Most of the non- white student population is concentrated in a band of states that begins in New York, stretches southward down the Atlantic coast, and then westward, ending in California. Black enrollment is highest in the District of Columbia, Mississippi, South Carolina, Alabama, and Georgia; Hispanic enrollment, meanwhile, is highest in New Mexico, Texas, California and Arizona. (See Figure 15 - Minority Enrollment as Percent of Public Elementary/Secondary School Enrollment, by State).

California now has a "majority of minorities" in its elementary schools; 46 percent of the students in Texas are Black and Hispanic. In the 25 largest city school systems, the majority of students are minorities.

As Hodgkinson (1986) states, "*How tolerant will we be of the racial and ethnic diversity coming into the system? Each part of the country will have to deal with that.*"

Understanding this diversity in our country should be viewed from two perspectives. First, socially, what is your personal viewpoint with regard to our diversity in the United States? Second, from an educational perspective, what should be the role and responsibility of our schools

Figure 15

Minority Enrollment as Percent of Public
Elementary/Secondary School Enrollment, by State

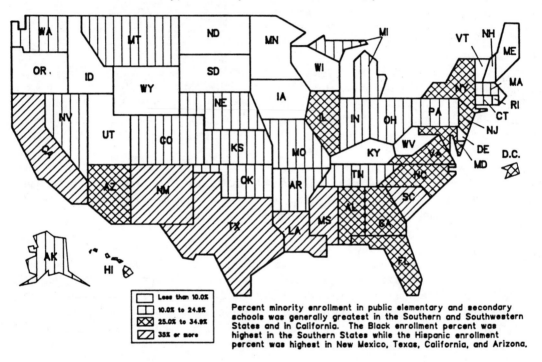

Less than 10.0%

10.0% to 24.9%

25.0% to 34.9%

35% or more

Percent minority enrollment in public elementary and secondary
schools was generally greatest in the Southern and Southwestern
States and in California. The Black enrollment percent was
highest in the Southern States while the Hispanic enrollment
percent was highest in New Mexico, Texas, California, and Arizona.

in addressing the diverse nature of our students? And, from both perspectives - how much diversity are we willing to recognize and accept - socially and educationally? Because of the heterogeneous character of the American population, the education of diverse or non-traditional groups has been a controversial subject. Consideration of the various diverse groups in American history suggests the broad diversity of problems and responses that has characterized educational efforts. There have been (and are) racial minorities, religious minorities, linguistic minorities, and national minorities. Each has had its own social and educational needs, which have been met or not been met in different ways.

Everyday we are exposed to these differences through radio, television, newspapers, our schools, our families, and the communities in which we live. Distorted messages about people who are "different" than we are, are not uncommon. Chinn and Gollnick (1983) state, "we may learn that Italian Americans control organized crime, Blacks are on welfare, Hispanics are illegal aliens, old people are senile, females are too emotional, hard hats are racists and handicapped individuals must be in constant pain and need to be taken care of. These stereotypes, and that is what they are, totally neglect the majority of individuals within each of these groups. Decisions made by employers, educators, politicians and neighbors are often based on such misconceptions."

As educators, it is our responsibility to assist our students, at all levels, with the interpretation and analysis of these cultural cues that are forced on them daily.

Chapter 5 - **Pluralism in America: Diversity in Our Schools** is intended to help focus our direction and planning with regard to one dimension of equity - ethnicity in the United States. There are three fundamental questions that this chapter is designed to raise:

(1)   What should be the role of the school in addressing ethnicity? Should we highlight the differences or minimize the differences?

(2)   How much "diversity" are we willing to allow in our society? In our schools?

(3)   What is the future of ethnicity in this country? Do we want it to remain a part of our American culture? Or, do we believe it is better to discourage it?

Certainly, as educators, how we address these three questions, would seem to dictate how we will perceive these differences within our society and specifically, within our schools and classrooms.

The nation's population will continue to grow, reaching 265 million by the year 2020, and much of that growth will be among the minority groups in this society. Although there is growing recognition of the importance of such demographic changes, there is also apprehension that this society's major education institutions are not responding quickly or adequately enough in developing policies that will maximize the contributions made by the escalating numbers of minorities in the population.

These findings are a result of a forum sponsored by the American Council of Education, the Forum of Educational Organization Leaders, and The Institute of Educational Leadership (Hodgkinson, 1988). The data portrays the dramatic change in the pattern of children entering our schools. For example, in the Fall of 1989, more than 3.6 million children began their formal schooling in the United States. These children are highlighted below:

---

1 out of 4 are from families who live in poverty.

14 percent are children of teenage mothers.

15 percent are mentally or physically handicapped.

15 percent speak a language other than English.

14 percent are children of unmarried parents.

40 percent will live in broken homes before they reach 18 years of age.

10 percent have poorly educated, even illiterate parents.

25 percent or more will not finish school.

The report goes on to say that by 1990, minorities of all ages will constitute 20 to 25 percent of our total population, while the percentage among the youth will be over 30 percent. *The conclusion for American education is inescapable: American public schools are now very heavily enrolled with minority students, will continue to be, and an increasing number of minority students will be eligible for college.*

A problem in studying the diversity within the United States, in particular, is its complexity. This complexity, coupled with the rapid changes of particular groups from generation to generation, makes the task more difficult. In a diverse nation such as the United States, the indigenous population, American Indians, makes up less than 1 percent of the total population; the other 99.4 percent are recent immigrants or have ancestors who were immigrants. According to the Harvard Encyclopedia of American Ethnic Groups (1980), at least 106 different ethnic groups compose this nation, excluding the 170 different American Indian groups. Thus it is possible, that we could trace our ancestry to one or more nations that existed independently at one time in history.

The fact that many people continue to maintain this ethnic identity over generations is the most remarkable quality of ethnicity in the United States. What is this phenomenon, *ethnicity* to which there are references in such diverse arenas as political elections, folk festivals, intergroup conflicts, desegregation, and federal forms?

What is an Ethnic Group?

An ethnic group is defined as a group of people within a larger society that is socially distinguished or set apart, by others and/or by itself, primarily on the basis of racial and/or cultural characteristics, such as religion, language, and tradition (DeVos, 1975). Ethnicity applies to everyone; people differ in their sense of ethnic identity. Everyone, however, has an ethnic group. Banks (1979) wrote:

All Americans are members of an ethnic group, since each of us belongs to a group which shares a sense of peoplehood, values, behaviors, patterns, and cultural traits which differ from those of other groups. However, one's attachment and identity with his or her ethnic group varies greatly with the individual, the times of his or her life, and the situations and/or settings in which an individual finds himself or herself. Ethnicity is extremely important for some individuals within our society and is of little or no importance to others.

DeVos (1975) describes ethnicity as an attribute of membership in a group that is set off by its ethnic or racial uniqueness. It is a sense of social belonging and ultimate loyalty to that group. Individuals in the groups share a history, a language (whether or not they can speak the language), the same value system and structure, and the same customs and traditions. To maintain the group identity throughout the generations, the attitudes, values, behaviors, and rituals are practiced in the family, the church, and social clubs.

According to Bennett (1986) in the United States, boundaries of ethnicity are mainly psychological in nature rather than territorial. A person does not have to live in the same community with other members of the group in order to identify strongly with the group. The boundaries are maintained by ascription from within as well as from external sources that place persons in a specific group because of the way they look, the color of their skin, the location of their home, or their name. Although all members of society can identify with one or more ethnic heritages, not all members choose to emphasize their ethnicity. In fact, some even choose to function as non-ethnics. The degree of identification with the ethnic group varies from person to person. This is certainly the cause of great debate concerning ethnicity in this country. There are individuals who prefer not to identify with any ethnic group, while others do. *Why do some individuals maintain their ethnicity and others chose not to identify with their ethnic background?*

Ethnic Minority Group.

The label minority group is confusing; today, many individuals prefer not to be labeled a "minority." The term connotes inferior or lesser status in relation to the majority. Furthermore, minority is often confused with numerical minority, when in fact a numerical minority may control a numerical majority (Wirth, 1945). Wirth defined minority group in terms of subordinate position, as "a group of people who, because of their physical or cultural characteristics, are singled out from others in the society in which they live for differential and unequal treatment and who therefore regard themselves as objects of collective discrimination."

The degree to which an ethnic group (*microculture*) retains ethnic minority group status depends upon how it is received by and/or receives the host society (*macroculture*). Does it experience long-term segregation? Is it quickly absorbed into the mainstream? Does it wish to retain its own cultural traditions?

The Melting Pot

America has always been a nation of immigrants. Many citizens believe the resulting ethnic and cultural diversity has given this society a distinctive quality. Others may argue that the sooner one rids himself/herself of these distinct qualities and becomes American - the better off he/she will be - and the better the country would be. Thus these opposing philosophies have sometimes strained the social fabric of this country even as it has strengthened it.

The first great period of immigration in this country was between 1910 and 1930, when the number of foreign-born Americans reached a peak of 14.2 million. In 1984, some 544,000 people immigrated legally to the United States - roughly as many as the annual average during the 1920s. Add the estimated 300,000 to 500,000 people who entered the country illegally and 1984 becomes the greatest year for immigration in our history. Immigrants entering the United States each year account for two-thirds of all the immigrants in the world. If the nation continues to allow 750,000 immigrants to settle here annually, by 2030 the population will be about 18 percent larger than it would be otherwise (Hodgkinson, 1986).

During the early part of this century, the majority of immigrants to the United States were of European heritage, and the color of their skin undoubtedly eased their assimilation into the predominantly white American mainstream. Today, however, most are Hispanic and Asian. About 40 percent of all legal immigrants come from Asia and another 40 percent from Mexico, Central and South America, and the Caribbean. Three out of four of the illegal immigrants come from Latin America - 50 percent from Mexico and 25 percent from other Central and South American countries.

Most parts of the nation feel little impact from this wave of immigrants because the majority of newcomers are choosing to settle in relatively few places. But in those areas, the effects have been astounding.

The concept of the melting pot was proposed by the playwright Israel Zangwill in his 1909 play The Melting Pot. In that work, a Russian-Jewish immigrant described the United States in this speech:

America is God's crucible, the great Melting Pot, where all races of Europe are melting and reforming! Here you stand, good folk, think I, when I see them at Ellis Island, here you stand in your fifty groups with your fifty hatreds and rivalries, but you won't be long like that, brothers, for these are the fires of God. A fig for your feuds and vendettas! Germans, and Frenchmen, Irishmen and Englishmen, Jews and Russians - into the Crucible with you all! God is making the American. . . the real American has not yet arrived. He is only in the Crucible, I tell you - he will be the fusion of all races, the coming superman. (Zangwill, 1909)

The melting pot, according to Pratte (1979), was quickly adopted as a promising ideal for fusing persons from various new and old immigrant groups into a new common American society. One of the problems or disadvantages (depending upon your perspective) of the melting pot was that it never proposed to melt all ethnic and cultural groups. Even in Zangwill's speech there is no mention of adding American Indians, Blacks, and/or Hispanics other than immigrants from Spain, or Asians to the crucible.

Although the prospect of being a part of the pot that would create the "real American" seemed an attractive idea to many immigrants, other groups, particularly American Indians, fought against becoming the *One Model American*. To melt into the American society required abandoning customs, dress, and language so that one would think, feel, and act like an American. However, there were many immigrants who strived to rid themselves of their accents and often anglicized their names. Although the unmeltable groups might anglicize their names and show no signs of an accent, they were unable to rid themselves of their skin color or physical characteristics that marked them as different from the idealized model American who was supposed to emerge from the melting pot. Even when these unmeltable groups chose to be the fused American, they were not accepted primarily because they were not white.

In an important sense, then, the ethnic diversity factor in the United States has been given a particular view by the ideology of the melting pot. By tying ethnic diversity to the melting pot, the basic direction given was that the immigrants were to intermarry on a large scale, denounce their Old World heritage by changing cultural patterns to those of the dominant or majority group, and impart positive meaning to an otherwise chaotic and highly fluid social situation (Pratte, 1979).

Thus, to the immigrant and the established American, the ideology of the melting pot gave support to the belief that the American experience was a new historical epoch for humanity; human history was being given an entirely new direction by the melting pot of America.

First, it was believed that the process called for was totally a biological one, the fusion of races by interbreeding and intermarriage. Second, it was believed that the melting pot meant a process by which persons or groups who were unlike in their social heritage somehow came to share and cherish the same body of tradition, loyalties, and attitudes. The first belief is commonly referred to as *amalgamation* ; the second as *assimilation*. Some ideologists of the melting pot looked at both of these as called for, and many older Americans as well shared this view. The melting pot was thus an ambiguous ideology for shaping thought and action regarding ethnic diversity, but the ambiguity was no obstacle and allowed for a number of groups to work together to direct social change in a particular way (Cubberly, 1909).

The fact remains, however, that the melting pot was a passionate belief by which many people lived by and continue to believe in and live by today.

The Role of the School.

What role, if any, did the schools play in the ideology of the melting pot? The mixture of the myth and reality in America has produced numerous legends, not the least of which is found in public education. If one were to ask the so-called *individual on the street* what role, if any, does schooling play in the success of the melting pot, the answer would most likely be that the public school was the prime factor. Indeed, many Americans look on schooling as the chief vehicle for assimilation.

As was so vividly expressed by the educational historian Cubberly (1909):

Everywhere these people (immigrants) tend to settle in groups or settlements and to set up their own national manners, customs and observances. Our task is to <u>break up</u> their groups and settlements, to assimilate or amalgamate these people as a part of the American race, and to implant in their children, so far as can be done, the Anglo-Saxon conception of righteousness, law, order, and popular government, and to awaken in them reverence for our democratic institutions and for those things which we as people hold to be of abiding worth.

According to Pratte (1979), the success or miracle of the melting pot was accomplished with schooling serving as the prime agent in the process. The legend has it that an enlightened body of teachers and administrators led the immigrants in establishing themselves as 100 percent Americans. The school, without hesitation, did its best for the immigrants and the country by making a new American out of the 'wretched refuse.' For some, the public school legend makes of schooling the primary means of Americanization.

While a core of reality lies behind the legend (myths usually have some basic connection with reality), the legend, as it stands, simply is not true. The twin elements of melting pot magic and public schooling alchemy are largely pseudo-historical, tending to ignore the fact that the school was, after all, only one institution that stood ready to meet the melting pot's demands for amalgamation. Moreover, the schools were not supported on a grand scale, and in large cities where the crush of immigrant children was heaviest, teachers were hard put to teach the basic three R's, let alone socialize the students in terms of the melting pot ideal. If ethnics were Americanized, the school did so in terms of imposition of *White Anglo-Saxon Protestant (WASP)* values and standards, not the ideal of the melting pot (Hunter, 1974). The main point is that although most Americans have assumed that schooling was essential to the success of the melting pot, the fact is that immigrants were not educated with the melting-pot ideal at all - they were indoctrinated in the schools with the values of the dominant White Anglo-Saxon Protestant (WASP) culture.

The common view offered with regard to ethnic diversity is that American schooling was a highly effective vehicle in achieving the success of the melting pot. But whether we recognize the fact or not, most immigrants and their children experienced little of the melting pot ideal. The myth continues, but the reality is that schooling promoted an Anglo-conformism that virtually denigrated the ancestral heritage of immigrants. Moreover, some groups were never allowed to melt into the American pot. And it is largely the latter groups who are now determined to be more self-assured, more proud of themselves and better prepared to be more self-determining about their own fate.

The Anglo-Conformity Theory

As mentioned earlier, many educators believe that schooling promoted more of an Anglo-Conformity perspective. For many researchers, primarily Milton Gordon (1954), the *Anglo-Conformity* theory better describes what was actually expected of immigrants and ethnic groups during this period. Distinct ethnic groups were not expected to contribute equally to the making of a new American as idealized in the melting pot theory. Instead they were expected to adopt the WASP culture that historically molded most of the political and social institutions of the country. They were required to attend school to learn the language, values, traits, dress, and customs of the dominant culture. To be accepted as Americans, members of these immigrant groups had to conform to the patterns of thinking, feeling, and behaving of the WASP culture.

The Anglo-Conformity theory described what was expected of immigrant and ethnic minority groups, but it did not describe how these particular groups were actually behaving as members within the larger society. Although some members of these groups chose to adopt the WASP culture as their own, many refused to assimilate into the dominant culture and maintained separate ethnic communities and enclaves within the society. They developed within-group institutions, agencies, and power structures for services within their ethnic communities (Banks, 1981).

This is also often referred to as **Separatism.** In virtually all sizes of cities across this country, pockets of ethnic groups still remain vital links to maintaining group cohesion and a sense of kinship. Obviously, the actual amount of isolation within all these separate entities depends upon the amount of language, customs and traditions that are maintained and lived by on a daily basis. My point being, we still have large numbers of ethnic groups, in many cities and towns across this country, that are living and functioning in a separatist manner, for a variety of reasons.

As Banks (1981) suggests in all probability, neither the Anglo-Conformity nor the melting pot concept adequately describes the complex process which occurred and is still occurring in the development of American society. Both concepts are in some ways incomplete or misleading because non-Anglo ethnic groups have had (and are still having) a much more cogent impact on American society than is reflected by either theory. WASP culture in the U.S. has been greatly influenced by other ethnic and immigrant cultures. Such ethnic groups as Italian-Americans and Polish Americans retain many more ethnic characteristics than are often acknowledged and or recognized.

The rather strong ethnic cultures existing within many Hispanic and Black communities are usually more often recognized by scholars and practitioners. As Novak (1973) has insightfully pointed out, however, ethnicity within White ethnic communities is often subconscious and subtle. Ethnic individuals themselves, especially White ethnic group members, are often unaware of the extent to which they are ethnic. Glazer and Moynihan (1975) recognized the tenacity of ethnicity within modern American society, writing in their classic book, Beyond the Melting Pot, *Individuals, in very considerable numbers to be sure, broke out of their mold, but the groups remained. . . The point about the melting pot is that it did not happen.*

Cultural Pluralism

The melting pot concept has been highly criticized and challenged because of its inaccuracy and how it has been misleading. The Anglo-Conformity concept suggests that the WASP culture changed very little in America and that other ethnic groups did all the changing.

Following World War II, ethnic minority groups became increasingly powerful, both politically and socially, and refused to tolerate discrimination by the dominant WASP cultural group and its political and social institutions. In the 1960's, the concept of *cultural pluralism* became popular in education circles. However, according to Higham (1978) this idea of cultural pluralism was born near the turn of the century when great numbers of European immigrants were entering the United States at the same time that Nativism, designed to stop the massive flow of immigrants, was becoming pernicious and widespread· Philosophers and writers, such as Horace Kallen, Randolph Bourne, and Julius Drachsler, strongly defended the rights of the immigrants, arguing that they had a right to maintain their ethnic cultures and institutions in the United States, and used the concepts of cultural pluralism and cultural democracy to describe their philosophical positions.

Ravitch (1985) states the principle of cultural pluralism is as thoroughly American as the melting pot idea. What pluralism means in practice is that diverse groups have the right to be left alone, so long as their members fulfill the basic obligations of citizenship. John Dewey (1939) described the American concept of pluralism as:

. . . a complete separation of nationality from citizenship. Not only have we separated language, cultural traditions, all that is called a race, from the state - that is, from problems of political organization and power. To us language, literature, creed, group ways, national culture, are social rather than national, political interests."

Like the concepts of the Melting Pot and Anglo-Conformity, however, Cultural Pluralism may not adequately describe the complex nature of ethnic relations and cultural development in the United States. When Americans urge one concept or the other on the public schools, they usually have in mind a certain kind of society that the schools are supposed to produce. Since American society is made up of hundreds, perhaps thousands, of different cultures and subcultures, the schools are incessantly torn between pressures to enforce unity and pressures to reinforce diversity (Chinn & Gollnick, 1983). Some members of cultural groups strongly support the development of identity and commitment with their cultural group almost to the exclusion of influence from the dominant culture. Under such a pluralist ideology, the rights of the group membership are more important than the rights of the individual. These particular groups assume that an ethnic group can attain inclusion and full participation within a society only when it can bargain from a powerful position and when it has little or no influence from competing groups. In its strongest form, the cultural pluralist idea suggests that ethnic groups live within tight ethnic boundaries and communities and rarely, if ever, participates within the universal American culture and society. To this extent, cultural pluralism denies the reality of a universal American culture and national identity which every American, regardless of ethnicity and ethnic group membership, shares to a large extent. I believe that most Americans highly value their national identity and significant ethnic behaviors and characteristics. This common national culture and identity should be accepted, respected, appreciated and promoted by the schools in any reform effort related to ethnicity.

While some members of cultural groups strongly support a pluralist ideology, there is little overall support for a cultural entity separate from the dominant culture of the United States. If we were to develop a continuum that defined assimilation theories, we could place the Melting Pot at one end of the continuum, and Separatism at the other end, with cultural pluralism between, as shown below:

Melting Pot	Cultural Pluralism	Separatism

If a representative sample of the U.S. population were asked to indicate whether citizens should be expected to conform to cultural patterns, values, and traits of the dominant culture or be allowed to maintain a separate Cultural identity, they would probably indicate that neither end of the continuum is desirable. Somewhere between the two ends of the continuum is desirable, although responses would be likely to favor the Melting Pot. If we were to study the cultural patterns of individuals in the United States, we would again find individuals scattered across the continuum. Such findings would support the idea that ethnic attachments exist simultaneously with shared cultural traits. How culturally diverse we are does not seem to matter as long as we agree on certain basic values, one of which is respect for one another's cultural differences. As Gollnick and Chinn (1983) state, *We need to learn to live together, not how to become alike.*

Summary

The demographic data and the theories offered in this chapter indicate that America's population is becoming more diverse, not more homogeneous. There seems to be an increasing resistance to the old, majority American philosophy of assimilation reflected in the melting pot ideology.

In addition to a more diverse population, the nation will have larger numbers of minorities in proportion to the majority population. In many larger cities, minorities already are in the majority, and the trend will continue.

The minority population grows younger and increases at a faster rate, while the majority population ages and slows down in growth. In education, the wave of declining enrollments now rolling through the system will reverse itself, but a very different education environment will emerge regionally, racially, and economically.

As Hodgkinson (1985) states, demographic forecasts can permit policy makers to peer into the future to discern the kinds of problems and opportunities that await. The challenge to the schools is less clear. What policies, what programs, will ensure an excellent educational system for the generation now growing up and for the future generations? Clearly, a program that seeks to treat all alike will end up continuing to benefit some more than others and to leave still others with no benefits at all. An educational policy that focuses on the needs laid out by the demographics will have to be more targeted and tailored than has been the case up to now. Based on the demographic data and the changing nature of the economy, it seems clear that much greater attention will have to be paid to the needs of an ever-growing minority population. The demographic future is rather predictable: Much less predictable is the nation's capacity (the schools in particular), or willingness, to initiate changes in policy, practices and resource allocation patterns to cope with that future.

Schools will have to answer some important questions. First, what is or will be the policy addressing the diversity within our society in general? Second, what is or will be the policy and practices of their school in addressing diversity of individual students or groups?

Today's education must include the development of skills and concepts students can use to form their own cultural perspective to allow them to function actively and effectively in our ever-changing society. Raw knowledge of ethnic or cultural differences will not be enough. Tomorrow's adults will need constructive attitudes toward the differences which exist between people and cultures. They will require a set of values which will allow them to deal effectively with change in our diverse society. As the self-interests of one group interacts with the self-interests of persons from other segments of our society, there will be a search for common ground so the interest of both parties will be protected.

Tomorrow's citizens will find differences between themselves and other people, and they will have to look for strength in those differences. They will have greater opportunities to interact with people whose values do not match their own; and as a result, they will need attitudes that will help them build strong working relationships. They will need an appreciation of the interdependency of the people in our diverse society which goes beyond knowledge of contributions, holidays, and cultural characteristics. Students must now begin to learn to respond positively and easily to change because change is the only thing we can promise them in the future. In short, leaders of business, industry, government, science and education will be most effective in the future if they who can cope with change, deal with a society as a system, and appreciate and accept human diversity.

WORKSHEET 1

Define the following terms:

1. Ethnic group: a group of people w/in a larger society socially disting. or set apart, basis of racial/cultural characteristics: rel., lang., trad.

2. Ethnic minority group: gp of people who for phys/cult char., singled out from others in soc'ty for diff'l/ unequal treatm't, reg. selves as obj. of coll. discrim.

3. Macroculture: the host society of the min. gp.

4. Microculture: the ethnic gp itself

5. Anglo-Conformity Theory: conformity to the traits, expec'ns of Anglo America, not of one's ethnic groups

6. Melting Pot Theory: all people from various ethnic gps would be combined to create Americans — generally don include groups today considered oppressed

7. Cultural Pluralism: sep'n of nationality from citizenship — of cult'l traditions from political power
   e.g. Italian & American simultaneously

8. Assimilation: those unlike in social heritage somehow come to cherish, share same body of tradn/lgy's/attit. — social melting pot

9. Amalgamation: biological vers. of melting pot: fusion of races by interbreeding/marriage

10. WASP: White Anglo Saxon Prot., the predom. culture

11. Separatism refusal of gp. to assimilate into predom. culture, maint'g its own cultural enclave w/in U.S. physically

WORKSHEET 2

1. What are the demographic projections for the near future - in terms of the children entering our schools?

They'll be less white, less trad'l nuclear family, poorer, less nurtured at home, fewer native speakers of English, more learning impaired

What are the implications for educators with the above demographics? Explain.

Since educators tend to have not suffered from the above as children, they're not as intimately familiar with these problems -- adjustment of teaching style, add'n of resources

What are the implications for teacher training programs?

They'll need to train students to und. these problems, introduce strategies for working with them.

2. In your opinion, what should be the role of the public school in addressing the diversity of students that are presently enrolled and for those who will be entering our schools? Explain.

The school needs to get the facts first — demogr. data of its students. Relevant literature should be consulted. Staff should design own strategies, meeting as gp/teams to monitor implementation

3. Are all ethnic groups defined by the same factors? Explain. (Provide an example.)

Not really. Most "white" ethnic groups are defined by lang. (their own or use of English), appearance, cuisine, cust. occup. modes of living: Italians, Poles. Black, Hispanics, Asians, N-A have race involved as well, which in common excludes them

4. Why do some ethnic groups isolate themselves from the mainstream of American society? Explain.

Some just don't buy into our ways of life. The Amish, for example, reject most of our technology, fashion, religious, ways of earning a living. They only submit to this society to the extent they must for practicality and the law.

5.   How does a school promote the melting pot theory? Provide examples.

It can reward mainstream ways of speech, phys. conduct, dress, activity — ie., std. English over Black English. It may even prohibit actions contrary to norm: English only, dress codes, expulsions/suspensions for rule breaking.

In what ways can a school promote cultural pluralism? Provide examples.

By tolerating and celebrating difference, insofar as it's possible. I would pair up 2 kids of diff. social or ethnic or racial bkgds and have each report on the other's way of life, aspects of it, etc.

WORKSHEET 3

Different Viewpoints on America's Ethnic Composition

Directions: Each of the following items presents a particular view of the nature of American society with regard to its ethnic composition. Some clearly illustrate a belief in the melting pot while others represent a separatist point of view, and still others may represent a middle ground between these two extremes, cultural pluralism. Under each item place an **X** on the continuum to indicate the perception of America's ethnic character as the individual makes the statement.

1. "My parents decided never to teach us Spanish. They hoped that by not doing so, we would gain a generation in the process of becoming full Americans."

| Melting Pot | Cultural Pluralism | Separatism |

2. "Outwardly I lived the life of the white man, yet all the while I kept in direct contact with tribal life. While I had learned all that I could of the white man's culture, I never forgot that of my people. I kept the language, tribal manners and usages, sang the songs and danced the dances."

| Melting Pot | Cultural Pluralism | Separatism |

3. "That's right! I was ashamed of my name. Not only that, I was ashamed of being a Jew. There you have it! Exit Abraham Isaac Arshawsky. . . enter Art Shaw! You see, of course, how simple this little transformation was."

| Melting Pot | Cultural Pluralism | Separatism |

4.   "I am not referred to as our seventh-grade math teacher, but as our minority math teacher."

Melting Pot   Cultural Pluralism   Separatism

5.   "It makes no difference to me whether my students are Black, Hispanic or Asian. They are
      students and I treat them all the same, I don't see any differences."

Melting Pot   Cultural Pluralism   Separatism

6.   "There are many regions of the United States where the third generation of Americans do not
      speak English."

Melting Pot   Cultural Pluralism   Separatism

7.   "Why all the attention to the "minorities?" "Why not include and emphasize Irish Americans,
      German Americans and Swedish Americans?"

Melting Pot   Cultural Pluralism   Separatism

8.   "Americans who do not speak English should learn it or go back to where they came from!"

Melting Pot   Cultural Pluralism   Separatism

9. "The Amish want to keep to themselves - a separate people. They are tied together by their religion and its values, by kinship (most are related), and by customs that make them appear different from everyone else."

Melting Pot   **Cultural Pluralism**   **Separatism**

10. "What the United States needs at this time, more than at any other time in our history, is an official language-English."

Melting Pot   **Cultural Pluralism**   **Separatism**

11. "More and more, I think in family terms, less ambitiously, on a less than national scale. The difference in being Slovak, Catholic, and lower-middle class, seem to be more important to me."

Melting Pot   **Cultural Pluralism**   **Separatism**

12. "I am not a 'minority,' I am a Japanese-American."

Melting Pot   **Cultural Pluralism**   **Separatism**

13. "We demand that Spanish be the first language of the school and that the textbooks be rewritten to emphasize the heritage and the contributions of Hispanics in the United States."

Melting Pot   **Cultural Pluralism**   **Separatism**

14. "Black people just don't want to help themselves. They just keep together in their groups and they will never learn what it takes to make it in this country."

Melting Pot   **Cultural Pluralism**   **Separatism**

15. "Bilingual education is detrimental to the progress a student can make in school and in society. Teach them English as quickly as possible because that is what they will need to learn in order to succeed in American society."

Melting Pot   **Cultural Pluralism**   **Separatism**

16. "I don't consider myself 'ethnic,' I am an American. The only traditions we maintain in my family are the major holidays, birthdays, family reunions and the importance of our religion."

Melting Pot   **Cultural Pluralism**   **Separatism**

17. "My grandparents came to America not knowing a word of English, with no formal education and made a pretty good life for themselves. I don't understand why the new immigrants are not able to adapt and become Americans like my grandparents did."

Melting Pot	Cultural Pluralism	Separatism

18. "There is nothing wrong with an all Black school - as long as the programs meet state requirements for graduation and accreditation standards. As a matter of fact, they will probably get along better with their own kind."

Melting Pot	Cultural Pluralism	Separatism

REFERENCES

Banks, James A. Multiethnic Education: Theory and Practice. Allyn and Bacon, Inc., Boston, MA, 1981.

Banks, James A. Teaching Strategies for Ethnic Studies. Allyn and Bacon, 2nd Edition, Boston, MA, 1979.

Bennett Christine I. Comprehensive Multicultural Education - Theory and Practice. Allyn and Bacon, Boston, MA, 1986.

Chinn, Philip A. & Gollnick, Donna M. Multicultural Education in a Pluralistic Society. The C. V. Mosby Company, St. Louis, MO, 1983.

Cubberly, Ellwood P. Changing Conceptions of Education. Houghton Mifflin, Boston, MA, 1909. p. 16.

De Vos, G. Ethnic Pluralism: Conflict and Accommodations. Mayfield Publishers, In G. De Vos and L. Romanucci-Ross (Eds.), In Ethnic Identity: Cultural Continuities and Change, Palo Alto, CA, 1975.

Dewey, John Freedom and Culture. Putnam, New York, NY, 1939.

Glazer, Nathan & Moynihan, Daniel P. (Eds.) Ethnicity: Theory and Experience. Harvard University Press, Cambridge, MA, 1975.

Higham, John (Ed.) Ethnic Leadership in America. The John Hopkins University Press, Baltimore, MD, 1978.

Hodgkinson, Harold L. All One System - Demographics of Education, Kindergarten through Graduate School. The Institute for Educational Leadership, Inc., Washington, D.C., 1985.

Hodgkinson, Harold L. "The Patterns in Our Social Fabric are Changing." Education Week, May 14, 1986. p. 16.

Hodgkinson, Harold L. "Today's Numbers, Tomorrow's Nation - Demography's Awesome Challenge for Schools." Education Week, May 14, 1986. p. 14.

Hunter, William A. Antecedents to the Development and Emphasis on Multicultural Education. American Association of Colleges for Teacher Education (AACTE), Washington, D.C., 1974.

McNett, Ian Demographic Imperatives: Implications for Educational Policy American Council on Education, Forum of Educational Organization Leaders and The Institute for Educational Leadership, September, 1983.

Novak, Michael The Rise of the Unmeltable Ethnics. MacMillian Publishing Co., Inc. New York, NY, 1973.

Pratte, Richard Pluralism in Education: Conflict, Clarity and Commitment. Thomas Books, Springfield, IL, 1979.

Ravitch, Diane The Schools We Deserve Basic Books, Inc., New York, NY, 1985.

Thernstrom, S. (Ed.) Harvard Encyclopedia of American Ethnic Groups. Harvard University Press, Cambridge, MA, 1980.

Wirth, Louis "The Problem of Minority Groups." In The Science of Man in the World Crisis, ed. Ralph Linton. Columbia University Press, New York, NY, 1945.

Zangwill, Israel The Melting Pot MacMillian Publishing Co, New York, NY, 1909.

SUGGESTED READINGS

Reimers, D. M. Ethnic Americans: A History of Immigration and Assimilation. Harper and Row Publishers, New York, NY, 1975.

Uncertain Americans: Readings in Ethnic History. Oxford University Press, New York, NY, 1977.

Allport, Gordon The Nature of Prejudice. Doubleday, Anchor Books, Garden City, NJ, 1954.

Bahr, Howard, Chadwick, Bruce A. & Stauss, Joseph J. American Ethnicity. D.C. Heath Publishers, Lexington, MA, 1979.

Cortes, Carlos Understanding You and Them: Tips for Teaching about Ethnicity ERIC Clearinghouse for Social Studies, Boulder, CO, 1976.

Dinnerstein, Leonard & Jaher, F. C. (Eds.) The Aliens: A History of Ethnic Minorities in America. Oxford University Press, New York, NY, 1970.

Gelfand, Donald E. & Kutzik, Alfred J. (Eds.) Ethnicity and Aging: Theory, Research and Policy. Springer Publishing Company, New York, NY, 1979.

Hall, Edward T. Beyond Culture. Doubleday, Garden City, NJ, 1978.

Kinloch, Graham C. The Sociology of Minority Group Relations. Prentice-Hall, Englewood Cliffs, NJ, 1979.

Novak, Michael Further Reflections on Ethnicity. Jednota Press, Middletown, PA, 1977.

Ravitch, Diane The Troubled Crusade - American Education 1945 - 1980. Basic Books, Inc., New York, NY, 1983.

United States Commission on Civil Rights. The Tarnished Door: Civil Rights Issues in Immigration. The Commission, Washington, D.C., 1980.

Wynar, Lubomyr R. Encyclopedia Directory of Ethnic Organizations in the United States Libraries Unlimited, Littleton, CO, 1975.

CHAPTER SEVEN

A Host of Languages: Policies and Issues

Introduction

Language variation in the United States has evolved out of a long history of cultural diversity. If equity in education is to succeed either in cultivating understanding and respect for social and cultural diversity, or in providing a truly effective learning experience for all students - especially for students from diverse socio-cultural backgrounds - it must be concerned with the diversity in language form and use.

Before Europeans began to colonize this country, native people spoke hundreds of different languages. Colonists brought with them Spanish, French, English, Dutch, and German, as well as slaves who spoke a number of distinct West African languages. In the nineteenth and twentieth centuries, massive immigration has continued to replenish our linguistic resources with a host of tongues from virtually every other nation in the world. Some of these languages have disappeared with hardly a trace, but a surprising number have either continued to be spoken in the United States or have left their mark on American English (Conklin & Lourie, 1983).

As we know, Americans are a diverse group of people, speaking many languages and many varieties of English. But for the most part, we have conducted our public life as if we were all monolingual English speakers. Only in the last three decades have we begun - often reluctantly - to respect linguistic diversity and minority rights enough to validate nonstandard dialects, offer bilingual education, or make public information available in non-English languages. Since the late 1970s, our non-English speaking population has increased because of legal immigrants, a large number of illegal immigrants, and refugees from Indochina, the Soviet Union, and Latin America. Consequently, the question of how to treat and address our non-English speakers is more pressing now than it has been at any time since World War I. In the Fall of 1989 - approximately 10-15 percent of our students beginning school - spoke a language other than English.

In this decade, the United States will confront a complex set of issues that will focus on languages other than English and their speakers. We will have to decide: (1) whether to keep admitting more non-English speakers into the United States, (2) how to plan for the education of those who are already in our schools, (3) which approach best meets the needs of limited English proficient students (bilingual education or English as a second language), and (4) whether we wish to encourage or discourage the continued use of languages other than English.

Chapter 6 - **A Host of Languages: Policies and Issues,** is intended to provide a variety of viewpoints on the special educational needs of linguistically different students and the most popular methods used in addressing those needs. In order to better understand how we have arrived at such a dilemma in this country, it will be necessary to provide a brief historical and judicial overview. We must be sensitive and understanding to the special needs these particular students bring to our schools. It is the intent of this section to convey the message that we have a significant number of limited English proficient students in our schools. Given the demographics presented earlier in this book, those numbers will more than likely increase. What concerns me is that a significant number of students in our schools have not been recognized, identified or are not being provided for.

The issue of linguistically different students in our schools, the current drive to get English recognized as our nation's "official" language and the heated debate about which program best serves our youth have become national headlines. As educators, we need to have an understanding of the policies, practices and issues facing the schools.

Historical Overview

In assessing the needs of limited English speaking students today, it may be helpful to understand the evolutionary pattern of language treatment that has occurred in the United States. (See Figure 16 - Evolutionary Pattern of Language Treatment in the U.S).

Figure 16

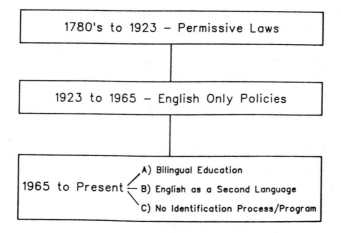

EVOLUTIONARY PATTERN OF LANGUAGE TREATMENT
IN THE U.S.

1780's to 1923 — Permissive Laws

1923 to 1965 — English Only Policies

1965 to Present
- A) Bilingual Education
- B) English as a Second Language
- C) No Identification Process/Program

During the first period, 1780s to 1920s, there was no explicit designation of English as the official language and there was a great tolerance for the use of other languages in the schools. Bilingual education had been part of the immigrant experience in America since the Colonial period, when native- language schooling was the rule rather than the exception. By the late 17th century, at least 18 different tongues were spoken by European ethnic groups, and many more were spoken by Indian tribes. While English was most prevalent, German, Dutch, French, Swedish, and Polish were also common(Castellanos, 1983). New arrivals fought vigorously to preserve their native customs, and language loyalties were strong. Indeed, the Pilgrims had left Holland in part because they feared their children were losing English. Where immigrant groups settled in enclaves, they naturally taught their children in their own languages, despite some attempts to impose English instruction. With mounting pressures for political unity, English became more common at ethnic schools - sometimes as a class and sometimes as a medium of instruction. Still, no uniform language policy prevailed during the 19th century. Bilingual education was accepted in areas where ethnic groups had influence and rejected where anti-immigrant sentiment was strong. By the mid-1800s, public and parochial German- English schools were operating in such cities as Baltimore, Cincinnati, Cleveland, Indianapolis, Milwaukee, and St. Louis. Wherever immigrant groups possessed sufficient political power - whether it was Italian, Polish, Czech, French, Dutch, or German - foreign languages were introduced into elementary and secondary schools, either as subjects or as languages of instruction. A resurgence of nativism in the late 19th century, a backlash against the foreign-born, led by such organizations as the Know- Nothing-Party marked the beginning of a decline for bilingual education. St. Louis cancelled its German-English program in 1888 after redistricting watered-down German voting strength. Louisville, KY, and St. Paul, MN, soon followed suit, allowing German to be taught only as a foreign language in the upper grades (Crawford, 1987).

In 1916, the U.S. Commissioner of Education compromised and allowed Spanish instruction in grades 1-4, Spanish and English in grade 5, and English only thereafter - a policy that lasted until 1948. With the approach of World War I, anti-German feeling spelled trouble not only for German-language instruction, but for all bilingual-education programs.

During the second period, 1920s to 1965, specifically in response to massive immigration and a growing hatred to the "foreigner," fourteen states had passed laws requiring English as the medium of instruction. By 1923, *(Meyers v. Nebraska)* the number of states requiring English had soared to thirty-five (Anderson & Boyer, 1970). In its 1923 ruling, the Supreme Court struck down a Nebraska law prohibiting foreign-language teaching before the 9th grade. "The protection of the Constitution extends to all those who speak other languages as well as to those born with English on the tongue," the Court said. "Perhaps it would be highly advantageous if all had a ready under-standing of our ordinary speech, but this cannot be coerced by methods which conflict with the Constitution - a desirable end cannot be prompted by prohibited means" (1923). Still, the trend had been established: bilingual education was virtually eradicated throughout the nation by what has been described as "the anti-hyphenation, anti-foreign language, anti- immigration movement." According to Castellanos (1983), roughly during the same period, the study of foreign languages, including Latin, declined dramatically, from 83 percent of high school students in 1910 to 22 percent in 1948. "This linguistic equivalent of 'book burning' worked admirably well in forcing assimilation," Gonzales (1975) writes. "But, he added, "it worked best with the Northern European immigrants," who had a "cultural affinity" with American values and shared a Caucasian racial history." For other language minorities, English-only schooling brought difficulties. While their cultures were suppressed, discrimination barred these groups from full acceptance into society.

As a result of several pieces of legislation, the third period (1965 to the present) brought alternatives and different approaches to the language diversity in our schools. Presently, languages other than English are once again recognized in the schools and by the courts.

Most Americans take it for granted that English is the official language of the United States and even imagine that every American speaks it fluently. According to the 1980 Census, however, 11 percent of Americans come from non-English speaking homes, while in 1986, the percentage of children starting school - with a language other than English - was estimated at 15 percent (Conklin & Lourie, 1983).

Non-English speakers live in all fifty states of our union. (See Figure 17 - Number of Persons with Non-English Mother Tongues by State).

Figure 17

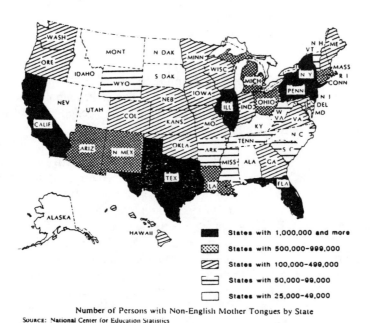

Number of Persons with Non-English Mother Tongues by State
SOURCE: National Center for Education Statistics

The figure displays their relative population densities. In two states - over 25 percent of the population is non-English speaking - Hawaii with its large proportion of Asian Americans and New Mexico with its many Spanish speakers and American Indians. In California, Arizona, Texas, Louisiana, New Jersey, Conneticut, Rhode Island, Massachusetts, New York, and North Dakota, between 16 and 25 percent of the population claims a non- English speaking background. In twenty-three states, the non- English language minority comprises 10 percent or more of the total population. Clearly, non-English languages can be heard today in every region of the country.

The Role of the Federal Government.

Historically, the federal government had played a limited role in the financing of public instruction. By the middle of the 1960s however, the pattern was to change drastically. This shift was clearly demonstrated with the introduction and passage of the Elementary and Secondary Education Act of 1965 (commonly referred to as Chapter 1). As mentioned in an earlier chapter these new programs were intended to provide financial assistance for schools in meeting the particular needs of impoverished and *educationally deprived* school-age children. The Elementary and Secondary Education Act supported reform, in that it provided recognition for the need of other types of educational and instructional approaches regarding the educational needs of students of limited English speaking abilities or students from low-income family backgrounds. Proper implementation of federally-sponsored educational programs was aided and regulated by the federal guidelines of the *Civil Rights Act of 1964. Section 601 of the Act states:*

No person in the United States shall, on the grounds of race, color, or national origin be excluded from participation in, be denied the benefits of, or be subjected to discrimination under any program or activity receiving federal financial assistance.

The political pressure of the 1960s further recognized the special needs of the many limited English speaking students in American public schools. These efforts culminated in 1967 with the introduction of the first bilingual education bill ever to be considered by Congress. Final passage of the bilingual bill was to create *Title VII of the Elementary and Secondary Education Act of 1965, better known as the Bilingual Education Act of 1968.*
Section 702 of the Bilingual Education Act asserts:

1 . *that there are large numbers of children of limited English speaking ability;*

2 . *that many such children have a cultural heritage which differs from that of English speaking persons;*

3 . *that the use of a child's language and cultural heritage is the primary means by which a child learns; and*

4. *that, therefore, large numbers of children of limited English speaking ability have educational needs which can be met by the use of bilingual education methods and techniques;*

5. *that in addition, all children benefit through the fullest utilization of multiple language and cultural resources.*

Furthermore, Congress thereby declares it to be the policy of the United States:

1. *to encourage the establishment and operation of educational programs using bilingual educational methods and techniques and;*

2. *to provide financial assistance to local educational agencies in order to enable such agencies to carry out such programs in elementary (including preschool), and secondary schools which are designed to meet the educational needs of such children (Bilingual Education Act, 1968).*

Legal Implications

The force which may have brought about the greatest recognition for bilingual education, and to which such national entities as the National Education Association (NEA) and the Civil Rights Commission contributed, were the education lawsuits. These lawsuits challenged the disproportionate placement of Hispanics and other linguistically and culturally different students in special education programs.

In considering the developmental history of bilingual education, it is vitally important for all educators, at all levels, to be aware of the significant lawsuits that have taken place and that have set school policy in many instances. These lawsuits were the first legal challenges to early testing, standardized testing, the selection process, and the caliber of instruction in special education classes. *In essence, they found that standardized tests were used to measure the capacity to know and speak English, rather than to measure a student's general achievement.*

The first of these special education lawsuits - *Arreola v. Board of Education* - was in Santa Ana, California and was argued in the state court. Although this particular cases did not have the significant impact that followed, the Santa Ana case broke new legal ground. It focused blame where, up to this point it had not been placed; it brought about significant state legislation and subsequent state education policies; and it generated important awareness of this type of educational neglect and damage to school children. Most significantly, the Santa Ana case helped to pave the way for *Diana v. State Board of Education*.

Unlike the Santa Ana case, *Diana v. State Board of Education* was argued in Federal court. The judgment of the court was that Hispanic and Chinese speaking students already in special education classes must be retested in their primarily language and must be re-evaluated only as to their achievement on nonverbal tests or sections of tests. Although this case was concerned with special education classes, it became clear that it was the teachers, counselors, and administrators who were referring linguistically and culturally different students to such classes because, to quote one Administrator at the trial, "we just do not know what to do with them." The basis for most of the judgments which placed these students in special education classes was their inability to speak or to function well in English, which had nothing to do with their mental or psychological capacities. It was evident that in too many instances, the language and culture of the schools could not or would not adapt to the language and culture of a significant community of students.

The special education lawsuits made their own impact on educational reform. Specifically, they contributed to an acceptance of the notion that there was a serious problem, that it started very early in the student's life, that it had to do mainly with the student's language and culture, and that what the schools were doing was not working. If anything, what the schools were doing was educationally and psychologically damaging the student, and a new educational strategy had to be developed. The special education cases, especially *Diana v. State Board of Education*, led to the development of what was commonly referred to as the *May 25th Memorandum.*

The *May 25th Memorandum* (1970), is the official policy of the Office for Civil Rights (OCR) regarding responsibility of the public schools to provide for the educational needs of linguistically and culturally different students. It was the direct result of the Diana v. State Board of Education. This memorandum was intended to expand educational concerns and issues elaborated in the special education cases. Until 1974 it became apparent that the majority of school district reviews by the Office of Civil Rights concentrated on one issue - the special education student. The four points of the memorandum were as follows:

1. *Where inability to speak and understand the English language excludes national origin-minority group children from effective participation in the educational program offered by a school district, the district must take affirmative steps to rectify the language deficiency in order to open its instructional program to these students.*

2. *School districts must not assign national origin-minority group students to classes for the mentally retarded on the basis of criteria which essentially measures or evaluates English language skills; nor may school districts deny national origin-minority group children access to college preparatory courses on a basis directly related to the failure of the school system to inculcate English language skills.*

3. *Any ability grouping or tracking system employed by the school system to deal with the special language skill needs of national origin-minority group children must be designed to meet such language skill needs as soon as possible and must not operate as an educational dead-end or permanent track.*

4. *School districts have the responsibility to adequately notify national origin-minority group parents of school activities which are called to the attention of other parents. Such notice, in order to be adequate, may have to be provided in a language other than English.*

These four points set forth the Executive Branch's interpretation and illustrate the application of the 1964 Civil Rights Act as it relates to the education of linguistically distinct students who are unable to read, write, or comprehend English.

In addition to the special education cases, a number of other education lawsuits have contributed significantly to the rise in bilingual education and English as a Second Language (ESL) programs throughout the country.

Lau v. Nichols.

Following the desegregation of the San Francisco school system in 1971, there were 2,856 students of Chinese ancestry in the school system who did not speak English. Of these, about 1,000 received supplemental courses in the English language. The remaining 1,800 did not receive supplemental or bilingual instruction.

The class action suit was brought by 13 non-English speaking Chinese American students who alleged that they were being denied an education because they could not comprehend the language in which they were being taught. They argued that the failure either to teach them bilingually or teach them English should be prohibited on the grounds that (1) failure to do so was a violation of equal protection under the Fourteenth Amendment, and (2) it was a violation of the Civil Rights Act of 1964.

The facts clearly supported the claims that the non-English speaking Chinese were not benefiting from their educational experience. Indeed, the school district noted the frustration and poor performance created by the students' inability to understand the regular work. Predictions were made that substantial numbers would drop out and become another unemployable in the ghetto (1974). The district argued, however, that discrimination was not being practiced because the students were being taught in the same facilities, by the same teachers, and at the same time as everyone else.

The district court and the circuit court of appeals both ruled in favor of the school district. The arguments in support of this ruling focused primarily on the fact that the alleged violation was not based on prior segregation. More importantly, the appeals court stated, there is no showing that appellants' lingual deficiencies are at all related to any such past discrimination(1974). The court suggested then, that the students' failure was of their own making, not state-related, and thus of little consequence when school resources were limited. The court further observed:

Every student brings to the starting line of his educational career different advantages and disadvantages, caused in part by social, economic and cultural background, created and continued completely apart from any contribution by the school system. That some of these may be impediments which can be overcome does not amount to a "denial" by the school district of educational opportunities. . . should the district fail to give them special attention. . . . .

On appeal to the Supreme Court, (*Lau v. Nichols*), the lower court's decision was reversed. The High Court's opinion supported the arguments presented at trial by the Chinese- speaking students:

Basic English skills are at the very core of what these public schools teach. Imposition of a requirement that before a child can effectively participate in the educational program he must already have acquired these basic skills is to make a mockery of public education. We know that those who do not understand English are certain to find their classroom experience wholly incomprehensible and in no way meaningful.

Under these state-imposed standards,there is no equality of treatment merely by providing students with the same facilities, textbooks, teachers, and curriculum; for students who do not understand English are effectively foreclosed from any meaningful education (Lau v. Nichols, 1974).

While the court laid to rest the argument that equal access to facilities provides equal treatment and equal educational opportunity, it did not base its decision on the constitutional requirement; rather, support was found in the *Civil Rights Act of 1964*. The act forbids discrimination on the grounds of race, color, or national origin by any agency receiving federal financial assistance. Because the support for the ruling came from the Civil Rights Act, there is still not a constitutional right to a bilingual education or even an education from which one can benefit. Thus, a district that does not receive federal funds would not be compelled to offer non-English-speaking students bilingual education. The constitutional issue has been raised elsewhere, however, with some support.

Serna v. Portales Municipal Schools.

The Serna case was remarkably similar to Lau and was working its way through the courts at approximately the same time. The city of Portales, New Mexico, was residentially segregated; Mexican Americans inhabited the north side of the city and Anglos inhabited the south side. The focal point of the action was the education offered in one of the Mexican American elementary schools. Plaintiffs asserted that educational discrimination existed throughout the Portales school system as a result of an educational program tailored to the middle-class child from an English-speaking family, without regard for the educational needs of the child from an environment in which Spanish was the predominant language spoken. Such a program, it was claimed, denied equal educational opportunity to Spanish-speaking children.

As in Lau, the plaintiffs presented evidence that the Spanish-speaking students' achievement was consistently lower than that of the students at the other schools. They did not claim that this difference was caused by the differential treatment in regard to facilities, teachers, or program; to the contrary, they argued that lower achievement resulted because school programs were substantially the same. The Portales School District basically defended its position in the same manner as did San Francisco: Because the needs of the non-English speaking students did not result from state action and because the district did not create these problems through any classification or racially motivated discrimination, they were under no legal obligation to provide compensatory programs.

161

The district court that tried the case, unlike the trial court in Lau, was not interested in the fact that the situation of these Mexican American students did not result from state action. Placing its decision squarely on the constitutional issue, the court concluded that when children are placed in a school atmosphere that does not adequately reflect the educational needs of the minority, the conclusion is inevitable that the students do not, in fact, have equal educational opportunity and that a violation of their constitutional right to equal protection exists. The court ordered the formulation of a bilingual education plan which would accommodate the language, history, and culture of Mexican American students in Portales.

Keyes v. School District 1.

In the decision of *Keyes v. School District 1* (Denver, 1976), the Tenth U.S. Circuit Court ordered the Denver schools to desegregate "root and branch." However, a federal judge allowed several elementary schools to remain segregated upon the request of parents. In support of this move, the judge stated, *Some representatives of the Mexican-American community. . . have expressed a desire not to desegregate. . . during the period that the desegregation program is developing. The court can see advantages in this and therefore holds that desegregation is not in its best interests.* In the same decision, the judge continued: *In some of the schools which have a preponderant Chicano population it has seemed to the court more desirable to pursue a bilingual and bicultural program rather than to change the numbers.*

On the surface, the separation allowed by Keyes seems inconsistent with the *Lee* decision, in which Chinese Americans were forced to integrate. However, we need to recall the guidelines set down in Swann, wherein the Supreme Court recognized that in some instances, certain schools could remain one-race schools. Inaccessibility was one such instance and served as one of the justifications in *Keyes*.

While the constitutional right to bilingual education would serve as a stronger base to support programs, the Civil Rights Act and the Constitution have basically the same implications for pluralism. In no court case was bilingualism/biculturalism supported on the grounds that it contributed to the development or preservation of a group's cultural heritage. On the contrary, where bilingual programs have been mandated by the courts, the purpose has been to enhance assimilation. (See Figure 18 - Dates and Outcomes of Court Cases Involving Language Diversity).

In 1978 the *Bilingual Education Act* was further amended and this became *P. L. 95-561*. Through these amendments the definition of the target population changed from Limited English Speaking Ability (LESA) to Limited English Proficient (LEP). This expanded the population of eligible participants. Limited English proficiency was defined to include children with limited English reading, writing, speaking, and understanding. The 1978 statute formally included the American Indian and Alaskan Native language groups. The new law also instructed grant recipients to use native-language instruction "to the extent necessary" for children to become competent in English. In order to promote a multicultural environment and to protect LEP students from segregation, the law set up a 60:40 ratio requirement. This meant the monolingual English speaker could participate in the program but only up to a maximum of 40 percent of the total number of students.

Figure 18

DATES AND OUTCOMES OF COURT CASES
INVOLVING LANGUAGE DIVERSITY

CASE	DATE	OUTCOME
Meyers v. Nebraska	1923	English Only Policy
Arreola v. Board of Education	1967	First Special Education Lawsuit (Broke New Legal Ground)
Diana v. Board of Education	1968	Must Test Students in Dominant Language of Student
Lau v. Nichols	1974	Affirmative Steps must be taken by the School District to Rectify Language Deficiency
Serna v. Portales	1974	Mandated Bilingual Programs
Keyes v. School District #1	1976	Established Bilingual Education as Compatible with Desegregation

The uses of the native language and culture in bilingual education were maintained in the 1978 legislation, but as Leibowitz pointed out, they were subordinated to a stronger English language emphasis.24 Title VII came under increasing fire after the Lau regulations were withdrawn in 1982. Soon after taking office, Former President Reagan declared that it was *absolutely wrong and against American concepts to have a bilingual education program that is now openly, admittedly dedicated to preserving native language and never getting adequate in English.* In the fall of 1981, an Education Department review of bilingual education research concluded that *the case for the effectiveness of transitional bilingual education is so weak that districts should be encouraged to experiment with alternative methods.* With the bilingual act up for reauthorization in 1983, opponents were optimistic that they could get the law changed or block an extension of the program. But the Congress postponed the battle by moving Title VII's expiration date up to the fall of 1984. Under a compromise, 4 percent of Title VII funds were authorized for *special alternative instructional programs* - those using no native language. For example, if total appropriations exceeded $140 million, half of the excess would go to the alternative programs, up to 10 percent of total grant awards. The Reagan administration cut Title VII funding from a high of $171.7 million in 1980 to $133.3 million in fiscal 1986 and grants for English-only programs remain capped at 4 percent. In the Fall of 1985, the Secretary of Education, William Bennett, had called for a more flexible, national bilingual education policy. The consensus at that time seemed to indicate that the *native language* component in a bilingual program was being slowly phased out and a stronger move toward *English as a Second Language(ESL)* was being encouraged by the Department of Education. For example, the Commissioner suggested that bilingual education had failed. Federal policy, he said, *had lost sight of the goal of learning English as the key to equal educational opportunity instead, native-language instruction had become an emblem of cultural pride.* With this assault, he initiated a three-part plan. First, the Education Department issued new regulations for bilingual education grants, which gave preference to programs that moved children as quickly as possible from native-language instruction to mainstream classes. Second, it informed the 498 districts that had adopted bilingual education as part of Lau plans that they were free to renegotiate the agreements with the Office of Civil Rights. Finally, the Administration, citing the inconclusiveness of research, proposed legislation to remove all restrictions on Title VII funding for English-only approaches (Crawford, 1987).

The *Bilingual Education Act of 1968* has had and appears to be continuing to have a number of significant changes over the past 21 years. The changes have gradually expanded the population of eligible students, but as noted, the most recent changes have put more emphasis on the acquisition of English language proficiency through *English-only* approaches.

In terms of financial support, the program has gone from an initial appropriation in 1968 of $7.5 million, serving 76 school districts and 25,521 students, to a high of $171 million, serving 564 school districts and 350,000 students in 1980. The 1981-84 Congressionally authorized ceiling of $139 million marked the beginning of a gradual decline in federal funding for all of education, including bilingual education. (See Figure 19 - Federal Spending for Bilingual Education).

Figure 19

FEDERAL SPENDING FOR BILINGUAL EDUCATION

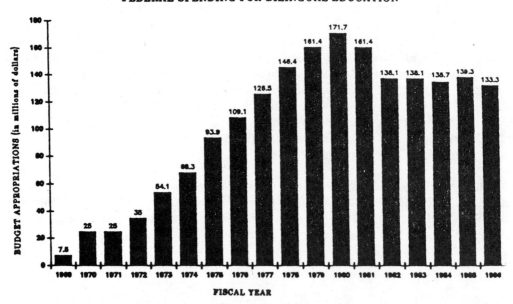

State Involvement.

In compliance with federal legislation and regulations, many state governments have adopted measures to fund and otherwise encourage bilingual education. By 1981, twelve states had stipulated conditions under which bilingual education was mandatory: Alaska, California, Connecticut, Illinois, Indiana, Iowa, Massachusetts, Michigan, New Jersey, Texas, Washington, and Wisconsin. Eleven other states had laws permitting bilingual education, and twenty-six had no provisions regarding language of instruction. Only one state, West Virginia, still required instruction to be exclusively in English.

The English-Only Movement.

English-only or English-plus? That's the question currently being debated in several states and considered by some members of Congress. In the fall of 1986, Californians voted by a 3-to-1 margin to declare English the state's official language. In the Fall of 1988, Arizona, Colorado and Florida also declared English as the official language of their states'. However, in the Spring of 1990, Arizona repealed the legislation and declared it unconstitutional.

In a national context, the measure's approval has been a boon to the *English-only* movement, the best organized opposition that bilingual education has yet faced. In 1987, 31 states had considered official language laws. There are now 16 states that have English as their official language. (See Figure 20: Where English is Official)

Figure 20

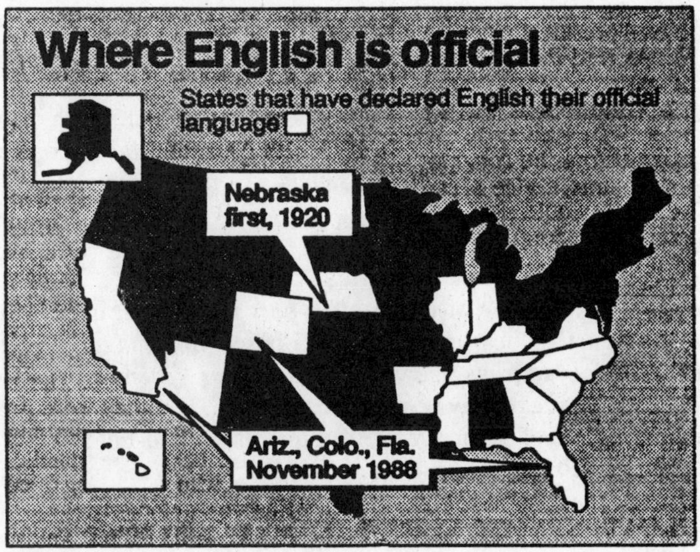

Where English is official

States that have declared English their official language ☐

Nebraska first, 1920

Ariz., Colo., Fla. November 1988

165

Legally, these statutes and constitutional amendments may have no direct effect on bilingual programs. But voter enthusiasm for such measures - as well as the letter writing campaigns that the issue has generated, usually featuring attacks on native language instruction - has not gone unnoticed by politicians.

The drive to get English recognized as our nation's "official" language began in 1981, when S. I. Hayakawa, then U.S. Senator from California, introduced a congressional proposal for an *English language amendment* to the U.S. Constitution. The amendment has been reintroduced as a joint resolution in each succeeding Congress but has never received action. Hayakawa, is now chair of U.S. English, the organization he created in 1983. The group's premise is that bilingualism poses a growing *threat to English* as the unifying force in American society. The group warns that the nation is being *divided along language lines,* as ethnic minorities, particularly Hispanics, insist on retaining their native languages and cultures instead of joining the English-speaking mainstream (Crawford, 1987).

While the current publicity about California had implied that the U.S. English movement was a national ground-swell, the movement had been successful in only three other states recently. The following states have enacted state legislation recently: Arizona (1988—repealed Spring/1990), Colorado (1988), Florida (1988), Arkansas (1987), California (1986), Georgia (1986), Indiana and Tennessee (1984). The current U.S. English movement had nothing to do with the nation's four other English-only state laws: Virginia (1981); and Illinois, Kentucky and Nebraska have been on the books for over 60 years.

Fishman (1987) questions the sudden concern for the "functional protection of English." *How*, he asks, *is English endangered in a country where it is spoken by 97 percent of the population; where "linguistic minorities overwhelmingly lose their mother tongues by the second or, at most, the third generation" and where "no ethnic political parties or separatist movement exists*? Fishman maintains that U.S. English and like-minded groups have a 'hidden agenda' of equating cultural differences with disloyalty, of seeking scapegoats for social ills that have little to do with language, such as terrorism abroad and economic dislocations at home. The English only movement, he argues, *is a displacement of middle-class fears and anxieties from difficult, perhaps even intractable, real problems in American society, to mythical, simplistic, and stereotypic problems.*

English-Plus.

To counter the growing influence of the *English only* movement, in late 1985, the League of United Latin American Citizens and the Miami-based Spanish American League Against Discrimination launched a campaign known as *English- plus.* There is no question that English is the nation's common language, says Soto, president of Spanish American League Against Discrimination, and the groups favor every effort to help limited-English-proficient children become proficient in it. *But English is not enough, we don't want a monolingual society. This country was founded on a diversity of language and culture, and we want to preserve that diversity.*

166

The English-plus campaign has concentrated on urging states and municipalities to declare themselves officially multilingual and multicultural. Such measures have passed in Atlanta, Tucson, and Oscelola County, Florida, and are pending in Arizona and New York State (Crawford, 1987).

Bilingual Education

Few programs are as poorly understood as bilingual education. So stubborn is the resistance to this concept that it has now permeated the press and other popular media to a degree that baffles many observers.

Certainly, the reasons for this lack of understanding and support for programs of bilingual education have been debated and have been centers of controversy for years. However, given the current demographic projections and the numbers of limited English proficient students currently in our schools - the issue becomes more critical, and perhaps more controversial. Some are deeply rooted in history and tradition, and in habits of thought that are difficult for society to break. Other reasons can be traced directly to the lingering effects of racism, discrimination (as in the cited court cases mentioned earlier) and ethnocentrism.

A commonly accepted definition of bilingual education is Cohen's (1975) definition, which is as follows:

Bilingual education is the use of two languages as a media of instruction for a child or a group of children in part or all of the school curriculum.

Gonzales (1975) defines bilingual education as:

The use of two languages, one of which is English, as a means of instruction.

The basic definition of bilingual education, generally agreed upon by scholars and laypersons is the use of two languages as a medium of instruction. In other words, there is an agreement regarding what the process of bilingual education is, but confusion arises when the philosophy and goals of bilingual education are discussed.

The Goals of Bilingual Education.

The goals of bilingual education may be organized into four categories: cognitive development, affective development, linguistic growth and culture. According to Blanco (1977), the consensus of experts in the field of bilingual education agree that the primary goals of bilingual education are the areas of cognitive and affective development rather than in the linguistic and cultural realms. In other words, it is not to teach English or a second language per se but to teach children concepts, knowledge, and skills through the language they know best and to reinforce this information through the second language.

When educators, legislators, or parents lose sight of cognitive and affective development as the primary goals of bilingual education, then confusion, controversy and disagreement are likely to be the outcome. What occurs most often is that the linguistic and cultural goals are taken out of context and made the primary purpose of the program. As Baca and Cervantes (1984) have stated, *Legislators might say: The main purpose of this program is to teach them English as soon as possible and get them into the mainstream of education.* On the other hand, parents might say: *The main purpose of this program should be to maintain their native language and culture while they learn English.* The issue of transition versus maintenance is certainly an important one, but it should not become the central issue when discussing the primary goals of the program.

Baca and Cervantes (1984) view four different philosophical perspectives with regard to the linguistic and cultural goals of bilingual education. They are: transition, maintenance, restoration, and enrichment.

Transitional. A bilingual program with a transitional linguistic and cultural goal is one that utilizes the native language and culture of the student only to the extent that it is necessary for the student to acquire English and thus function in the regular school curriculum. This program approach does not teach the student to read or write in the native language. The majority of bilingual programs in this country are transitional.

Maintenance. A bilingual program with linguistic and cultural maintenance as a goal also promotes English acquisition. In addition, it endorses the idea that there is value to linguistic and cultural diversity. Therefore linguistic and cultural maintenance encourages students to become literate in their native language and to develop bilingual skills throughout their schooling even into their adult lives.

All state and federal legislation supports the transitional approach to bilingual education. These laws, however, do not prohibit local districts from going beyond the law into a maintenance program using local resources. Although legislation favors the transitional approach, local school districts are free to implement a maintenance approach if they so desire.

Restoration. This is a bilingual program with linguistic and cultural restoration as a goal that would restore the language and culture of the students and ancestors, which may have been lost through assimilation. For example, if a group of Japanese American students had lost the ability to speak Japanese, an appropriate bilingual program could help them revitalize their ancestral language and culture. It should be noted that such programs are usually rare, and that the funding and impetus behind such programs come within the local school districts. No federal or state rules and regulations encourage this approach.

Enrichment. A bilingual program with linguistic and cultural enrichment as a goal concerns itself with adding a new language and culture to a group of monolingual students. A good example would be a program for mono-lingual English-speaking students that is designed to teach them the

Spanish language and culture simply as an enrichment of their education. Again, this type of program is usually a local decision and initiative.

No bilingual program should be designed without a comprehensive needs assessment of the students who will be involved in the program. This needs assessment should focus on first and second language proficiency, on academic needs, and on affective needs. This information should be provided for both the linguistically different as well as the non-linguistically different students who wish to participate in the program. Once the school district knows the needs of its students, it can then begin to review and select an appropriate dual language instruction schedule model. There are numerous models available and these models can be found in several of the books listed in the suggested readings section at the end of this chapter.

In summary, the program design is selected when compatibility exists between the needs of the students, the linguistic ability of the staff, and the philosophy of the school district.

English as a Second Language

One approach to remedying the school problems of linguistically different students has been instruction in *English as a Second Language* (ESL). English as a Second Language is a component of virtually all bilingual education programs in the United States. And because of a shortage of bilingual teachers, for many limited-English-proficient students it is the only special assistance available. Especially in school districts where many language groups are represented, students may receive ESL instruction only through *pull-out classes* a few times each week. Critics contend that the student plays catch-up all the time, trying to learn both a new language and new subject material.

With ESL, as with bilingual instruction, methods vary tremendously. The most common approaches remain Grammar-Based, such as the Audio-Lingual Method, which emphasizes memorization of vocabulary and drills in the structure of the week. The *Grammar-Translation Approach*, an older, less-used method, concentrates on learning a language by perfecting reading and writing skills, with less attention to listening and speaking.

While Grammar-Based ESL has produced students who can formulate grammatically perfect sentences - given enough time - it has often failed to make them proficient communicators, according to many researchers. And the tedious content of instruction, for students and teachers alike, appears to impede learning (Baca & Cervantes, 1984).

Increasingly, *Communication-Based ESL,* is superseding the old methods. The new approaches are grounded in the theory that language proficiency is acquired through exposure to comprehensible messages, rather than learned consciously through the study of syntax and vocabulary. Representatives of such innovative methods, *The Natural Approach* and *Total Physical Response* stress simplified speech and visual or physical cues to help students comprehend second-language input. Also, they aim to create low-anxiety environments that lower *the affective fiber* that prevents comprehensible input from getting through. For example, teachers focus on meaningful and interesting communication, resist the impulse to correct students' errors overtly, and avoid pressuring students to "produce speech" in the second language before they are ready (Carlos & Collier, 1985).

The ESL model for educating students with limited English proficiency is an attractive remedy for several reasons. It is less expensive than a full bilingual program and requires fewer specially trained teachers. It can accommodate students from a large number of language backgrounds in a single class. It allows minority language students substantial opportunity to improve their English skills by interacting with native-English speaking teachers and peers in regular classes. And in many cases, *ESL is the best and only viable alternative available for many school districts.*

The major criticism of ESL is that it ignores the student's language and culture. Also, the ESL model usually fails to teach minority language students enough English to keep up in other classes - unless they are also getting ample practice in using English at home and in the community. In addition, the pull-out methods segregates children with limited English in a way that invites their English-speaking classmates to stigmatize them, particularly if the non-English speakers are also economically and socially disadvantaged (Garcia, 1982). There is also mounting evidence that students who feel alienated from school are highly prone to academic failure.

Summary

The surprising multiplicity of U.S. languages has direct ramifications for public policy. As the institution that most embodies and perpetuates our language attitudes and policies, public education requires particular attention. What happens in this nation's schoolrooms will largely determine whether we continue efforts to homogenize the American language or view this linguistic diversity as a valuable and enriching asset.

Throughout its first century, the United States was an openly multilingual nation. There were treaties, public notices, and education in a variety of indigenous and immigrant languages. Subsequently, in the latter half of the nineteenth and first half of the twentieth centuries, the rights of non-English speakers were eroded by anti-foreigner and racist sentiment and action. In recent years, however, the Supreme Court, and federal court rulings and legislation have reinstated many minority language rights. In the 1980s, we are witnessing large-scale legal and illegal immigration from Mexico, resettlement of Southeast Asian refugees, and an influx of refugees from various Caribbean and Central American countries. What will be the reaction from the federal government? The public schools? The '80s have also produced a new surge of an English-only policy in many states and discussions of a national language are beginning to become more frequent.

As we witnessed the recent developments surrounding the government-sponsored ESL and bilingual education programs - both approaches still suffer from uncertainty about their effectiveness, and widespread confusion remains about their differing aims and implications. Clearly, however, they represent the largest legal, moral, and financial commitment this country has ever made to minority languages and their speakers.

Language variation in the United States has evolved out of a long history of cultural diversity. Chapter 7 was intended to provide a variety of viewpoints on the special educational needs of linguistically different students and the proposed methods of addressing those needs. In order to understand the current debate on which approach should be endorsed, it was necessary to provide a brief historical and judicial review. Politically, the issue of limited-English proficient students has recently taken on a new opponent - the English-only policies - from national and state levels. As we have learned, each of the two approaches - bilingual education and ESL - may be the best solution, given the particular variables within a community and school system.

Misunderstandings about the nature of language evolution and negative attitudes toward linguistic diversity make rational debate of such matters extremely difficult. As long as attitudes of any individual or group are the sole basis for policy making, it will remain impossible to discover the most effective means of meeting the needs of limited English proficient students.

WORKSHEET 1

1. What are the three evolutionary periods of language treatment that the United States has experienced?

   First: _Permissive laws -- communities used the predominant language of an area -- e.g. German, Norwegian_

   Second: _English-only -- xenophobia, anti-German sentiment_

   Third: _Bilingual/ESL/ignored problem_

What are the differences between the first and third periods? Explain.

The most important would have to be the attention paid to the issue -- before it was all local, the comm'ty set the standards -- today there's a feeling that the whole society, the whole nation has an interest

2. Why were the *special education* cases so important? Explain.

Very often students were assigned to SPED classes
on the basis of testing in English only where
they were non-native speakers. All SPED &
tracking must include testing in their
language. Also, not knowing English can
lead to other dev'ntl. problems here.

3. What is the significance of the *Lau v. Nichols* case?

When Chinese-~~language~~ speaking students brought suit
against the school district, the Supreme Court
found that although prior segregation did
not exist, students not being brought up
to speed in Basic English had been denied
access to an education.

What were the arguments presented by the San Francisco school district?

Past discrimination was not related to
students' linguistic deficiencies. Also,
the violation was not based upon
prior discrimination or segregation.

What was the Supreme Court's interpretation of *equal treatment*?

If the students do not understand the language of instruction, equal access to facilities or materials is not enough to constit equal treatment.

4. English-only or English-plus? Define each and then explain your preference.

English-only: Attempts to declare English the country's (or particular state's) official language and ending bilingual education.

English-plus: Attempts to have states declare themselves multilingual/cultural in an attempt to preserve diversity.

What is your preference? Neither. English-only represents xenophobia and bigotry, while English plus could result in Balkanization. I'm not against people using their native languages, but I don't want a Quebec either.

5. What is bilingual education?

The use of two languages — in the U.S., one is always English — as the means of instruction for a group of students for all or part of their education.

What are the goals of bilingual education?

Cognitive & affective development are more important than linguistic growth or imparting of culture i.e., concepts/knowledge/skills taught to children in language they know best over getting them to know English.

What are the advantages of bilingual education?

① Maintenance of native language ② students learn in lang. they're most comfortable with ③ ease transition into English

What are the disadvantages of bilingual education?

Does not specifically mainstream students into english, that is, students may or may not learn English in the process of learning other things into the other language.

6. What is English as a Second Language (ESL)?

A method of teaching English to non-native speakers without regard to native language, usually as a "pull-out" class in elementary school.

What are the goals of ESL?

To get students up to speed in English, but in a non-threatening way. Most methods concentrate on listening and speaking.

What are the advantages of ESL?

It's cheaper than bilingual ed. It doesn't require harder-to-find bilingual ed teachers. There's lots of interaction w/ native-speaking teachers & classmates, i.e. no isolation in bilingual classes.

What are the disadvantages of ESL?

Ignores child's lang. and culture. Doesn't teach enough English to insure proficiency by itself. Pull-out classes isolate, stigmatize students. ESL students already alienated from school prone to failure.

7. How should programs for limited English proficient students be defined - according to local schools, state departments of education or the federal government? Explain your position.

I would use the basic ESL model. If I'm in a district with majority English speakers, I would have those students tutor their classmates. If the majority are ESL students, I would divide the class into groups, with at least one student who is native speaking in each class.

Who will monitor or evaluate your position stated above? Explain.

My administrator. My school will develop its own measurement tools to evaluate the progress of ESL students, their proficiency, as well as the work of native-language tutors. It's my hope that each student can learn something from the other — e.g.: an ESL student who is good in math can help a native-speaker who isn't quite so good —

8. Where should the funding for limited English proficient students come from? Explain your response.

Same place it always has: property tax, sales tax, lotteries. Those who resist paying for it should be made to understand that these students are the future of their communities.

9. In what type of school system would bilingual education be more effective and beneficial for all students involved? Explain.

In these schools and areas where the non-native speakers speak 1 or 2 languages and represent a majority. It's easier to customize for such a group—such a group it homogeneous enough that the same things can be done for several students.

In what type of school system would ESL be more effective and beneficial for all students involved? Explain.

In areas where non-native speakers are a distinct minority and/or several different languages are spoken. Too many bilingual classes would have to be set up, or such classes would be too small to justify.

REFERENCES

Anderson, Theodore, & Boyer, Mildred, (Eds.) Bilingual Schooling in the United States U.S. Government Printing Office, Washington, D.C., 1970.

Arreola v. Board of Education, Santa Ana Unified School District, 150577, California.

Baca, Leonard M. & Cervantes, Hermes T. The Bilingual Special Education Interface. Times Mirror/Mosby Publishing Co, St. Louis, MO, 1984., p. 64.

Bilingual Education Act, P. L. 90-247, 81 Stat. 783 816 January, 1968.

Blanco, G. Bilingual Education: Current Perspectives. Center for Applied Linguistics, Arlington, VA, 1977.

Carlos J. & Collier, Virginia P. Bilingual and ESL Class- rooms: Teaching in Multicultural Contexts. McGraw Hill, New York, NY, 1985.

Castellanos, Diego The Best of Two Worlds: Bilingual- Bicultural in the U.S. New Jersey State Department of Education, Trenton, NJ, 1983.

Cohen, A. A Sociolinguistic Approach to Bilingual Education. Newbury House Publishers, Rowley, MA, 1975.

Conklin, Nancy Faires & Lourie, Margaret A. A Host of Tongues - Language Communities in the United States. Free Press, New York, NY, 1983.

Crawford, James "Bilingual Education: Language, Learning and Politics." Education Week, Washington, D.C., April 1, 1987.

Department of Health, Education, and Welfare. Office of the Secretary, Washington, D.C., May 25, 1970.

Diana v. State Board of Education, Soledad, C70-37-RFP, California.

Garcia, Ricardo L. Teaching in a Pluralistic Society: Concepts, Models, and Strategies Harper and Row, New York, NY, 1982. p. 142.

Gonzales, J. "Coming of Age in Bilingual Bicultural Education: A Historical Perspective." Inequality of Education, February, 1975.

Gonzales, Josue M. Coming of Age in Bilingual/Bicultural Education: A Historical Perspective. Inequality in Education, February, 1975, pp. 5-17.

Guey Heung Lee v. David Johnson, 404 U.S. 1215 (1974).

Keyes V. School District 1, 380 F. Supp. 673 (1974).

Lau v. Nichols, 94 S. Ct. 786 (1974).

Leibowitz, A. H. The Bilingual Education Act: A Legislative Analysis. National Clearinghouse for Bilingual Education, Rosslyn, VA, 1980.

Meyer v. Nebraska, 43 S. Ct. 625 (1923).

Serna v. Portales Municipal Schools, 351 F. Supp. 1279 (1972).

SUGGESTED READINGS

Alatis, James E., ed. Current Issues in Bilingual Education. Georgetown University Round Table on Languages and Linguistics 1980. Washington, D.C.: Georgetown University Press, 1980.

Alatis, James E., ed. International Dimensions of Bilingual Education. Georgetown University Round Table on Languages and Linguistics, 1978. Washington, D.C.: Georgetown University Press, 1978.

Anderson, Theodore, & Mildred Boyer,(Eds.) Bilingual Schooling in the United States, 2 Vols. Washington, D.C.: U.S. Government Printing Office, 1970.

Association for Supervision and Curriculum Development. Building an Indivisible Nation: Bilingual Education in Context. A.S.C.D., Alexandria, VA, April, 1987.

Baker, Keith A. & De Kanter, Adriana A. (Eds.) Bilingual Education: A Reappraisal of Federal Policy. Lexington Books, Lexington, MA, 1983.

Christian, Donna. Language Arts and Dialect Differences. Center for Applied Linguistics, Arlington, VA, 1979.

Hakuta, Kenji Mirror of Language: The Debate on Bilingualism. Basic Books, New York, NY, 1986.

Krashen, Stephen D. Inquiries and Insights: Second Language Learning, Immersion & Bilingual Education, Literacy Alemany Press, Hayward, CA, 1985.

Ovando, Carlos J. & Collier, Virginia P. Bilingual and ESL Classrooms: Teaching in Multicultural Contexts. McGraw-Hill, New York, NY, 1985.

Stein, Colman B. Jr. Sink or Swim: The Politics of Bilingual Education. Praeger, New York, NY, 1986.

Troike, Rudolph C. "Synthesis of Research on Bilingual Education." Educational Leadership, March, 1981. pp. 498 - 504.

"When Children Speak Little English: How Effective Is Bilingual Education? Harvard Education Letter, November, 1986.

Zamora, Gloria R. "Understanding Bilingual Education." National Coalition of Advocates for Students, Backgrounder Series. Boston, MA, 1987.

CHAPTER EIGHT

Equity and the Courts:
Selected Laws and Case Examples

Introduction

Today's schools exist and function in the midst of a complex legal environment, and it is difficult not to be aware of a wide range of legal issues that influence the lives of teachers, students, parents and administrators. Those in public education are well aware that the courts, over the past several decades, have played a significant role in establishing educational policy. In fact, the U.S. Supreme Court ruled in *Wood v. Strickland* (1975) that teachers and administrators may be held personally liable in money damages for violating students' clearly established constitutional rights.

Decisions in such areas as desegregation, the role of prayer in the public school, student rights, sex discrimination, linguistically-different students, students' rights, teachers' rights, exceptional students' rights and personnel issues attest to the extent and magnitude of the court's influence. These court decisions and those pending, have produced and likely will continue to produce a sizable body of school law that educators should be familiar with. It is generally believed that unlawful school practices are generally not intentional, but simply result from a misunderstanding of the law. Why are educators so poorly informed about the law that affects schools? The answer may be the fact that much of this law did not exist when they were students, and as a result, they learned very little, if anything, during their education.

Chapter 8 - **Equity and the Courts: Selected Laws and Case Examples,** is about teachers and the laws which affect them, laws established by state and federal statutes, constitutions and court decisions. These laws will have little significance, however, unless educators know about them and are willing to make an effort to see that they are carried out.

This chapter is intended to highlight the laws that are most central to the theme of this book - equity in education. Much of the law examined in these pages is neither simple nor unchanging. Many of the cases are as difficult to resolve for lawyers and judges as they are for educators. This is because cases involving school law often do not address simple conflicts of right against wrong but complex issues encompassing the conflicting interests of teachers, parents, administrators and students. Moreover, educational law is constantly changing. New legislation is passed, regulations are changed, school boards revise their practices, and the Supreme Court may declare a policy unconstitutional. Because of this diversity and change, my discussion of the cases and laws is intended to be illustrative, not exhaustive.

What Laws Affect Schools?

It is important to have a common understanding of the definition for a discriminatory act or policy. Discrimination exists when a person or organization makes decisions that result in denying benefits to people or in treating them differently. Both students and employees of federally-funded educational institutions are covered by these laws. With the categories of student and employees, persons are protected by legislation against discrimination on all of the following bases:

* *Race*   * *Sex*   * *Handicap*

* *National Origin*   * *Age*   * *Marital Status*

* *Religion*

Figure 21 - Formula for Discrimination, is a general overview of how one may look at a specific act or policy and determine if the act or policy is discriminatory. Although Figure 21 may seem simple, it is important to understand: 1) the formula, and 2) the process, when examining any specific case or situation. The following specific pieces of legislation have affected our actions in schools today.

Figure 21

FORMULA FOR DISCRIMINATION

WHO	BASED ON	IN A COVERED SUBJECT AREA	THAT ENDS IN A RESULT PROHIBITED BY LAW
ANY SCHOOL POLICY/ PRACTICE OR STAFF ACTION	AGE EXCEPTIONALITY NATIONAL ORIGIN RACE RELIGION SEX MARITAL STATUS	• ACCESS TO COURSE OFFERINGS • STANDARDS OF MEASUREMENT OR PROGRESS • EMPLOYMENT ASSISTANCE OR EMPLOYMENT PLACEMENT • ATHLETICS • COUNSELING AND APPRAISAL • FINANCIAL ASSISTANCE AND SCHOLARSHIPS • HEALTH AND INSURANCE BENEFITS/SERVICES	• DIFFERENT TREATMENT ON THE BASIS OF SEX, RACE, RELIGION, EXCEPTIONALITY (i.e. Having different requirements for male and female students) • DIFFERENT AIDS, BENEFITS OR SERVICES (Providing scholarship opportunities for males, but not for females) • DENIAL OF AID, BENEFITS OR SERVICES (Preventing a handicapped student from going on a field trip) • SEPARATE RULES OF BEHAVIOR, SANCTIONS OR TREATMENT (Reprimanding certain students based on background etc., and suspending others based on their background) • DISCRIMINATING IN APPLYING RULES OF APPEARANCE (Sending females home for wearing patched jeans to school, but not sending males who do the same) • LIMITING ANY RIGHT, PRIVILEGE ADVANTAGE, OR OPPORTUNITY

There are nine United States anti-discrimination laws and one Presidential Executive Order enforced by different agencies (see code below), that require different remedies if violations are proven. However, they are very similar in the educational activities which they affect and the types of discrimination they prohibit. They are as follows:

Codes for Enforcing Agencies

> OCR = **Office for Civil Rights**
> USDE = **United States Department of Education**
> EEOC = **Equal Employment Opportunities Commission**
> DOL = **Department of Labor**

TITLE VI OF THE CIVIL RIGHTS ACT OF 1964 (P.L. 88-352)

prohibits discrimination on the basis of race, color, or national origin against students of any school receiving federal financial assistance. (OCR/USDE)

TITLE VII OF THE CIVIL RIGHTS ACT OF 1964 (P.L. 88-352)

prohibits discrimination on the basis of race, sex, color, national origin, and/or against employees of a school receiving federal financial assistance. (EEOC)

TITLE IX OF THE EDUCATION AMENDMENTS OF 1972 (P.L. 92-318)

prohibits discrimination on the basis of sex against students and employees of a school receiving federal financial assistance. (OCR/USDE)

EQUAL PAY ACT (as amended in 1972) (P.L. 88-38)

prohibits discrimination on the basis of sex in wages and fringe benefits by any employer in the United States. (DOL)

THE VOCATIONAL EDUCATION ACT OF 1963 (as amended by the Educational Amendment of 1976).

requires states to make new efforts to overcome sex discrimination and stereotyping in vocational education. (OCR/ USDE)

THE REHABILITATION ACT OF 1973 (P.L. 93-112)

promotes and expands opportunities available to individuals with handicaps. Section 502 requires complete accessibility in all buildings constructed after 1968 and financed with federal funds. Section 503 requires federal contracts valued over $2,500 to include affirmative action and non-discrimination clauses. Section 504 and its regulations provide equal educational opportunity for "otherwise qualified handicapped individuals" in all educational programs. Equal Educational

Opportunity requires program accessibility, identification of needs for educational assistance and provision for financial assistance to allow participation in the school. (OCR/USDE)

THE EDUCATION FOR ALL HANDICAPPED CHILDREN ACT OF 1975 (P.L.94-142)

requires that students with a handicap be educated in the "least restrictive environment." The school must provide each identified student with an individualized educational program (IEP). Schools are required to search for students with a handicap, rather than waiting for students to identify themselves to the school. (OCR/USDE)

PREGNANCY DISCRIMINATION ACT OF 1978 (P.L. 95-555)

is an amendment to Title VII of the Civil Rights Act of 1964. This law makes clear that discrimination on the basis of pregnancy, childbirth or related medical conditions constitutes unlawful sex discrimination under Title VII. (EEOC)

AGE DISCRIMINATION IN EMPLOYMENT ACT (as amended in 1978)

prohibits employers, employment agencies and labor organizations with 20 or more employees from basing hiring decisions on a person's age when the person's age is between 40 and 70 unless an age limit is a necessary qualification for the performance. (DOL, OCR, USDE)

EXECUTIVE ORDER 11246 (amended by 11375 in 1968)

prohibits discrimination against employees on the basis of race, color, religion, sex, or national origin in all schools with federal contracts or subcontracts of $10,000 or more. These orders also require written affirmative action programs for schools holding federal contracts of $50,000 or more. (OCR/USDE)

(See Figure 22 - Federal Law Summary Sheet).

Constitutional Provisions for Education

The educational system of the United States, both public and nonpublic, is governed by law. The United States Constitution provides the law for the nation, and State Constitutions provide the law for each state. Since the U.S. Constitution was created by the people, a state legislation has no right to change that Constitution. State legislatures make laws that apply to education; these laws must be in accordance with both the U.S. Constitution and the applicable state constitution.

FEDERAL LAW SUMMARY SHEET

LAW OR EXECUTIVE ORDER	PROHIBITS	COVERS	*enforced*
Title VI: Civil Rights Act of 1964	Race, Color, National Origin Discrimination	Students	OCR, USDE
Title VII: Civil Rights Act of 1964	Race, Sex, Color National Origin & Religious Discrimination	Employees	EEOC
Title IX: Education Amendments of 1972	Sex Discrimination	Employees & Students	OCR, USDE
Equal Pay Act of 1963	Sex Discrimination (in pay only)	Employees	DOL
P.L. 94-142	Handicapped Discrimination	Students	OCR, USDE
Vocational Educational Act: 1963	Sex Discrimination in Vocational Education	Students	OCR, USDE
Executive Order 11246 (as amended by Executive Order 11357), 1968	Race, Sex, Color, National Origin & Religious Discrimination	Employees	OCR, USDE
Rehabilitation Act of 1973 (Section 504)	Handicapped Discrimination	Employees & Students	OCR, USDE
Pregnancy Discrimination Act of 1978	Sex Discrimination (Pregnancy)	Employees	EEOC
Age Discrimination In Employment Act, 1978	Age Discrimination	Employees	DOL, OCR, USDE

Figure 22

Education is legally considered a function of the individual states but, as such, must be practiced in accordance with other provisions of the Constitution; the First and Fourth Amendments have been applied to the operation of education in various states. The *Fourteenth Amendment* protects speci- X 14th fied privileges of citizens. It reads in part:

No state shall make or enforce any law which shall abrogate the privileges or immunities of citizens of the United States; nor shall any state deprive any person of life, liberty or property without due process of law; nor deny any person within its jurisdiction the equal protection of the laws.

The *First Amendment* ensures freedom of speech or religion, of the press, and the right to peti- X 1st tion. It specifies:

Congress shall make no law respecting the establishment of religion or prohibiting the free exercise thereof; or abridge the freedom of speech or of the press; or the right of people peaceably to assemble and to petition the government for redress of grievances.

Significant Court Cases Affecting Schools

School Desegregation.

The equal protection clause of the Fourteenth Amendment has been the major legal vehicle used to challenge various aspects of racial discrimination in public life. Early in the history of the amendment, it was determined that since public schools are state institutions, actions by public school officials and employees are state actions. However, the famous case of *Plessy v. Ferguson* established the principle that separate but equal facilities satisfy the equal protection clause of the amendment. Though Plessy involved public transportation facilities, the Supreme Court used it as a precedent in a public school conflict in 1927 (Lum v. Rice, 1927) A successful challenge to the *separate but equal doctrine* did not arise until 1954 in the landmark case of *Brown v. Board of Education*. The Supreme Court said, *Separate but equal has no place in public education. And that. . separate facilities are inherently unequal.*

Must all one-race schools be eliminated? Not necessarily. Geographic factors, population concentrations, location of schools, traffic patterns, and good-faith attempts to create a unitary school system must all be taken into consideration. The Supreme Court addressed this question in the *Swann (1971)* case.

The North Carolina schools in this 1965 case had adopted a desegregation plan that was being challenged during the 1968-69 school year as inadequate. Chief Justice Burger, in writing for a unanimous Court, recognized that in large cities minority groups are often concentrated in one part of the city. In some situations, certain schools remain all or largely of one race until new schools can be built or until the neighborhood changes. Thus the mere existence of such schools is not in itself proof of unconstitutional segregation. Nevertheless, the courts will carefully scrutinize such arrangements, and the presumption is against such schools. District officials have the burden of showing that single-race schools are genuinely nondiscriminatory.

Does the Brown case apply to teachers and staff? Yes. While *Brown I* dealt with the general constitutional principles related to desegregation, the Court addressed the question of judicial remedy a year later in *Brown II*. The decision generated several guiding principles - requiring school districts to "make a prompt and reasonable start toward full compliance - with all deliberate speed. It also meant that courts may consider "the physical condition of the school plant, the transportation system, personnel," and other factors in supervising good-faith compliance (*Brown v. Board of Education,* 1954). Courts have relied heavily on Brown II in the breadth of their discretionary powers and in considering the role of teachers, administrators, and staff in efforts to desegregate schools. In the fall of 1986, *Brown v. Topeka Board of Education*, returned to the courtroom for a trial to determine whether the vestiges of de jure segregation had been eliminated. The court issued its ruling in April, 1987, in favor of the Topeka Board of Education.

Teacher Rights.

Pickering v. Board of Education,(1968) was a leading case which partially clarified a teacher's right to freedom of speech under the First and Fourteenth Amendments. Marvin Pickering was a high school teacher from Will County, Illinois, who published a long, sarcastic letter in the local newspaper about the way his superintendent and school board raised and spent school funds.

Angered by the publication of the letter, the board of education charged that it contained false and misleading statements, "damaged the professional reputations" of school administrators and the board, and was "detrimental to the efficient operation and administration of the schools." Pickering argued that his letter should be protected by his right of free speech, but an Illinois court ruled against him. Since Pickering held a position as teacher, the state court wrote that he "is more en-titled to harm the schools by speech than by incompetency."

Pickering still believed his letter was protected by the First Amendment, so he appealed to the U.S. Supreme Court. The Court rejected the board's position that critical comments by a teacher on matters of public concern (allocation of funds) may furnish grounds for dismissal. In sum, Pickering unintentionally made several incorrect statements (in the article) on current issues that were critical of his employer but did not impede his teaching or interfere with the regular operation of the schools. The Court therefore concluded that "absent proof of false statements knowingly or recklessly made by him, a teacher's exercise of his right to speak on issues of public importance may not furnish the basis for his dismissal for public employment."

When are teacher complaints not protected? When they are not matters of public concern. In 1983, the U.S. Supreme Court ruled in *Connick v. Myers (1983)* that "when a public employee speaks not as a citizen upon matters of public concern, but instead as an employee upon matters only of personal interest. . .a federal court is not the appropriate forum in which to review the wis-dom" of the public agency's personnel decision.

Academic Freedom.

Academic freedom includes the right of teachers to speak freely about their subjects, to experiment with new ideas, and to select appropriate teaching materials and methods. Courts have held that academic freedom is based on the First Amendment and is fundamental to our democratic society. It protects a teacher's right to evaluate and criticize existing values and practices in order to allow for political, social, economic, and scientific progress. Academic freedom is not absolute, and courts try to balance it against competing educational values (Fischer, 1987).

Students and Free Speech.

In 1965, when the debate over American involvement in the Vietnam war was becoming heated, a group of students in Des Moines, Iowa decided to publicize their antiwar views by wearing black armbands. On learning of the plan, principals of the Des Moines schools established a policy prohibiting armbands in order to prevent any possible disturbance. Although they knew about the policy, several students nevertheless wore armbands to school and refused to remove them. They were suspended. The students argued that the school policy was unconstitutional, and they took their case to court. After the trial, a federal judge ruled that the anti-armband policy was reasonable. But the students appealed their case all the way to the Supreme Court, presenting it with a conflict between their rights and the rules of the school.

Writing for the majority, Justice Forbes stated:

First Amendment rights applied in light of the special characteristics of the school environment are available to teachers and students. It can hardly be argued that either students or teachers shed their constitutional rights to freedom of speech or expression at the schoolhouse gate (Tinker v. Des Moines, 1960).

In sum, the *Tinker v. Des Moines (1968)* case held that school officials cannot prohibit a particular opinion merely "to avoid the discomfort and unpleasantness that always accompany an unpopular viewpoint." On the contrary, unless there is evidence that the forbidden expression would "materially and substantially" interfere with the work of the school, such a prohibition is unconstitutional. Thus this landmark decision established guidelines to help educators understand the scope and limits of student free speech. Since Tinker clearly recognized that teachers as well as students have a constitutional right to freedom of expression, it has been used as precedent by both groups in almost all subsequent cases in this area.

Do students have a right to academic freedom? No. Fischer (1987) states that although student choices in courses, curriculum materials, assignments, and even teachers is increasing in many school districts, this is a matter of educational policy and not a legal right. Courts have not ruled that students have a constitutional right to determine courses, texts, or teaching methods. Thus a federal appeals court held that students have no constitutional right to challenge a school board's decision to eliminate a popular course or remove certain books from the curriculum.

Can schools remove controversial books from a school library? After obtaining a list of *objectionable* books from a conservative parents' organization, a New York school board removed 10 books from their school libraries because they were *anti-American, anti-Christian, anti-Semitic and just plain filthy.* But a group of students and parents claimed that the board's action was unconstitutional, and a majority of the U.S. Supreme Court agreed (*Board of Education v. Pico,* 1982). Judge Brennan emphasized that student's First Amendment rights are applicable to the school library, and that a school board's discretion "may not be exercised in a narrowly partisan or political manner" because "our Constitution does not permit the official suppression of ideas."

If board members *intended by their removal decision* to deny students access to ideas with which the board disagreed and if this intent was "the decisive factor" in the board's decision, then the board's action was unconstitutional. On the other hand, Justice Brennan indicated several legitimate motivations for removing library books, including pervasive vulgarity, educational suitability, "good taste," "relevance," and "appropriateness to age and grade level."

In sum, to avoid violating the First Amendment, "boards may not remove books from school library shelves simply because they dislike the ideas contained in those books." Rather, they should establish and follow constitutional criteria and reasonable procedures before removing controversial material.

Role of Religion.

Controversies concerning the appropriate place, if any, of religion in the schools have occurred periodically in our history of education. Though the First Amendment states that *Congress shall make no law respecting the establishment of religion, or prohibiting the free exercise thereof*, the interpretation of these general provisions and their application to public schools have been problematic. Religion tends to be so important in the lives of people, and so surrounded by powerful emotions, that many want to use the schools to maintain their religious beliefs at the same time that others insist on the complete exclusion of religion from public schools.

Can a teacher refuse to follow the curriculum if the refusal is based on religious objections? No. This question was raised in the Chicago public schools when a kindergarten teacher, who was a member of Jehovah's Witnesses, informed her principal that because of her religion she would not be able "to teach any subjects having to do with love of country, the flag or other patriotic matters in the prescribed curriculum." The U.S. Court of Appeals ruled in favor of the school board, and the Supreme Court upheld the ruling (*Palmer v. Board of Education*, 1980). The decision basically stated that while her right to her religious beliefs must be respected, she has no "right to require others to submit to her views and to forgo a portion of their education they would otherwise be entitled to enjoy."

Can public schools start the day with prayers? No. Historically, many public schools began each day with a required prayer, Bible reading, or both. In 1959 Pennsylvania enacted a law requiring daily Bible reading in the schools but exempting children who had written requests for exemption from their parents. The Schempp children, who were Unitarians, challenged the law (*Abington School District v. Schempp*, 1963). Their case eventually reached the Supreme Court, which ruled in their favor.

Can students receive religious instruction during school hours? Yes. The instruction must take place away from school, however, not on school grounds, and must be conducted by teachers or religious figures independent of the school and not paid by the school. This "released time" religious education is used in some communities in the country, and the Supreme Court (_Zorach v. Clausen_, 1952) has ruled that the arrangement does not violate the Constitution.

In 1984, a situation arose in Lubbock, Texas, where pursuant to school board policy students could gather before and after school hours, under school supervision, for voluntary moral, religious, or ethical activities led by students. When the policy and practice were challenged, the court of appeals also applied the three-pronged _Lemon_ test: (1) Does the policy or practice have a secular purpose? (2) Is the primary effect of the policy or practice one which neither advances nor inhibits religion? (3) Does the policy or practice avoid an excessive entanglement with religion? To satisfy the Constitution, the answer must be in the affirmative for each of these questions. In the Lubbock (_Lubbock Civil Liberties v. Lubbock Independent School District_, 1984) case the policy and practice failed on all three grounds. The facts showed the purpose was clearly to advance religion and that its primary effect would do the same. Furthermore, school supervision of the activities is precisely the kind of entanglement that is impermissible under constitutional precedents.

Sex Discrimination.

The history of sexual discrimination among teachers is well documented. In recent years, there have been a variety of challenges to such discrimination, and many school policies have been revised in the light of court cases, legislation, and a new public concern for equal treatment of men and women. I will only highlight some of the more popular questions related to the issues of sex discrimination in our schools.

How has Title IX affected the schools?

In several areas _Title IX_ covers virtually every aspect of a school system, excluding curriculum materials and textbooks. The impact of Title IX and its regulations is the most important law to achieve equal treatment of the sexes in public schools. Sex discrimination and stereotyping in the school life of students have also been challenged in recent years. It is no longer legally acceptable to exclude girls or boys from parts of the curriculum, though in practice cultural pressures remain influential. Preferential treatment of boys in school athletics has created many lawsuits as well as new legislation. As a result, girls and boys must have equal access to noncontact sports, on separate teams if the schools provide them, and on integrated teams if only one team is available in the particular sport. Schedules, coaching, equipment, and other support must be comparable for girls' and boys' teams.

Different admission standards for girls and boys to selective public schools are unconstitutional, but separate facilities are currently acceptable if they are genuinely equal. Married and/or pregnant students may not be excluded from school nor compelled to attend separate classes, separate schools, or evening classes. Similarly, courts now tend to protect the rights of such students to participate in extracurricular activities, though health and safety considerations may always be used to exclude an individual from a particular activity.

Laws today generally require employers to treat pregnancy disability the same way as any other disability. Are teachers on maternity leave able to receive these disability benefits? Yes. Do teachers on maternity leave have a right to use their sick- leave pay? Yes. Congress passed the *Pregnancy Disability Bill* in 1979. The law now provides that pregnancy-related disabilities receive the same insurance coverage and sick-leave benefits as other disabilities. This law is an amendment to Title VII of the Civil Rights Act of 1964.

Can male coaches receive more pay than female coaches? The principle of equal pay for equivalent work has been difficult to apply in the area of coaching. Historically, significant disparities existed in favor of male coaches. While Title IX has equalized some aspects of the funding of athletics, it has not been applied to coaching because Congress intended this particular law to apply to students and not to coaches (Fischer, 1987). The federal *Equal Pay Act of 1963* and similar state laws have been used to challenge unequal pay. The Department of Labor claims that regardless of the sport in question, coaches perform substantially similar duties. If this proposed policy becomes law, pay differentials among different kinds of coaches and between male and female coaches will disappear. In the meantime, some discrepancies continue, based on the differences in assigned duties.

[handwritten margin note: murky: what about male coaches of girls teams, & vice versa?]

Does coupling a teaching position with coaching constitute sex discrimination? This is a interesting and widespread practice. Basically, there are two legal theories under which employment discrimination cases are decided: the disparate treatment and disparate impact theories. *Disparate treatment* means the employer treats certain people less favorable because of their race, color, religion, sex, or national origin. The burden of proof is always on the plaintiff in such claims. *Disparate impact* is involved when the employment practice appears neutral but in fact has the effect of excluding a group protected by the Civil Rights Act. Once the plaintiff establishes there is such a negative impact on a protected group, the employer must prove business necessity (*Civil Rights Division v. Amphitheater Unified School District,* 1984). In light of the widespread practice of coupling academic teaching positions with coaching, it becomes very important for school districts to consider the disparate impact theory of discrimination and the stringent requirements of the defense of business necessity.

[handwritten margin note: ?]

Due Process for Students.

The Supreme Court addressed this issue in *Goss v. Lopez (1975)* Dwight Lopez and several other students were suspended for up to ten days from school in Columbus, Ohio, during the 1970-71 academic year without receiving a hearing. Some of the students were suspended for documented acts of violence, but others, Lopez among them, were suspended even though they claimed to be innocent bystanders of demonstrations or disturbances. Moreover, they were never informed of what they were accused of doing. The students went to court and claimed that their right to due process was violated. When the federal district court agreed with them, the administrators appealed to the U.S. Supreme Court. In a 5-4 opinion, the Court ruled in favor of the students.

The Court reiterated the key principle of the *Tinker* case, that *young people do not 'shed their constitutional rights' at the schoolhouse door*. Clearly, said the Court, the Constitution protects students in cases of expulsion from the public schools. Furthermore, some degree of due process is required even in cases of short term suspension. Thus it is clear that the law requires schools to respect students' constitutional rights to due process in both serious and minor disciplinary matters that might lead to either expulsion or suspension from school. It is generally accepted by the courts, that as a minimum, students facing suspension "must be given some kind of notice and afforded some kind of hearing." Notice of the charges may be oral or written, and a student who denies the charges must be given "an explanation of the evidence the authorities have and an opportunity to present his/her side of the story."

Serious disciplinary cases, by contrast, may require extensive and thorough procedures. *Serious cases* means those cases that might lead to long-term suspension or expulsion. Cases involving serious disciplinary violations call for a written notice specifying the charges, the time and place of the hearing, and a description of procedures to be followed at the hearing. Students should know what evidence will be used against them, the names of witnesses who will testify, and the substance of witnesses' testimony. Students should have the right to cross-examine witnesses, as well as to present witnesses and evidence on their own behalf. The right of appeal should also be clearly stated.

Do "Miranda rights" apply to school situations? No, they do not. In 1966 the Supreme Court held in *Miranda v. Arizona* (1966) that the *Fifth Amendment* privilege against self-incrimination applies to those under questioning while in official custody related to a criminal investigation. This means that the person "deprived of his freedom of action in any significant way" must be informed of his right to remain silent, that anything he says may be used against him, and that he has a right to the assistance of a lawyer. Such rules, however, do not apply when school officials detain students for questioning - they have no right even to have their parents present. Since the Miranda rule derives from the Fifth Amendment provision that a person shall not be "compelled in a criminal case to be a witness against himself, "and since public school disciplinary proceedings and inquiries are not criminal proceedings, Miranda does not apply.

Are there disciplinary situations where due process is not required? Yes. In two situations teachers or school administrators may proceed without first observing any formal due process procedures. First, in situations involving minor infractions of rules or nonperformance of required tasks, students are given a variety of "punishments" ranging from brief detentions to extra work, verbal chastisement, being sent to the principal's office, and so forth. The second exception involves emergencies in which educators must act quickly to preserve the safety of persons or property. The Supreme Court recognized in *Goss* that emergencies occur in school that would make notice and hearing prior to action impracticable because the situation presents danger to persons or property. In such situations, the only legal requirement is that fair procedures be followed "as soon as practicable after removal of the danger or disruption."

Dress Codes.

All courts recognize that schools have authority to regulate student clothing. But not all dress codes are constitutional (*Cronin v. Moody*, 1979). In New Hampshire, for example, a federal court held that a rule prohibiting the wearing of blue jeans or dungarees was unconstitutional (*Bannister v. Paradis,* 1970). The court rejected the argument that wearing jeans "detracts from discipline and a proper educational climate" because the school presented no evidence supporting this position. However, in a subsequent North Carolina case, the Courts held that a student was properly excluded from his graduation ceremony for violating a rule requiring men to wear "dress" pants, as opposed to jeans under their graduation gowns (*Fowler v. Williamson,* 1979).

Can students wear anything they desire to school? No. In the New Hampshire case, the judge wrote that a school "can and must. . .exclude persons who are unsanitary, obscenely or scantily clad." Good hygiene may require that dirty clothing be prohibited. And a school may prohibit scantily-clad students "because it is obvious that the lack of proper covering, particularly with female students, might tend to distract other students" and disrupt the educational process.

School boards have the authority to regulate dress for reasons of safety, order and discipline, but have no authority to enforce regulations not related to those factors. In New York, a "no jeans rule" applied only to female students. This was clearly not related to the educational process and was found to be unconstitutional (*Scott v. Board of Education*, 1969).

Students' Grooming.

Can students wear their hair as they wish? Surprisingly, only about half of the U.S. circuit courts of appeals answer yes to the question. A case arose in Indiana's Wawasee High School where a committee of students, teachers, and administrators developed a dress code *to insure the best possible overall appearance of the student body.* The code was adopted by a vote of the students, and they and their parents were notified of its provisions. Nevertheless, Greg Carpenter, with his parents' consent, chose to violate the code's "long hair provision" and was punished. As a result, Greg's father sued on his behalf to prohibit enforcement of the code's hair length regulations. The school board argued that because the code was adopted by a majority of the students, it was not an unreasonable interference with Greg Carpenter's constitutional rights, but the Seventh U.S. Circuit Court of Appeals disagreed (*Arnold v. Carpenter,* 1972). It held that "the right to wear one's hair at any length or in any desired manner is an ingredient of personal freedom protected by the United States Constitution." To limit that right, a school would have to bear a "substantial burden of justification." In this particular case, the school board did not meet that burden. What about the issue that this code was adopted by the majority of students? The court concluded that the democratic process by which the code was adopted did not justify the denial of Greg's constitutional right to wear his hair as he chose. The U.S. Constitution, said the court, cannot be amended by majority vote of any school or community.

Nine of the thirteen U.S. circuit courts of appeals have clearly ruled on the constitutional right of students to choose the length of their hair. Some circuits hold that grooming is a constitutional right, and others do not. The arguments used on each side are varied and vigorous, and no final decision establishing a uniform law has been reached because the Supreme Court has refused to rule on the issue.

Those states in which the Circuit Courts have decided that grooming is a constitutional right are: First Circuit (Maine, Massachusetts, New Hampshire, Rhode Island), the Fourth Circuit (Maryland, North Carolina, South Carolina, Virginia, West Virginia), the Seventh Circuit (Illinois, Indiana, Wisconsin), the Eighth Circuit (Arkansas, Iowa, Minnesota, Missouri,

Nebraska, North Dakota, South Dakota), and the Second Circuit (Connecticut, New York and Vermont). In these states, courts will hold grooming regulations unconstitutional unless school officials present convincing evidence that they are fair, reasonable, and necessary to carry out a legitimate educational purpose.

In the following states, the circuit courts have decided that grooming is not a significant constitutional issue and that federal courts should not judge the wisdom of codes regulating hair length or style. Basically, this means that the federal courts will generally not consider such cases. Those states are: Louisiana, Mississippi, Texas, Kentucky, Michigan, Ohio, Tennessee, Alaska, Arizona, California, Hawaiian Islands, Idaho, Montana, Nevada, Oregon, Washington, Colorado, Kansas, Oklahoma, New Mexico, Utah, Wyoming, Alabama, Florida, Georgia, Delaware, New Jersey, Pennsylvania, and the District of Columbia (Fischer, 1987).

Student Searches.

In *New Jersey v. T.L.O.* (1985) the Supreme Court rendered an opinion related to the authority of school officials to search students for contraband.

The facts accepted by the Court were that a teacher, upon entering the girls' restroom found T.L.O. and another student holding lighted cigarettes. Since school rules forbade smoking there, the girls were escorted to the assistant vice principal's office. When questioned, T.L.O. denied smoking at all. At the request of the official she opened her purse, where, in addition to cigarettes, there was drug paraphernalia and evidence that she had sold drugs. After examining the purse, the assistant vice principal summoned T.L.O.'s mother and the police.

A divided Supreme Court said school searches are justified "when there are reasonable grounds for suspecting that the search will turn up evidence that the student has violated or is violating either the law or the rules of the school." The Court rejected the *Fourth Amendment* requirement of probable cause as inapplicable to school situations. Justice White, writing for the majority, said that the proper standard for searches by educators is "reasonableness, under all circumstances." Reasonableness "involves a twofold inquiry: first, one must consider 'whether the. . .action was justified at its inception';. . .second, one must determine whether the search as actually conducted was 'reasonably related in scope to the circumstances which justified the interference in the first place." Justice White concluded that the initial search for cigarettes was reasonable, since finding the cigarettes in the purse "would both corroborate the report that she had been smoking and undermine the credibility of her defense to the charge of smoking." Since the first search for cigarettes was reasonable, the second search for marijuana was also considered reasonable by the Court.

While the Court was divided in its analysis, educators can be guided by the standard applied by the Court. As Justice White indicated, the Supreme Court has not yet ruled on: (1) the search of lockers, desks, and other storage areas provided by schools, and what standards should be used for searching such areas; (2) searches by educators at the request of law enforcement officials; (3) whether or not "individualized suspicion" is an essential part of the standard of reasonableness; and (4) whether or not the "exclusionary rule applies to the fruits of unlawful searches conducted by school authorities.

Generally, school lockers may be searched by appropriate school officials if they have reasonable suspicion that unlawful or dangerous materials are hidden there. Similarly, the Supreme Court held that students' purses may be searched. The search of students' clothing, or "strip searches," are more invasive, and therefore merit greater protection. While the Supreme Court has not ruled on such cases, lower courts indicate that a standard related to "probable cause" must be used by educators.

Censorship of Student Press.

The U.S. Supreme Court ruled in January of 1988, _Hazelwood School District v. Kuhlmeier_, that school administrators have sweeping authority to regulate student speech in school-sponsored publications and activities. The _Hazelwood_ case began in May of 1983 when the principal of Hazelwood East High School in suburban St. Louis ordered the deletion of two pages from _Spectrum_, a student newspaper produced as part of the school's journalism course, because he objected to a pair of article - one on girls at the school who had become pregnant and another on the effects of divorce on students.

The principal said he prevented the stories from being printed to protect the privacy of students and parents referred to in them, to avoid the appearance that the school endorsed the sexual mores of the preganant girls, and to shield younger students from "inappropriate" material. He also said he had "serious doubts" that the articles comported with the journalistic rules of fairness and privacy taught in the course.

Three editors of _Spectrum_ filed suit against the principal and the district, charging that the principal's action violated their First Amendment right to freedom of expression.

A federal district judge held in May 1985 that because the paper was produced as part of the school's curriculum, the student journalists were not entitled to the same degree of First Amendment protection as professional reporters.

A federal appellate court over-turned that ruling in July 1986, holding that the paper was constitutionally protected public forum for student expression. Applying the standard set by the High Court in _Tinker_, it ruled that official censorship is justified only if articles threaten to result in substantial disruption or to subject the school to a lawsuit.

In sum, the Supreme Court ruled in January 1988 that educators may exercise editorial control over the contents of a high school newspaper produced as part of the school's journalism curriculum.

Corporal Punishment.

Specifically, spanking of students, has been permitted by the Supreme Court in the _Ingraham v. Wright_ decision in 1977. In Dade County, Florida, James Ingraham and Roosevelt Andrews, junior high school students, were severely paddled during the 1970-71 school year. In fact, Ingraham was so harshly beaten that the resulting hematoma required medical attention, and he missed ll days of school. The paddling Andrews received including being struck on the arms, depriving him the use of an arm for a week.

At the time of the paddling, Dade County schools used corporal punishment as one means of maintaining discipline. Simultaneously, a Florida law forbade punishment that was "degrading and unduly severe" or that took place prior to consultation with the principal or the teacher in charge of the school. The students filed suit against several school administrators and claimed that the severe beating they received constituted cruel and unusual punishment. The district court, the court of appeals, and finally the Supreme Court all ruled that the beating, although excessive and unreasonable, did not violate the Eighth Amendment, which prohibits cruel and unusual punishment.

Whether school children and youth ought to be physically punished is not a legal matter. The Constitution is silent on this matter, as it is silent on education in general. Thus courts have held that education is a function of the state governments and that states may further delegate power over schooling to local governments. At this date, nine states prohibit the use of corporal punishment: Hawaii, Maine, Massachusetts, New Hampshire, New Jersey, New York, Rhode Island, Vermont and California.

Child Abuse and Neglect.

Child abuse and neglect are social problems affecting thousands of children each year in all socioeconomic levels and from a variety of problem family situations. Recently, there appears to be great deal of attention directed toward problems of child abuse and neglect in the United States. Social service agencies have been aware of the problem of child maltreatment for a number of years. Now medical personnel, educators, law enforcement officers and the general public are becoming aware of child maltreatment and its effects on the child and the family.

As of 1980, 43 states and the District of Columbia specifically mention educators in their laws. The other seven states require any person suspecting child abuse or neglect to make a report. As educators, we have a legal responsibility to report any and all cases of suspected abuse or neglect. There are myths surrounding who abuses and neglects their children. Research has indicated that the problem knows no ethnic boundaries, socioeconomic levels or religious backgrounds.

While there is no single, generally accepted authoritative definition of child abuse or neglect, the *National Child Abuse Prevention and Treatment Act (P. L. 93-247)*, passed in 1974, defines child abuse and neglect as:

Physical or mental injury, sexual abuse or exploitation, negligent treatment, or maltreatment of a child under the age of eighteen or the age specified under the child protection law of the state in question, by a person who is responsible for the child's welfare, under circumstances which indicate that the child's health or welfare is harmed or threatened thereby.

Each state has its own definition of what constitutes abuse or neglect, but they all tend to use a combination of two or more of the following elements: (1) physical injury, (2) mental or emotional injury, and/or (3) sexual molestation or exploitation. Although there is a federal definition as well, child abuse or neglect is not a federal offense but a state crime.

Can teachers be penalized for failure to report child abuse or neglect? Yes. Most states provide criminal penalties for failure to act by persons mandated to report child abuse or neglect. Penalties range from a 5-to-30 day jail sentence and a fine of $10 to $100, to as high as a year in jail and a fine of $1000. Furthermore, because many teachers do not report suspected cases (only 12 percent of all cases), some states have imposed civil liability for failure to report. This means that such teachers may be sued for money damages. Among these states are Arkansas, Colorado, Iowa, and New York, where the law requires that there be evidence of willful misconduct, whereas Michigan and Montana require only that simple negligence be shown (Aaron, 1981).

Education and the Handicapped.

When Congress enacted the _Education of All Handicapped Children Act (P.L. 94-142)_ in 1975, it found that there were more than 8 million handicapped children in the country and that over half of them were not receiving an appropriate education. Furthermore, approximately one million were completely excluded from the public schools. Congress stated that the main purpose of the act was to assure that states provide all handicapped children with "a free appropriate public education and related services designed to meet their unique needs." While Congress recognized that education remains a state responsibility, it also acknowledged that federal assistance was necessary to "assure equal protection of the law."

Who are the handicapped?

Federal regulations define _handicapped children_ as those who are mentally retarded, hard of hearing, deaf, speech impaired, visually handicapped, seriously emotionally disturbed, orthopedically impaired, other health impaired, deaf-blind, multihandicapped, or who have specific learning disabilities and who, because of these impairments, need special education and related services. The main features of the Act are:

* _All handicapped learners between the ages of three and twenty-one are to be provided with a free public education._

* _Each handicapped child is to have an individualized education program, developed jointly by a school official, a teacher, the parent(s) or guardian, and if possible, the learner._

* _Handicapped children are not to be grouped separately unless they are severely handicapped, in which cases separate facilities and programs would be deemed more appropriate._

* _Tests for identification and placement are to be free of racial and cultural bias._

* _School districts are to maintain continuous efforts at identifying handicapped children._

* _School districts are to establish priorities for providing educational programs in compliance with the law._

* _Placement of the handicapped is to require parental approval._

* _Private schools are to comply with the Act._

* _Retraining or in-service training of all workers with the handicapped is required._

* _Special federal grants are available for modifying school buildings._

* *State departments of education are to be designated as the responsible state agency for all programs for the handicapped.*

Individualized Education Program (IEP).

An individualized education program (IEP) must comprise written statements developed by the school, the child's teacher, one or both of the child's parents or guardians, and the child when appropriate. Other specialists may be involved if the parents or school so desire. Each written IEP must include:

* *the student's present level of educational performance*

* *annual goals, including short-term instructional objectives*

* *specific special education and related services to be provided to the student, and the extent to which the student will be able to participate in regular educational programs*

* *projected dates for initiation and anticipated duration of special services*

* *objective criteria, evaluation procedures, and schedules for determining, on at least an annual basis, whether or not the short-term instructional objectives are being met*

Due Process.

Parents or guardians of handicapped students must be notified in writing before a school initiates, changes, or refuses to initiate or change the identification, evaluation, or placement of the student or the provision of a free appropriate public education to the student. This notification in the parents' native language or other mode of communication (e.g., braille, oral communication, sign language) must include:

* *a full explanation of the parents' due process rights*

* *a description of the action proposed or refused by the school; why the school proposes or refuses to take the action; and a description of any options considered by the agency and reasons why they were rejected*

* *a description of each evaluation procedure; that is, a test, record, or report the school uses as a basis for the proposal or refusal*

* *any other factors relevant to the school's proposal or refusal*

School Records

In 1974, Congress passed the *Family Educational Rights and Privacy Act* (also known as FERPA or the *Buckley Amendment*) to define who may and may not see student records. The main features of the act are:

* It requires school districts to establish a written policy concerning student records and to inform parents of their rights under the act each year.

* It guarantees parents the right to inspect and review the educational records of their children.

* It establishes procedures through which parents can challenge the accuracy of student records.

* It protects the confidentiality of student records by preventing disclosure of personally identifiable information to outsiders without prior parental consent.

* It entitles parents to file complaints with the FERPA Office concerning alleged failures to comply with the Act.

The act applies to all schools receiving federal education funds either directly or indirectly (*United States Code 20*, 1979). Parents may assert their children's rights of access and consent until they become 18 years old or begin attending a post-secondary institution; after this, these rights will "only be accorded to . . .the student."

Education records include any information compiled by a school that is directly related to a current student regardless of whether the record is in handwriting, print, tape, film, microfilm, or microfiche. Do parents have the right to see teachers' personal notes about their students? No. The *Buckley Amendment* does not give parents that right. If these records are in their sole possession and are not revealed to any other individual except a substitute teacher, parents have no right to their access. Also, eligible students do not have the right to see records of a physician, psychologist, or other recognized professional used only in connection with their treatment. Parents have no right to see records of the law enforcement unit that the school maintained solely for police purposes; or job- related records of students who are employees of the school.

Three areas of misunderstanding have regularly occurred concerning the Buckley Amendment. First, many educators are still unaware that access applies to all student records, not just to the cumulative file. Second, many parents believe the act gives them the right to challenge the fairness of a student grade. Although the act does allow parents to question whether a teacher's grade was recorded accurately, it does not allow them to challenge the reasonableness of the grade that was assigned (Fischer, 1987). Third, many administrators are not aware that the parental right to inspect and review the educational records of their children applies equally to noncustodial parents who do not live with their children (unless their access has been prohibited by a court order).

Summary

Court cases that deal with issues related to the rights and responsibilities of students and teachers provide the basis for more and more discussion in newsletters, newspapers, professional journals, magazines, radio and television across the country. The range and scope of the education-related court decisions have become so broad that concentration in school law is becoming a more recognized field of preparation in the legal profession, as well as the teaching profession.

As I had indicated in the beginning of this chapter, the objective was not to cover all cases involving student and teacher rights, but to provide an overview of the more significant cases that have evolved and will continue to evolve in the courts. The cases that were outlined in this chapter have had a direct impact on many of our school policies and practices today. Obviously, there are other issues that could be covered, for example on the teachers' side: teacher certification, teacher contracts, tenure, academic freedom, right to bargain collectively, right to strike, liability and negligence and educational malpractice. On the students' side: right of an education for children of illegal aliens, loco parentis doctrine, marriage and censorship. Other issues that have been and will continue to find their way through the courts and certainly have an impact on our schools will be: prayer and religious activities in the public schools, tuition tax credits (private v. public schools), vouchers, intelligence testing, ability grouping, busing, magnet schools, school finance, affirmative action guidelines and comparable worth issues.

It is important that we not fear the laws and courts and simply react to court decisions. We must take the initiative on certain legal issues, and we must *put our own house in order* to assure equity in education from a legal standpoint.

WORKSHEET 1

1. What is the difference between Title VI and Title VII of the Civil Rights Act?

   Both cover discrimination on basis of race/color
   nat'l origin, VI for students, VII for employees.
   VII also prevents discrimination on basis
   of sex.

2. What was the significance of the <u>Plessy v. Ferguson</u> decision and <u>Brown v. Board of Education (Topeka)</u>?

   <u>Plessy v. Ferguson</u>: *covered "separate but equal," allowed it*
   in public transport, has been applied to other
   areas incl. education

   <u>Brown v. Board of Education</u>: *ruled that separate was in-*
   herently unequal in education

3. What are the implications for teachers according to the <u>Pickering v. Board of Education</u> decision?

   Teachers are still citizens and still have
   the right to free speech in matters
   of public concern. Cannot be fired
   for exercising this right.

4. What are the implications for students according to the <u>Tinker v. Des Moines</u> decision?

Students have free speech too, in light of special characteristics of school enviro. "Disruption" or unpopularity cannot gag students.

5. What are the implications of the <u>Hazelwood v. Kuhlmeier</u> case for teachers and students? What do you think of this 1988 Supreme Court decision?

~~Because student~~ Because student news papers are often part of a school course ~~(or~~ or paid for by school, educators can censor them. I have no real problem if the character of teachers/admin is good & reasons are valid -- on the surface, case in q. might have better been resolved by aliases in stories rather than deletion of stories.

6. Do "Miranda rights" apply to school situations? Why or why not?

No, only if student is subject on criminal investigation. School is its own world and admin. may maintain order within it. Minor punishments for minor infractions do not have their own "due process" here. School discipline ≠ criminal proceeding.

7. What did the 1985 Supreme Court case of New Jersey v. T.L.O. concern itself with?

Search and seizure. Reasonable grounds for search of students belongings are easily established and search may commence. Is action justified? Is search scope appropriate?

What are the implications for classroom teachers? Explain.

Compared to police, teachers have more leeway, not having to establish probable cause to search a student for contraband.

8. What information must be included in an Individualized Education Program (IEP)?

① students current level of ed perf ② annual goals incl s-t instr obj ③ spec. SPED + rel. serv. provided, extent will partic. in reg. prog. ④ proj. initiation dates, antic dur. of spec serv ⑤ obj crit/eval proc/ sched for deter if objectives being met

9. What does the Family Educational Rights and Privacy Act pertain to?

Who may or may not see students educ records. Parents allowed full access, outsiders only w/ parent permission.

WORKSHEET 2

Case Analysis 1

Mr. Suarez, a social studies teacher in Flagstaff, Arizona has approached the principal about the state-adopted textbooks used in his classes. According to Mr. Suarez, they are biased against women and minorities. The accomplishments of these groups are not recognized, the language is sexist, and accurate representation of the American family is not present. Mr. Suarez demands that supplementary funds be made available to provide him and other concerned teachers with materials that are more equitable.

VIOLATION OF THE LAW: _____ Yes   No ✔

If yes, which laws apply? _____curriculum_____

_____

_____

If no, provide a reason(s) for your decision: _The ~~district~~ state has_
academic freedom, but so does Mr.
S. -- he can propose or even write
new texts.

Corrective action recommended: _____

_____

_____

_____

_____

1st amend v. Title IX

cross

Case Analysis 2

The parents of an tenth-grade girl have requested that their daughter be removed from the co-educational physical education class that is required for graduation. Her wearing the prescribed gym shorts in a coed setting violates the family's religious beliefs. Because of Title IX, the school district has a firm policy on co-educational P.E. classes.

VIOLATION OF THE LAW: _____ YES __✓__ NO

If yes, which laws apply? _____

_____

_____

If no, provide a reason(s) for your decision: *An exception could be made for the uniform rule, e.g. the girl could be allowed to wear a skirt. The district*

Corrective action recommended: *has a right to require students to meet grad requirements, so such exceptions to minor rules should make it possible for these requirements to be met.*

Case Analysis 3

West High School provides a variety of academic and extra-curricular activities for the 1,857 students attending the recently established magnet school. As a result of a court order, more than 600 Black students from East High School, which had been attended primarily by Black students, were assigned to West High School. All Black students were assigned to one semester of remedial English and were required to demonstrate proficiency in English before they could enroll in other English courses. This requirement did not involve those students currently enrolled at West High School.

VIOLATION OF THE LAW: ✓ YES _____ NO

If yes, which laws apply? Title VI _____

_____

_____

If no, provide a reason(s) for your decision: _____

_____

_____

Corrective action recommended: Only those students who need remedial English should be enrolled in it; this rule was applied to all black students regardless and thus violated separate Brown v. Topeka BE std'z'd testing for all *fine line: acad. freedom*

Case Analysis 4

A tenured kindergarten teacher in the New York City public schools has been informed that her contract will not be renewed next year because of her refusal to teach certain parts of the required curriculum. Ms. Herriot, a Jehovah's witness, plans to file suit against the district, claiming her rights to religious freedom have been violated. Her religious beliefs prohibit her from teaching students the pledge of allegiance, patriotic songs, or conducting activities connected with holidays, such as Halloween, Thanksgiving and Christmas. Ms. Herriot believes these activities are forms of idolatry and worship of artificial images banned by the Bible.

VIOLATION OF THE LAW: _____ YES __✓__ NO

If yes, which laws apply? _____

_____

_____

If no, provide a reason(s) for your decision: *Ms. Herriot is denying her students the right to partake of the common curriculum.*

Corrective action recommended: _____

_____

_____

_____

_____

Case Analysis 5

May Chao, a Laotian-American student, had been placed in the elementary school program for handicapped children. Her parents complained to the school district that they didn't believe she was either physically or mentally handicapped. The teacher, who recommended that May be placed in the program for the hearing impaired, explained that he felt May should stay in the program until she learned English well enough to transfer to a regular class. The teacher believed that this environment would have allowed the child to make the most rapid progress as there was a low teacher-pupil ratio. He strongly believed that there would be more time for the individual attention she needs.

VIOLATION OF THE LAW: ✔ YES ____ NO

If yes, which laws apply? _Title VI, PL 94-142, Rehab._
Act
test/placement/IEP

If no, provide a reason(s) for your decision: _____

_____

Corrective action recommended: _She should be tested, and if any handicaps do exist, she'll receive a specific, not indefinite, time to be enrolled in it, and will be placed in the least restrictive environment. Must be ESL or biling ed, not spec. ed._

Tonganoxie has severe dress code

Case Analysis 6

Jefferson High School has a dress code that was democratically ratified by 70 percent of the student body that prohibits "extreme non-conformity" in personal appearance. The principal has used this code to send the following students home:

1. Bill, who wears an earring in his left ear. *girls can wear*

2. Fred, who has a shoulder-length hair and a mustache. *girls long hair*

3. Sandy, who wore a halter-top and cut-offs. *yes: provocative -- distract, disrupt*

4. Jeff, who wore a shirt expressing a favorite beer.

VIOLATION OF THE LAW: __✓__ YES ____ NO

If yes, which laws apply? *Arnold v. Carpenter* _____
_____ *Sex discrim.* _____

_____

If no, provide a reason(s) for your decision: _____

_____

_____

Corrective action recommended: *A ~~cer~~ dress code should be established which defends clothing choices on the basis of hygiene, safety, order + discipline -- i.e. Sandy's wardrobe could be excluded because she distracts from lesson -- possibly even Jeff, since students not of drinking age? Nah!*

209

Case Analysis 7

Ms. Wright has taught for seven years at the elementary school in District 301. She is expecting a child in 7 months. She has accumulated 48 days of sick leave over the 7 years. She has informed the school district administrative office of her intention to use her sick leave as part of her maternity leave. The district has indicated that her sick leave is not the same as maternity leave and thus she is not entitled to use those 48 days. However, the district is willing to let her take a leave without pay and promise her position when she is ready to return.

VIOLATION OF THE LAW: __✓__ YES _____ NO

If yes, which laws apply? _Title VII, Title IX, Equal Pay Act, EO 11246, Preg Act 78_

If no, provide a reason(s) for your decision: _____

Corrective action recommended: _Let her use her sick leave -- a man would not face the loss of income & benefits she would._

doing something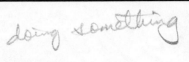

Case Analysis 8

Anthony Reyes is a 14 year-old Hispanic student who is limited English proficient. He is one of several students in the district receiving instruction in English as a Second Language (ESL). The district is hard pressed to find enough resources and materials, let alone a bilingual teacher. The district is providing ESL classes 2 days per week for 30 minutes each day.

VIOLATION OF THE LAW: _____ YES __✓__ NO

If yes, which laws apply? _____

_____

_____

If no, provide a reason(s) for your decision: *The school is doing the best it can with the resources it has. Try for federal grants!*

Corrective action recommended: _____

_____

_____

_____

_____

can be released from school 2 yrs./wk. for rel. observ. as long as d/n interfere w/ req. courses for grad'n

Case Analysis 9

For years, a small rural school district, where 95 percent of the population is Protestant, has provided release time for students to attend religious classes in an empty classroom at one of the elementary schools. An unsuccessful school board candidate has lodged a complaint against the district for this practice. The school district argues that no one objected when the church was used by the school for kindergarten classes and that sending the students to a church for the voluntary religious class would present a safety hazard because of the busy street.

VIOLATION OF THE LAW: __✓__ YES _____ NO

If yes, which laws apply? *Lubbock* _____

_____

_____

If no, provide a reason(s) for your decision: _____

_____

_____

Corrective action recommended: *Release times OK -- must be in another building, cannot use school employees. K is not the same unless that church taught religion to the students in that class.*

Lemon test --

Case Analysis 10

The Riverview School Board recently took several books off of the public school library shelves. They felt the books were racist, anti-American and "not the type of material that Riverview students should be exposed to." A sample of the books that were removed is listed below:

Huckleberry Finn
Lord of the Flies
Jaws
To Kill a Mockingbird
The Color Purple
Little Red Riding Hood
Hansel and Gretel
Charlie and the Chocolate Factory
The Diary of Anne Frank

VIOLATION OF THE LAW: __✓__ YES ____ NO

If yes, which laws apply? _BofE v. Pico_

1st Amend

supr. of ideas

If no, provide a reason(s) for your decision: _____

_____

_____

Corrective action recommended: _Put the books back on the shelf and come up with a concrete, constitutional basis for excluding works._

REFERENCES

20 U.S.C, 1401, 1402, 1411-20.

Abington School District v. Schempp, 374 U.S. 203 (1963).

Arnold v. Carpenter, 459 F.2d 939 (7th Cir. 1972).

Bannister v. Paradis, 316 F. Supp. 185 (D. N.H. 1970).

Board of Education, Island Trees Union Free School District No. 26 v. Pico, 457 U.S. 853 (1982).

Brown v. Board of Education, 347 U.S. 483 (1954).

Brown v. Board of Education, 349 U.S. 294 (1955).

Civil Rights Division v. Amphitheater Unified School District No. 10., 680 P. 2d. 517 (Ariz. App. 1983).

Connick v. Meyers, 461 U.S. 138 (1983).

Fischer, Louis et. al. Teachers and the Law. 2nd Edition. Longman, New York, NY, 1987. p. 120.

Fowler v. Williamson, 251 S.E.2d 889 (N.C. 1979).

Gong Lum v. Rice, 275 U.S. 78 (1927).

Goss v. Lopez, 419 U.S. 565 (1975).

Hazelwood School District v. Kuhlmeier (Case No. 86-836) 1988.

Ingraham v. Wright, 420 U.S. 651 (1977).

Lemon v. Kurtzman, 403 U.S. 602 (1971).

Lubbock Civil Liberties v. Lubbock Independent School District, 669 F. 2d. 1038 (5th Cir. 1984).

Miranda v. Arizona, 377 U.S. 201 (1966).

Moody v. Cronin, 484 F. Supp. 270 (C.D. Ill. 1979).

New Jersey v. T.L.O., 105 S.Ct. 733 (1985).

Palmer v. Board of Education of City of Chicago, 44 U.S. 1026 (1980).

Pickering v. Board of Education, 391 U.S. 563 (1968).

Plessy v. Ferguson, 163 U.S. 537 (1896).

Pollnow v. Glennon, 549 F. Supp. 220 (S.D. N.Y. 1984).

Scott v. Board of Education, Hicksville, 305 N.Y. S.2d 601 (1969).

See Aaron, Civil Liability for Teachers' Negligent Failure to Report Suspected Child Abuse, 28 Wayne L. Rev. 183 (1981).

Swann v. Charlotte-Mecklenburg, 402 U.S. 1 (1971).

Tinker v. Des Moines, 393 U.S. 503 (1960).

United States Code Title 20 1232g. Title 45, Part 9 (1979).

Wood v. Strickland, 421 U.S. 308 (1975).

Zorach v. Clausen, 343 U.S. 306 (1952).

SUGGESTED READINGS

Alexander, Kern & Alexander, David M. The Law of Schools, Students and Teachers in a
Fellman, David, (Ed.) The Supreme Court and Education. Teachers' College Press, 3rd Ed. New York, NY, 1976.

Fischer, Louis; Schimmel, David & Kelly Cynthia Teachers and the Law. Longman, New York, NY, 1987.

Hogan, John C. The Schools, the Courts and the Public Interest. 2nd. Ed., Lexington, Books, Boston, MA, 1985.

La Morte, Michael W. School Law: Cases and Concepts. Prentice- Hall, Englewood Cliffs, NJ, 1982.

Morris, Arval A. "Substantive Constitutional Rights: The First Amendment and Privacy - Legal Issues in Public School Employment." Phi Delta Kappan, Bloomington, Indiana. 1983.

Nutshell. West, St. Paul, MN, 1984.

Reutter, Edmund E., Jr. The Law of Public Education. 3rd Ed., The Foundation Press, Mineola, NY, 1985.

School Law News. Capitol Publications, Inc. Suite G-12, 2430 Pennsylvania Ave. N.W.
Valente, William D. Education Law: Public and Private. West, St. Paul, MN, 1985.

Washington, D.C., 20037.

CHAPTER NINE

Instructional Materials: Policies and Strategies

Introduction

Throughout the past three decades, there has been an increased research effort and acknowledgment to the role textbooks and instructional materials play in education. The conclusion of these efforts is that textbooks and instructional materials do play an important part in education - transmitting not only facts and figures, but ideas and cultural values. According to the Association of American Publishers (1976), the words and pictures students see in school influence the development of the attitude they carry into adult life - *these words and pictures not only express ideas, but are part of the educational experience which shape ideas.*

Today many educators continue to discuss the need for improving the quality of textbooks by including diverse perspectives and by excluding bias content. Bias and stereotyping in the content of textbooks and other instructional materials continue to stand in the way of educational equity at the national, state, and local levels. Many believe "state textbook adoption" policies can best achieve this goal, others point to the negative effects of state textbook adoption policies. What criteria are used to evaluate texts from an equity perspective? Who are the individuals or groups responsible for the text selection? Are state textbook adoption policies and equity education compatible?

Chapter 9 - **Instructional Materials: Policies and Strategies,** is intended to: (1) address the importance of instructional materials in education, (2) identify who selects textbooks and instructional materials, (3) examine state adoption policies, (4) identify criteria for the selection of materials, and (5) provide the opportunity to evaluate textbooks and instructional materials. In addition, suggestions are provided for individual classroom teachers and school district personnel in addressing the issue of equity in textbooks and instructional materials.

Because bias and stereotyping are frequently an unconscious practice, teachers-to-be, teachers, administrators and other school personnel limit a student's opportunities without intending to do so. They simply continue biased practices because "that is the way it has always been done." However, in order to make any significant changes in the school environment and build the school's capacity to provide instruction not limited by bias or stereotyping, educators need to make a conscious effort to learn new skills in identifying and compensating for bias.

Impact of Textbooks and Instructional Materials

American schools have been described as textbook dominated. Indeed, researchers have found that textbooks are primary determinants of what is taught in the U.S. classroom. One can easily become overwhelmed by the total number of instructional materials available for use in the classroom. The National Education Association (NEA, 1976) for example, lists 24 different kinds of instructional materials, including textbooks, films, and newspapers. There are over 500,000 different materials available for classroom use. How important are textbooks and instructional materials in the classroom? Goldstein (1978) suggests that textbooks are the focus of more than 75 percent of a pupil's classroom time. Other studies have shown that as much as 95 percent of all "teaching time" is spent on the use of some type of textbook or instructional material (EPII, 1984).

If this is an accurate portrait of life in U.S. schools, it follows that textbooks and instructional materials must be significant factors in determining the quality of U.S. education.

Who Selects the Textbooks and Instructional Materials?

Review committees are created in a variety of ways. In most adoption states, the state board of education appoints committee members at the state level. In several states, the state board appoints a special textbook committee or commission which in turn appoints the actual reviewers. In local districts, reviewers may be appointed by the superintendent or board or may represent constituent groups. Members of committees are usually appointed on the basis of their roles (teacher, supervisor, principal, parent) or on the basis of location - regions in the state, areas in a school district, etc. According to Cody, (1986) educators, especially teachers, make up most of the committee members at both the local and state levels.

Such variance demonstrates the lack of overall consistency with regard to textbook selection. Although local districts are, in general, responsible for identifying and rectifying weaknesses in instructional materials, a growing number of individuals believe states still need to take a more active role in providing bias-free textbooks in the classroom.

State Textbook Adoption Policies

What are state textbook adoption policies? How do they work? Observers often comment that state adoption procedures distort the market and allow pressure groups in adoption states to dominate. Although that may be true and in some cases may have a negative effect on the selection of books, centralized book selection can also permit states to have positive influences on the market. In any case, few states indicate that they are interested in changing the way in which books are selected.

In 27 states, local school districts make textbook decisions independently of any state control. These are referred to as *open states*. In 23 states, mostly in the south and west, districts select textbooks from a preliminary list created and approved at the state level. These are referred to as *adoption states*.

As of 1990, there were 23 states that had adopted the policy of "state approved" textbooks. They were: Oregon, California, Nevada, Idaho, Utah, Arizona, New Mexico, Texas, Oklahoma, Arkansas, Louisiana, Mississippi, Alabama, Georgia, Florida, Tennessee, North Carolina, South Carolina, Kentucky, West Virginia, Virginia ,Indiana, and most recently Hawaii.(See Figure 23 - State Textbook Adoption Policies). Most state textbook adoption policies are a result of legislation passed prior to the 1950s. Several states first enacted such policies just after the turn of the century (e.g., Utah, 1909), and of these, the majority seem to have revised their laws in the late 1970s and early 1980s.

Figure 23

STATE TEXTBOOK ADOPTION POLICIES
22 states take active role in approving texts

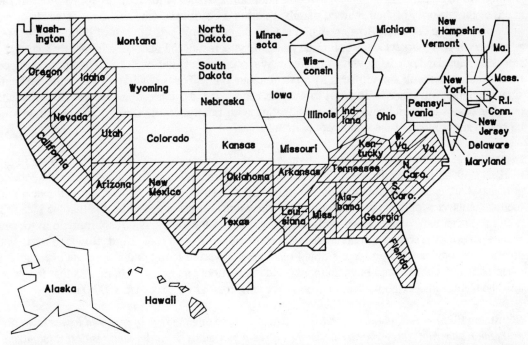

The original purpose of such policies on the part of the states was: (1) to ensure that every student had a book, (2) to screen out "inferior" texts and uphold high standards, and (3) to make efficient use of tax dollars via centralized purchasing arrangements (McCloud, 1974). More recently, due to an increased awareness of cultural pluralism in the country, state curriculum committees have also served to evaluate potential materials in light of equity education.

Disadvantages for State Adoption Policies

Tulley and Farr (1985) argue that the actual statutes mandating state textbook adoption policies show little evidence of pedagogic intent. Instead, say the researchers, *the data contained in these statutes suggest that the intent of state level textbook adoption may be to control the marketing practices of the publishing industry.* Categorizing the content of 23 different states' statutes reveals that out of 20 categories, nine deal with controlling costs and contractual obligations between publisher and state. Out of these nine categories dealing with the publishing industry, one category shows interest in pedagogic quality - to provide evidence of learner verification. But only two of the 23 states, California and Florida, have such a statute. On the other hand, 17 out of the 23 states have a statute requiring publishers to maintain the lowest price.

Adoption Policies and Equity

Bowler (1978) cites that the state textbook adoption systems tailor their textbooks to suit the needs of the majority of their market, mainly Texas and California, thus slighting the needs of the other parts of the country. Bowler explains why the economic self-interest of publishers in cornering the largest markets leads to limited choice for the rest of the nation's schools. He shares the story of a Maryland educator who wondered why a poem about Harriet Tubman had been dropped from a major textbook and replaced by a poem about White Texas cowboys. This editorial decision, of course, was made in an effort to woo the heart of Texas. Unfortunately, what Texas wants out of textbooks, Bowler says, are topics dealing with family, conflict, sex, love, hate, and violence - in short, much of the reality of children's lives.

In addition to the unreality and lack of diverse perspectives caused by publishers' pandering to big markets such as Texas, Bowler (1978) cites three other arguments against state textbook adoption policies. One is that state-level adoption implies that district educators, who know the needs of their students, cannot make intelligent textbook decisions. A second argument is that the idea of a uniform curriculum, which was a useful idea for states in the 1800s, is not appropriate in today's society where a diversity of materials is what most educators call for. Third, Bowler asserts that contrary to popular belief, a huge amount of money is wasted maintaining the state bureaucracy machine which chooses and buys textbooks and instructional materials. He reports that ten years ago, the California Textbook Commission's operating costs alone exceeded $800,000.

Bernstein (1985) writes, *publishers have tried to accommodate the lists of required topics from several major adoption states in order to have as large a market as possible. The result is a magazine-style book - filled with tidbits but lacking context, adequate explanations, or clarifying examples.* Thus, although put-downs based on gender and ethnic slurs have been virtually banished by state-mandated content guidelines, *textbook portrayals of oppressed groups are often trivial or mechanical.* The goal of helping young people achieve an equity perspective is not accomplished when publishers think only of satisfying the letter of the law and not the spirit of the law.

Perhaps the strongest argument for state textbook adoption policies is that in a few states, such as California, a statute mandates that all materials adopted must meet specific minimum criteria for including diverse points of view, multiple approaches, and so forth. For example, the California State Board of Education's (1984) list of instructional materials approved for legal compliance includes only those materials that fairly represent males and females, ethnic groups, the aged, and the disabled. However, many state-adoption guidelines do not include these criteria on their evaluation forms.

Advantages to State Adoption.

Proponents of state textbook adoption policies cite three areas of strength: (1) efficiency, (2) comprehensive public review, and (3) dollars saved. Efficiency in terms of the saving of time and money for local school districts is often cited (through lower freight costs and publishers maintaining at least one depository in the state). Another advantage cited is the fact that the public has more input - because books under consideration must be displayed at several locations throughout the state.

State Adoption - Sequence of Events.

Figure 24 - State Textbook Adoption Process, outlines the process in flowchart form. The sequence of events may be considered typical and is based upon the common denominators in states having textbook adoption policies.

Figure 24

STATE TEXTBOOK ADOPTION PROCESS

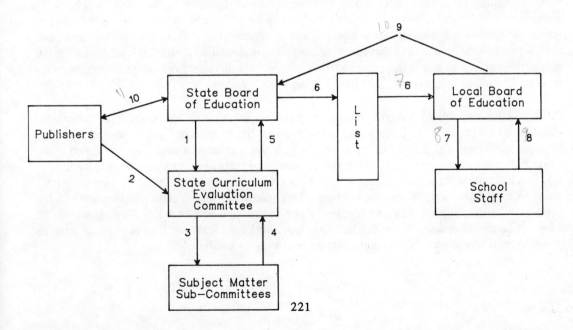

221

Reviewers.

Members of the State Curriculum Evaluation Committee are selected by the State Superintendent and the Board of Education. Usually, one person is appointed from each congressional district in the state. In several states, the state board appoints a special textbook committee or commission which in turn appoints the actual reviewers. In local districts, reviewers may be appointed by the administration or school board or may represent constituent groups. In some cases, anyone who volunteers may serve on the committee. Members of committees are usually appointed on the basis of their roles (teacher, supervisor, principal, parent) or as mentioned above, on the basis of location - regions in the state.

Educators, especially teachers, make up most of the committee members at both the local and state levels. Eighteen of the adoption states and most of the localities about which there is information include lay citizens on the review committees. About 25 percent of the local districts that have negotiated contracts with teachers include teacher participation on selection committees in the contract (Cody, 1986). In eighteen adoption states, the final adoption is made by the state board of education; in four adoption states, the final decision is made by the board- appointed state textbook committee. In most local districts, the local school board is the official adopting body.

Is the task of reviewing textbooks too large and too difficult for most committee members? Committees in adoption states can be responsible for reviewing hundreds of books. For example, over 1200 books were considered in Oklahoma in 1985, and 27 elementary reading series were considered in Texas (Cody, 1986). Adoption states reported that the amount of time allotted for the committee's work varied from a matter of days to an entire year. There is little data on the actual amount of time spent reading the books. Sixteen of the adoption states have some form of training program for committee members. Although most of the training has to do with legal requirements and logistics, committees are receiving more training in the application of criteria. About half of the local school districts reported that teachers on local committees are released from teaching to review books. In other locations, the time is contributed after school or during the summer. State committee members may receive some reimbursement for expenses; no states report that committee members are paid for their time.

Publishers are notified of hearing dates and are invited to submit their textbooks and instructional materials to the committee. During the review process, books are displayed at several locations throughout the state and public feedback is invited. Various subcommittees may be formed at the request of committee members, to aid in the evaluation of texts in assorted disciplines. All findings and evaluation forms are submitted to the committee members who then vote on each textbook. A two- thirds vote is commonly required for placement on the state adoption list. In the past, some of the adoption states selected only one book for the entire state. Now, however, all adoption states allow districts greater latitude. State-approved textbook lists may range from as few as three books in each subject and grade level to as many as 30 or 40.

The multiple listings are then finalized by the State Board of Education and sent to various local school boards. Texts are selected locally, but the contracts are usually made between the state and the publisher. All adoption states also have a procedure to allow districts to petition a state agency to use state funds to purchase a book not on the state list. In general, adoption states have established cycles for the adoption of books in the subject areas; for example, reading, literature, and language arts one year, mathematics the next year, science the following year. *Adoption cycles are commonly 5 to 7 years long.*

Funding.

How does funding for textbooks influence the textbook market? It is important for those of us who are not accustomed to thinking about marketing to understand that the books published will be only those that publishers believe will be profitable. Since publishers must decide what books to develop and print years ahead of actual sales, any clues to a future market - earmarked funding or a concentrated market such as those that large adoption states (California and Texas) can promise - will influence their decisions. Such was the case in the Fall of 1985, when the California Board of Education rejected all high school biology textbooks that publishers submitted on the grounds that they contained watered-down science, including little or no mention of evolution. Again, in the Fall of 1986, California rejected all the mathematics textbooks submitted by the publishers because of the *watered-down* content.

Fourteen of the adoption states and two open states provide earmarked funds for textbooks, usually by statute, and most commonly on a per pupil basis. States vary from $15 to over $50 per student per year. Texas and California, the largest state markets, each spend over $100 million each year on textbooks. Few states provide full funding for textbook purchases; full funding means to provide enough funding to remove old books and buy new books for each subject in the year of the adoption. In most adoption states, local districts supplement state funds with local funds to give every student a new book. It is more common, however, for districts to use both state and local funds and still replace only some of the books used in the classrooms. This means that many books in use are older than the cycle would indicate. The costs of books are influenced by funding legislation. Requirements by adoption states and some local districts require that publishers post performance bonds, provide free samples, maintain depositories, conduct learner verification, maintain on-site sales representatives, provide cross indexing to curriculum frameworks, etc. This involves large publisher investments in the adoption process and often affects book costs. All adoption states have a provision stating that they will not pay more for a book than is paid in other states. Working under such "most favored nation" price controls, publishers find new ways to negotiate with large purchasers. Although publishers may not negotiate price, they may offer to provide free inservice, more manuals, workbooks or other ancillary materials to encourage larger sales. Not surprisingly, such criticism does not sit well with the publishers who are, in all fairness, caught between powerful interest groups and, in all honesty, trying to make a buck.

Publishers Respond

In response to growing external pressures, textbook companies have developed formal policies that reflect guidelines for authors and editors that are aimed at reducing bias and stereotyping in textbooks. Since the middle 1970s, over 170 groups, including publishing companies, educational organizations and associations, have responded by developing guidelines for their staff. The growing consciousness of the industry is a result of both their concern with the current attitudes in the society and their awareness of the impact of instructional programs on young people's thinking.

The Association of American Publishers prepared a *Statement on Bias-Free Materials* (1976 and 1984)) in order to further the cause of fair and equitable treatment for all people. This position paper states that the publishing industry is responding today to the challenge of bias-free materials that reflect the contributions of all cultures and both sexes.

In evaluating learning materials for fair treatment of all people, three main areas — content, illustrations and language — require special attention. Different publishers approach these areas in a variety of ways, but a basic commitment is shared by all and is embodied in the individual publisher's guidelines from which the next three sections are drawn.

Content.

Specifically, bias-free educational materials are those that:

*   *represent different groups of people in varied activities and vocations, including positions of leadership, and show children aspiring to a variety of careers.*

*   *represent fairly and accurately the historic and current achievements of people, and include a balanced proportion of materials about or originated by women and minority people.*

*   *use material that honestly tells about the exploitation of people and the real hardships imposed on people through such exploitation.*

*   *depict men and women alike as having the full range of human emotions and behavior, and finding for themselves attributes that lead to self-esteem and success.*

*   *represent minority and majority groups in varied communities from urban to rural, and in all socio-economic levels.*

It is important to note that guidelines for the inclusion in school programs of selections from the recognized body of literature (poetry, fiction, drama, etc.) call for different criteria than those applied to newly written instructional materials. Because they frequently reflect the social and cultural values of times that have passed into history, literary selections must be assessed for their contributions to the overall education of the nation's youth.

Illustrations.

Specifically, bias-free illustrations should:

* *reflect a fair and reasonable balance of representation, whether regarding race, religion, ethnic groups, age, economic levels, sex, or national origins.*

* *provide positive role models for students of different ethnic and racial backgrounds and of both sexes.*

* *avoid stereotypes and caricatures of individuals and groups, portraying a realistic and broad view of physical characteristics.*

* *promote opportunities for depicting women and minority group members in positions of prominence, leadership, and high achievement.*

Language.

Bias-free language is language that includes all people and treats them with equal dignity and respect, whatever their race, sex, age, religion or national and ethnic origin. Bias-free language deals with people as individuals, not as members of stereotyped groups. It minimizes the cultural differences on which prejudice is often based, avoids insults and derogatory connotations, and does not trivialize or patronize, slight or slander, mock or deride whole classes of people.

Specifically, bias-free language is language that:

* *seeks to encompass members of both sexes by (1) avoiding the use of man and its derivatives to denote the average person or the human race; and (2) designating occupations by the work performed, not only by the gender of the worker.*

* *avoids excluding women by the use of the generic pronoun he by pluralizing, shifting to one, you, or we; rephrasing to eliminate gender pronouns altogether, or balancing he with she.*

* *employs generic terms such as doctor, lawyer, actor, teacher, secretary, and poet for both males and females and for all races or ethnic groups.*

* *reflects our cultural diversity by including a variety of ethnic names as well as the more common Anglo-Saxon ones.*

*   *avoids loaded words, biased connotations, and prejudiced assumptions. Particularly it expresses critical or negative judgments with words not associated with a particular race or sex.*

(This statement was developed in September 1976 by the AAP School Division Committee on Social Issues in Education and revised in October 1984 by the renamed Committee on Critical Issues in Educational Publishing. Reprinted with Permission).

Despite publishers' efforts, students continue to read many similar stories with little or no changes in series after series. When one considers that there is an average time lapse of approximately four years between textbook editions, and coupled with the fact that state laws may only require new textbooks every six or eight years, it may become apparent how an entire generation of students can pass through schools using biased textbooks even after it is evident to many that these texts limit the potential for many students. While the guidelines of textbook publishers for the promotion of fair policies have not been completely successful, publishers should not be considered solely responsible, either for the existence of bias in textbooks or for its elimination. It is important that other educational agencies and institutions take action on this issue.

Changing textbooks is a slow process. First of all, it is expensive, both to rewrite and to launch a new textbook series. A series is sometimes promoted as a new edition even though extensive changes have not been made. For a book or series to qualify as a new edition, copyright law only requires a 10 percent change, which may be made in the binding, by the addition of color plates or illustrations, by revising a teacher's guide, or by inserting a few new pages.

Local Strategies

The responsibility for selecting instructional materials is an important responsibility and one which needs to be addressed in a consistent and systematic fashion at the local level. Local communities are in the best position to assess and respond to the educational needs of their students.

Local authorities can take steps to make sure that instructional materials do not promote bias and stereotyping. If we are to improve textbooks and instructional materials, we must improve the review processes of each individual reviewer. That is, we must understand and help to improve the procedures that both individuals and committees utilize when they review textbooks. It is when a textbook is in the hands of a reviewer that the most important phase of the textbook evaluation process takes place. To improve that process, the following are suggestions:

*   *Develop a philosophy of textbook use.* The criteria for evaluating a textbook needs to be stated so they are understood by everyone involved in the process, and these criteria should be determined with an understanding of what a textbook can and cannot do as an adjunct to an instructional program. *We need to understand that textbooks are not total programs, nor do they establish curriculum; they are instructional aids to be used as part of a program.*

* *Develop a set of review and selection criteria on local situations.* Check the comprehensiveness of the list by comparing it to other lists developed by other educators. Evaluation techniques for reviewing books need to be developed, reviewed, and revised. Textbook review committees need to have practice in using these procedures prior to the time that the books are actually reviewed.

* *Provide adequate training and release time for the evaluation process.* Those who review textbooks must receive a significant amount of training in how to review a textbook. It is not a task that one should learn while engaged in the process. Teachers should be provided with ample release time to carry out their reviews. When review times are squeezed between scheduled classes and added to after-school demands, the result is usually a cursory review rather than an in-depth review.

* *Sampling techniques* must be developed so that a smaller number of specific items can be reviewed in greater depth. There is no way that every topic in a particular text can be reviewed thoroughly. Research (Farr, 1986) has demonstrated that random selection procedures have adequate validity. These techniques can help textbook evaluation committees to do a much more thorough evaluation.

* *Textbook reviewers must be trained* to provide specific information regarding each point that they review. It not enough to say that something is good or bad or to provide general summaries. The evaluation evidence must be specific to each point that is reviewed.

* *Feedback to publishers* from the results of textbook reviews must be specific and thorough. Publishers must learn what it is about their books that reviewers like and dislike. Publishers need to be convinced in very specific ways that books aren't adopted because they are not acceptable.

Biased and stereotyped instructional materials continue to find their way into our classrooms for a variety of reasons. It is important for us as teachers and administrators to develop criteria for accurately assessing bias in existing classroom textbooks and supplementary materials. In this way we can make a conscious effort to compensate for bias when it does occur. In addition, through constructive use of biased materials, we can teach students about bias in textbooks, and give them the skills and tools necessary to counteract the biased images they may confront daily in the society around them.

Textbook Evaluation

Farr and Tulley (1985) conducted a study which indicated that the number of criteria on any one sheet is overwhelming. The average number of items included on the criteria sheets they studied was 73. The longest sheet included 180 items, and the shortest included 42 items.

Are the standards by which books are evaluated appropriate? There are many guides to textbook se-lection available; most provide a fairly standard list of the important features of textbooks, for ex-ample: (1) physical characteristics, (2) readability formulas, (3) pictures and graphics, (4) content - currency and accuracy, (5) content - difficulty, (6) curriculum and test alignment, (7) social issues, (8) instructional design - vocabulary, (9) instructional design - organizational features, (10) instruc-tional design - questions, and (11) ancillary materials - teachers' manuals, software, and workbooks.

Certainly, when one begins to consider all of the identified areas that are important aspects of in-structional materials - then one can understand the overwhelming number of criteria that can be generated for one text. As mentioned above, there is a need to generate "sampling techniques" in the review process - so that a smaller number of specific items can be reviewed in greater depth.

A Sampling Technique for Equity.

Specific items will be identified to analyze textbooks and instructional materials for equity. Although there are numerous guidelines for evaluating instructional materials for equity, Sadker and Sadker (1978) have identified six forms of bias that are useful to implement when examining materials. The following identified areas are not to be used as a template for evaluating equity, but rather as a guide. These biases include: 1) invisibility, 2) stereotyping, 3) selectivity and imbal-ance, 4) unreality, 5) fragmentation and isolation, and 6) language.

Invisibility.

Invisibility means that certain groups are under-represented in materials. This omission implies that these groups have less value, importance, and significance in our society. Invisibility in in-structional materials occurs most frequently for women, minority groups, handicapped individuals and older persons.

Materials can be examined for invisibility simply by counting the number of different groups rep-resented in illustrations, in various roles, occupations, in biographies, or as main and secondary characters. Additional factors to consider with invisibility include:

* *Do the materials include contributions and a variety of roles of our diverse population?*

* *Are a variety of socioeconomic levels and settings (urban, rural, suburban) included?*

* *Is diversity in terms of religion, cultures and family lifestyles included?*

* *It is important to remember that visual images (illustrations) should accurately depict physical images, lifestyles, cultural traditions and surroundings when portraying persons from diverse backgrounds. It is not enough to simply change skin color or names.*

Stereotyping.

The concept of stereotyping was mentioned in previous chapters, but since it is crucial to the expectations that we build up for our interactions with others, a closer examination will be provided.

The concept of stereotyping was first popularized by Lippman (1922). He defined a stereotype as a factually incorrect simple description of a person or group resulting from illogical, rigidly-held reasoning. Katz and Braly (1978) regard a stereotype as a fixed impression which conforms very little to the facts it is supposed to represent and is the result of defining first and observing after.

Stereotypes are commonly believed to be associated with hostility towards certain categories of people. In their analysis of stereotyping, Seccord recognized three components of stereotyping. He said that we first identify a category of people, like students or police officers. Then we agree that the people in that category share certain traits, like being liberals or exercising an authoritarian personality. Finally, we attribute those traits to everyone in that category, however conservative or benign they may be. Several arguments are developed in the literature against the process of stereotyping:

*   *Categorizing people is unacceptable.*

*   *Stereotyping is based on inaccurate data.*

*   *Stereotyping implies that the categories of people are based on inborn, unchangeable characteristics.*

*   *There is an implicit assumption that one's own cultural group represents the norm by which other groups should be judged.*

*   *Categorizing people becomes a self-fulfilling prophecy.*

*   *Stereotyping is often objectionable to individuals who are stereotyped.*

The most powerful criticism of stereotyping is that there is a hidden assumption that most stereotypes are based on inborn characteristics which cannot be changed. This silent assumption is probably the strongest with respect to ethnic and racial stereotypes. The hidden assumption is that "our" characteristics form the norm from which we judge all other groups, and the closer a group is to us in physical attributes, the greater our attraction to it in most respects and the more favorable the stereotype we hold for it (Seccord, Backman, Slavitt (1976), and Sadker & Sadker, 1978).

By assigning traditional and rigid roles or attributes to a group, instructional materials stereotype and limit the abilities and potential of that group. Not only are careers stereotyped, but so are intellectual abilities, personality characteristics, physical appearance, social status and domestic roles. Stereotyping denies all students a knowledge of the diversity, complexity, and variation of any group of individuals. Additional factors to consider when examining materials for stereotypes and stereotyping include:

* *Do men and women, boys and girls, show a wide variety of emotions?*

* *Are both sexes involved in active and passive activities, indoors and outdoors?*

* *Do visual depictions make clearly apparent the differences in appearance within a group as well as between groups?*

* *Does the plot or story line exaggerate the exoticism or mysticism of the various ethnic groups? For example: customs and festivals.*

* *Are older people shown in active as well as passive roles?*

* *Is old age and aging usually equated with death?*

* *Are disabled persons usually portrayed as members of problem ridden families?*

* *Must representatives from previously excluded groups have super hero/heroine characteristics?*

* *Do members of the aforementioned categories fill both support and leadership roles?*

Selectivity and Imbalance.

Selectivity and imbalance occurs when issues and situations are interpreted from only one perspective, usually from the perspective of the majority group. Many issues, situations, and events described in textbooks are complex and can be viewed from a variety of viewpoints or perspectives. However, only one perspective is often presented. For example, the relationship between the U.S. government and the American Indian is usually examined only from the government's perspective in terms of treaties and protection. An American Indian perspective may also examine broken treaties and the appropriation of native lands, but from a different perspective. This is an example of bias through selectivity and imbalance.

What can we do about this situation? As classroom teachers, we must be conscious of what textbooks and curriculum materials present. Although the materials we use may indeed be limited in their viewpoints, our sensitivity and understanding can then provide further research and discussion by our students to examine the issue or situation from another point of view. It is not necessary that each and every situation or event be examined with this in-depth scrutiny, but once students become aware and conditioned to look at situations or issues from a variety of perspectives, then the role of the classroom teacher can become one of facilitator in discussing the various alternatives that present themselves.

Unreality.

Textbooks frequently present an unrealistic portrayal of our history and contemporary life experiences. Controversial topics are glossed over or are not included in the textbook. As we saw earlier in the State Adoption Policy section, several "controversial" topics are being hotly debated between selection committees and textbook publishers. However, when sensitive and unpleasant issues such as racism, sexism, prejudice, discrimination, inter-group conflict(s), divorce and death are not included in instructional materials, students are then not provided any guidance or information in handling such complex and contemporary problems. Contemporary problems faced by the disabled or elderly are often disguised or simply avoided. American Indians, in discussions or illustrations, are often pictured in "historical" context rather than in a contemporary image. Most materials (where appropriate) do not consider sex bias and race bias that do exist in employment practices and in salary schedules. These avoided issues do include those that many students may very well have to face in their lives. This unrealistic coverage denies or prohibits students the information needed to recognize, understand and perhaps someday conquer the problems that plague our society (Sadker & Sadker, 1978).

This unreality issue appears to be taking a new added dimension. The two court decisions that were handed down in 1986 and 1987 are examples. The 1986 case, _Mozert v. Hawkins County Public Schools_, probed the issue of whether fundamentalist Christian students had a right to be free from exposure to concepts not compatible with their religious beliefs - concepts that may be as varied as idol worship, nontraditional sex roles, evolution, and secular humanism.

The lawsuit focused on the Hawkins County school board's decision before the start of the 1983-84 school year to adopt as part of its curriculum for Grades 1 through 8 - a reading series published by Holt, Reinhart and Winston. During the course of the academic year, several parents began scrutinizing their children's texts and found a host of stories and assignments that offended their fundamental Christian beliefs.

Eleven of the families filed suit against the district in December of 1983 after the school board denied their request to supply the children with alternative textbooks. Their suit sought unspecified monetary damages and a permanent injunction barring the Hawkins County Board from forcing the students to use the textbooks and from punishing them if they refused. U.S. District Judge dismissed all complaints against the Board in early 1984. But a Federal Appeals Court overturned the decision in June 1985 and instructed the lower court to schedule a trial to resolve the disputed fact in the case. In particular, the appeals panel directed the judge to decide whether the reading texts unconstitutionally impinged on the families' religious beliefs and, if so, whether "a compelling state interest" overrides the families' right to free exercise of religion.

In the Fall of 1986, the judge ruled in favor of the parents. The landmark decision sent shock waves around the country. The decision sent a clear message - parents do have a right regarding what their children are taught in public schools. What was at stake is whether people who have religious objections to certain ideas can force their public school to provide their children with a curriculum tailored to their own particular beliefs. On appeal, the Supreme Court ruled against the parents in the Fall of 1988.

In the Spring of 1987 _Smith v. School Commissioners of Mobile County, Alabama_, a federal judge in Mobile, Alabama ordered 44 textbooks removed from the Alabama public schools because they unconstitutionally promoted the "religious belief system" of secular humanism. This latest ruling was widely viewed as a major victory for fundamentalist Christians, many of whom have long contended that secular humanism is a religion that places an individual's values above any divine authority, and that its tenets pervade the public schools' curricula. This decision marked the first time that a federal court had ruled that humanism is the equivalent of a religion for First Amendment purposes.

"Teaching that moral choices are purely personal and can only be based on some autonomous, as yet undiscovered and unfulfilled inner self is a sweeping fundamental belief that must not be promoted by the public schools," Judge Hand wrote. "With these books, the State of Alabama has overstepped its mark, and must withdraw to perform its proper non-religious functions."

The chairperson of the civil liberty group that aided the State Board of Education in its defense of the textbooks characterized this decision as "judicial book burning." Buchanan, chairperson of "People for the American Way" - a lobbying group that monitors civil liberty issues - described the decision nothing less than "government censorship of the school curriculum" (Goldberg, 1987).

As with the Tennessee case, this Alabama decision by the federal court is being appealed. It appears that the two decisions will not be isolated instances and that this particular issue will run through the judicial court systems of this country for years to come.

Fragmentation and Isolation.

Fragmentation and isolation is a popular method in which many publishers include some of the ethnic groups, women, elderly and disabled, in their instructional materials. Issues, contributions, and information that we have previously discussed as being relevant are typically separated from the regular text and discussed in a "section" or "chapter" of its own. This add-on approach is easier to accomplish than trying to integrate the information throughout the text. There is nothing wrong with having some information separate from the regular text if it is not the only place students read about this added-on information. However, the isolation of particular information does often suggest negative connotations or mixed messages for students. This approach suggests that the experiences and contributions of these groups are merely an interesting diversion and not an integral part of historical and contemporary developments (Sadker & Sadker, 1978) The same analogy can be made with regard to our earlier discussion of ethnic studies, multiethnic education and the broader concept of equity education. As discussed earlier, our society is very diverse and pluralistic, and it is important that instructional materials and textbooks reflect this diversity as a part of the total text rather than discussing particular groups in a separate section or as an add-on.

Language.

Examples of linguistic bias in materials include the use of masculine pronouns or only Anglo names throughout the textbook. The lack of (1) Spanish, Polish, Filipino, African, and other non-Anglo names, and (2) feminine pronouns or names in materials will be evident to the sensitive teacher. When teachers are aware that linguistic bias blatantly omits female and many ethnic group references, they can develop strategies to correct the biases and ensure that these groups are an integral part of the curriculum Sadker & Sadker, 1984). In examining curricular materials for language usage, several questions should be considered:

*   *Is the language and terminology used up-to-date?*

*   *Is the language void of derogatory words or phrases?*

*   *Are the terms used to refer to an individual or group so broad they are inaccurate or non-descript? For example: Indian vs. American Indian or Native American vs. Dakota.*

*   *Is parallel language used when describing the sexes? For example: men - women, ladies - gentlemen, boys - girls, rather than men - ladies, or men - girls.*

Strategies to Counter Biased Material.

Individual awareness of bias and stereotyping in textbooks and instructional materials is an important *first* step in changing materials and their impact on all of us. Each of us has a responsibility for using our awareness to bring about some changes and support others who are working in this area.

*   *Look for and learn to recognize bias that may be found in textbooks, curriculum materials, supplementary materials, library books, television programs, magazines, etc.*

*   *Level with the students in your classroom. Point out bias and stereotyping in books and materials. Help them learn to identify sources of bias and important omissions in the materials.*

*   *Develop classroom instruction and activities around identifying bias and stereotyping found in television, textbooks, movies, library books, magazines, etc.*

*   *Identify or develop supplementary materials which can help "correct" some of the bias found in materials or their identification of supplementary materials.*

*   *Assign student research projects. These might include a study of their own textbook materials or their identification of supplementary materials.*

233

* *Ask students to rewrite materials, write their own materials on subjects omitted from the textbook, or rewrite the material from other persons' points of view.*

* *Use bulletin boards, posters, pictures, magazines and other materials to expose students to information commonly excluded from traditional materials.*

* *Develop a collection of non-biased reading materials for students. Identify books that students may be encouraged to seek out in their personal reading.*

* *Request and use funds available for instructional materials in building supplementary materials resources for your classroom(s) or school(s).*

* *Conduct a study and periodic review of the bias found in the textbooks and materials used in your course(s) or school program(s).*

* *Meet with the librarian or media specialist and ask him/her to assist faculty in the identification (non-biased) of equity books and materials. Urge him/her to order and provide resources for supplementary materials.*

* *Organize a central file in your department or school that will have supplementary materials, curriculum outlines, or other resources for identifying bias and supplementing the curriculum.*

* *Develop a "Yellow Pages" of resources for equity education which would be helpful to faculty; this might include a list of speakers, resource persons, organizations and places for good out-of-class learning experiences with the community (field experiences).*

* *Identify non-traditional publishing firms, alternative presses and other groups developing materials in this area. Distribute this information to all faculty members.*

* *Publicize studies, workshops, and other efforts to improve materials or reduce the impact of biased materials.*

Summary

The role models presented in textbooks are very important in helping children identify with and learn from the curriculum. The influence of materials on a student's sense of self-worth depends on the extent to which the student identifies with the characters and situations presented as he or she becomes emotionally involved with them (Hall & Sandler, 1982). Besides transmitting knowledge about the world around him/her, curriculum materials may also affect a student's career interests and expectations, especially through the role models presented. Interest and expectations, in turn, may influence a student's level of achievement and career choice in later years. For example, there is a significant amount of information concerning sex bias in education and its effect of students. For girls, as they progress through school, the research documents report losses of intellectual potential (especially in math and science), of self-esteem, and of occupational aspirations (Tetreault & Schmuck, 1985). For boys, there is the pressure of unrealistic and stereotyped expectations. It has also been found that the longer students are exposed to a sexist program (of materials), the more their attitudes conform to stereotyped sex roles and the more these attitudes are retained over time.

By inference, the content of textbooks has the institutional stamp of approval. Moreover, as mentioned earlier, textbooks often determine curriculum, since what is covered in a text is usually what ends up being taught, and what is left out of a text is usually not considered important to course content. Because, as we have seen, textbooks and other instructional materials are critically important, they must be designed to avoid the perpetuation of bias and stereotyping. They should foster for all people, regardless of their diverse backgrounds, a sense of personal worth and dignity and a respect for their abilities and rights.

There is little argument that school texts and supplementary materials help students identify possible future lifestyles, careers, and goals and provide learners with role models. However, as mentioned earlier, numerous studies have indicated that despite an increasing social awareness of bias and stereotyping, publishers are still producing books that portray a number of groups in a limited number of roles, a very limited number of skills, or not at all.

While deeply ingrained societal attitudes and habits cannot be changed overnight, policymakers must work toward eliminating bias and stereotyping in future publications. An effective step is for all those involved at local and state levels to take responsibility for what students read and work with in school. For the benefit of individuals as well as society, it is necessary to eliminate inequities in educational material.

QUESTIONS FOR DISCUSSION

1. Are classroom teachers, in your opinion, as dependent upon textbooks as the research indicated in this chapter?

2. How much influence do you believe textbooks have on curriculum development?

3. If publishers have gone on record against bias and stereotyping, why do we still have bias and stereotyping in current textbooks and instructional materials?

4. What is an adoption state? An open state? What are the advantages and disadvantages of each?

5. What suggestions were cited in this chapter that would improve the process of textbook evaluation at the local level?

6. What are the implications for classroom teachers with regard to the two recent court cases involving fundamental Christians (Tennessee) and the teaching of secular humanism (Alabama) in textbooks?

7. How can classroom teachers counter stereotyping and bias that exist in textbooks and instructional materials that they are presently using?

CLASS ACTIVITY

Evaluating Curriculum Materials

Objectives:

(1) To demonstrate the complexity of textbook adoption and selection.

(2) To experience a variety of perspectives in the process of textbook adoption.

(3) To develop a list of criteria for the evaluation of textbooks.

Task:

(1) Divide into eight sub-groups (3-4 to a group is ideal).

(2) Each group will randomly select one of the represented groups they will represent in the activity.

(3) To evaluate a series of textbooks i.e., elementary reading series. (Should include - Teacher's manual, teacher's guide, student workbooks and reading book).

(4) To prepare a summary of the textbooks to be presented to the class.

Represented Groups:

1. *Fundamental Christians for a Better Life*

2. *Black Caucus for Improving Schools*

3. *Local P.T.A.*

4. *Women for the American Way*

5. *West Side Parents for a Better School*

6. *Elementary Classroom Teachers*

7. *The Foundation for the Back to the Basics in Schools*

8. *The Coalition for Exceptional Students*

FUNDAMENTAL CHRISTIANS FOR A BETTER LIFE

(Founded 1981)

General Objectives and Beliefs:

About 10 percent of the community favors your position.

You strongly believe that curriculum materials in public schools should not perpetuate anti-Christian beliefs.

You believe in creationism.

You believe that evolution should not be evident or endorsed in public schools.

You favor the role of women in "traditional" roles.

You strongly favor a "voucher" system for public education.

You believe that schools should accommodate your children with special curriculum materials that are not offensive to your religious convictions.

Task:

Identify two (2) criteria that must be considered in the evaluation of curriculum materials (from your group's perspective):

1. _____

_____

_____

2. _____

_____

_____

Summary of evaluation:

_____ Recommended

_____ Not Recommended

Comments that will be made to the class supporting the above decision.

BLACK CAUCUS FOR IMPROVING SCHOOLS

(Founded 1970)

General Objectives and Beliefs:

About 21 percent of the community is Black.

You believe that curriculum materials either perpetuate stereotypes (negative) or omit the contributions of Blacks.

You believe that the school district has been extremely negligent in correcting these curriculum practices.

You are also sensitive to the lack of any "ethnic authenticity" in the district's curriculum materials (Hispanic, Asian, and American Indian perspectives).

The role of Black women is highly suspect in curriculum materials.

The diversity of Black people is non-existent in curricular materials.

Task:

Identify two criteria that must be considered in the evaluation of curriculum materials (from your group's perspective):

1. _____

_____

_____

2. _____

_____

_____

Summary of evaluation:

_____ Recommended

_____ Not Recommended

Comments that will be made to the class supporting the above decision:

LOCAL P.T.A.

(Founded 1967)

General Objectives and Beliefs:

About 34 percent of the parents in the district are active in the P.T.A.

You strongly believe that "competency" in subject areas should be a high priority.

You are concerned that today's textbooks are "watered down" in content and validity.

You are cautiously concerned that textbooks have gone "overboard" in their attempt to portray America's diversity.

You are very concerned about the "readability" levels that textbooks are being published today.

You believe that too many "special interest" groups have taken control of the textbook adoption/selection process.

Task:

Identify two (2) criteria that must be considered in the evaluation of curriculum materials (from your group's perspective):

1. _____

_____

_____

2. _____

_____

_____

Summary of evaluation:

_____ Recommended

_____ Not Recommended

Comments that will be made to the class supporting the above decision:

WOMEN THE FOR THE AMERICAN WAY

(Founded in 1983)

General Objectives and Beliefs:

A recent survey indicates that about 28 percent of the households in the community support your objectives and beliefs.

You believe the balance between males and females in curriculum materials is slanted toward the males.

You strongly believe that the role of females is very stereotypical.

You contend that most of the "content" concerning the role of women is superficial.

You would like to see a district policy that states no textbooks will be considered or adopted that contain sexist images, language and roles.

The roles of "minority" women are almost non-existent.

The lack of female authors is also disturbing to your organization.

Task:

Identify two (2) criteria that must be considered in the evaluation of curriculum materials (from your group's perspective).

1. _____

_____

_____

2. _____

_____

_____

Summary of evaluation:

_____ Recommended

_____ Not Recommended

Comments that will be made to the class supporting the above position.

WEST SIDE PARENTS FOR A BETTER SCHOOL

(Founded in 1979)

General Objectives and Beliefs:

About 45 percent of the community is low income.

You believe that curriculum materials totally neglect any "real- life" experiences for your children.

You believe that curriculum materials are geared toward middle- class students.

You believe that your libraries are less adequate than other schools in the district.

You believe that many materials neglect the one-parent family.

You believe that materials neglect the extended family.

You are concerned about the high drop-out rate of your children: currently 58 percent are not finishing school.

Task:

Identify two (2) criteria that must be considered in the evaluation of curriculum materials (from your group's perspective).

1. _____

_____

_____

2. _____

_____

_____

Summary of evaluation:

_____ Recommended

_____ Not Recommended

Comments that will be made to the class supporting the above position.

ELEMENTARY CLASSROOM TEACHERS

(Founded in 1957)

General Objectives and Beliefs:

You are concerned with textbooks that are "readable" with the age group you are working with.

You are concerned that the textbooks have a good format.

You are concerned with "content difficulty."

You want textbooks that have good instructional design: vocabulary, questions, workbooks.

You want good teacher manuals.

You want materials that have been classroom tested.

You want materials that are competency based.

Task:

Identify two (2) criteria that must be considered in the evaluation of curriculum materials (from your group's perspective).

1. _____

_____

_____

2. _____

_____

_____

Summary of evaluation:

_____ Recommended

_____ Not Recommended

Comments that will be made to the class supporting the above decision.

THE FOUNDATION FOR THE BACK TO THE BASICS IN SCHOOLS

(Founded 1978)

General Objectives and Beliefs:

You are strongly in favor of a sound "basic" education (reading, writing and arithmetic).

You believe that all students must pass a competency level before moving on to the next grade level.

You strongly believe that there are too many "frills" in today's textbooks that get away from the basics.

About 70 percent of the community is in favor of your objectives and beliefs.

You believe that subjects other than (math, reading, arithmetic and writing) are not appropriate for elementary children.

You strongly believe that students should have homework.

You believe that constant drilling and repetition is the most effective way to get competency in basic skills.

Task:

Identify two (2) criteria that must be considered in the evaluation of curriculum materials (from your group's perspective).

1. _____

_____

_____

2. _____

_____

_____

Summary of evaluation:

_____ Recommended

_____ Not Recommended

Comments that will be made to the class supporting the above position.

THE COALITION FOR EXCEPTIONAL STUDENTS

(Founded 1977)

General Objectives and Beliefs:

About 16 percent of the students in the district are handicapped.

You believe that curriculum materials are negligent in their fair and unbiased portrayal of exceptional populations.

The portrayal of any exceptionality is very narrow (usually a child in a wheelchair).

Curriculum materials are unfavorable for the truly gifted student. Materials are geared for the "average" student.

You are concerned that textbooks have responded more favorably to women and minorities than to exceptional populations.

You wish the enthusiasm for the "special olympics" would be as great for textbook selection and adoption for exceptional populations in curriculum materials.

Task:

Identify two (2) criteria that must be considered in the evaluation of curriculum materials (from your group's perspective).

1. _____

_____

_____

2. _____

_____

_____

Summary of evaluation:

_____ Recommended

_____ Not Recommended

Comments that will be made to the class supporting the above decision.

WORKSHEET 1

Introduction

As discussed in this chapter, there are numerous guidelines, charts and forms that could be used to evaluate curriculum materials in the field of education. Every educational organization, school district, publisher, and scholarly journal has at one time or another, proposed guidelines and suggestions for evaluating materials. These guidelines and evaluation instruments are all available from the sources mentioned above. In other words, the problem hasn't been one of the lack of an information base, but one of *how to go about it systematically*. Textbook analysis is neither a quick nor an easy task. I refer you to "Suggested Readings" for guidance and suggestions of sources that may be of benefit to you now and in the future.

As you will learn along the way, there are many curriculum materials that are very well done, but at the same time there are many materials that fall far short of an equitable perspective. If we can imagine the different levels of equity displayed in <u>Figure 25 - Rating the Level of Equity Input</u>, - this in fact, is the diversity of equity within textbooks and instructional materials found today. The following exercise will provide you with a first-hand experience in: 1) evaluating textbooks for equity concerns, and 2) acquaint you with how your specific area or level has responded to equity education from two distinct periods of time.

Figure 25

RATING THE LEVEL OF EQUITY INPUT

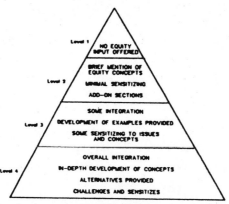

Task:

You are to locate <u>two</u> textbooks in your specific field or level. One book must have been published before 1975, and the second book must have been published after 1985. Based upon the evaluation forms provided on the following pages, you are to analyze the two texts.

EVALUATING CURRICULUM MATERIALS
IN YOUR SUBJECT AREA OR GRADE LEVEL

Name of Evaluator: _____

Title of Book:_____

Publisher: _____

Date of Publication: **(Before 1975)**: _____

Level: (Circle One)   Subject Area

Elementary _____

Middle Level _____

Secondary _____

Post-Secondary _____

Level of Equity

1 2 3 4	Criteria for Evaluation
	Diversity of Representation
	Positive Portrayal of Individuals or Groups
	Variety of Perspectives
	Realistic in Approach
	Integrated Material (No Add-On Sections)
	Terminology is fair and unbiased
	Total Number of Points (24 possible)

1. Why did you rate the material as you did? Explain your score.

    _____

    _____

    _____

    _____

    _____

2. Identify specific examples to support your evaluation. (page numbers, sample statements, illustrations)

    _____

    _____

    _____

    _____

    _____

    _____

    _____

3. Would you recommend the use of this particular material? Why or why not?

    _____

    _____

    _____

    _____

    _____

EVALUATING CURRICULUM MATERIALS
IN YOUR SUBJECT AREA OR GRADE LEVEL

Name of Evaluator: _____

Title of Book: _____

Publisher: _____

Date of Publication: (After 1985): _____

Level: (Circle One)   Subject Area

Elementary _____

Middle Level _____

Secondary _____

Post-Secondary _____

Level of Equity

1 2 3 4	Criteria for Evaluation
	Diversity of Representation
	Positive Portrayal of Individuals or Groups
	Variety of Perspectives
	Realistic in Approach
	Integrated Material (No Add-On Sections)
	Terminology is fair and unbiased
	Total Number of Points (24 possible)

1.   Why did you rate the material as you did? Explain your score.

_____

_____

_____

_____

_____

2.   Identify specific examples to support your evaluation. (page numbers, sample statements, il-
     lustrations)

_____

_____

_____

_____

_____

_____

3.   Would you recommend the use of this particular material? Why or why not?

_____

_____

_____

_____

_____

REFERENCES

Bernstein, Harriet T. *The New Politics of Textbook Adoption.* Phi Delta Kappan, Vol. 66, 1985.

Bowler, Mike *Textbook Publishers Try to Please All, but First They Woo the Heart of Texas.* Reading Teacher, February, 1978.

California State Department of Education. Instructional Materials Approved for Legal Compliance, Sacramento, CA, 1984.

Cody, Caroline B. A Policymaker's Guide to Textbook Selection. National Association of State Boards of Education. Alexandria, VA, 1986.

Eakins, B. & Eakins, G. *Sex Differences in Human Communication.* Houghton Mifflin,Boston, MA, 1978.

Educational Products Information Institute (EPII). Report of the Nature and the Quality of Instructional Materials Most Used by Teachers and Learners. New York, NY, 1977.

Farr, Roger *Do Our Textbook Selection Process Work?* In a Policymaker's Guide to Textbook Selection , by Caroline B. Cody. National Association of State Boards of Education. Alexandria, VA, 1986.

Goldberg, Kirsten. *Federal Court Finds Secular Humanism a Religion.* Education Week, March 11, 1987.

Goldstein, Paul *Changing the American Schoolbook.* D.C. Heath: Lexington, MA, 1978.

Hall, Roberta & Sandler, B. The Classroom Climate: A Chilly One for Women. Project on the Status and Education of Women, Association of American Colleges, Washington, D.C., 1982.

Katz, D. & Braly, K.W. *Racial Stereotypes of One Hundred College Students.* Journal of Abnormal Social Psychology, 1978.

Lippman, W. *Public Opinion.* Harcourt Brace New York, NY, 1922.

McCloud, Paul I. *A Survey of State Textbook Practices.* Educational Leadership, Vol. 31, 1974.

Mozert v. Hawkins County Public Schools, 1986.

National Education Association. Instructional Materials: Selection and Purchase. Washington, D.C., 1976.

Sadker, M. & Sadker, D. *The Teacher Educator's Role.* In S. McCune and M. Matthews, eds. Implementing Title IX and Attaining Sexual Equality: A Workshop Package for Post-Secondary Educators. Washington, D.C. 1978.

Sadker, M. & Sadker, D. Year III: Final Report. Promoting Effectiveness in Classroom Instruction, NIE Contract No. 400-80-0033, Washington, D.C., 1984.

Saunders, Malcolm. *Multicultural Teaching: A Guide for the Classroom*, McGraw Hill Publishing Co: London, 1982.

School Division - Association of American Publishers. Statement on Bias-Free Materials, New York, NY, 1976.

Seccord, P.F., Backman, C.W. & Slavitt, D.R. *Understanding Social Life*, McGraw Hill Publishing Co: New York, NY, 1976.

Smith v. School Commissioners of Mobile County, Alabama, 1987.

Tetreault, M. & Schmuck, P. *Equity, Educational Reform, and Gender.* Issues in Education, Vol. 3, 1985.

Tulley, Michael A. & Farr Roger *Do Adoption Committees Perpetuate Mediocre Textbooks?* Phi Delta Kappan, Vol. 66, 1985.

U.S. Commission on Civil Rights. *Fair Textbooks: A Resource Guide*, Washington, D.C., 1979.

SUGGESTED READINGS

Adams, A., Carnine, D., & Gersten, R. "Instructional Strategies for Studying Content Area Texts in the Intermediate Grades." Reading Research Quarterly, Fall 1982.

Apple, Michael W. *The Political Economy of Text Publishing.* Educational Theory.Vol. 34, 1984.

Bernstein, Harriett *The New Politics of Textbook Adoption.* Phi Delta Kappan , March 1985.

Blaunstein, P. *An Overview of State Textbook Selection Procedures.* In Brunelle, R., Eds. How Can We Improve Both the Quality of Textbooks and the Process for Selecting Them? National Forum on Excellence in Education Conference Papers, Washington, D.C., 1983.

Comas, J. *Review of Seventy Textbook Adoption Criteria Sheets from both Adoption and Non-Adoption States.* Unpublished paper, Indiana University, 1982.

Crane, B. *The California Effect on Textbook Adoptions.* Educational Leadership, Vol. 32, 1975.

Komoski, K. *Instructional Materials Will Not Improve Until We Change the System.* Educational Leadership, Vol. 42, 1985.

Muther, C. *What Every Textbook Evaluator Should Know.* Educational Leadership, Vol. 42, 1985.

Osburn, J., Jones, B. & Stein, M. *The Case for Improving Textbooks.* Educational Leadership, Vol. 42, 1985.

Tulley, M. *A Descriptive Study of the Intents of State-Level Textbook Adoption Processes.* Educational Evaluation and Policy Analysis, Fall, 1985.

U. S. Commission on Civil Rights. *Fair Textbooks: A Resource Guide.* Washington, D.C., 1979.

CHAPTER TEN

Stages and Strategies for Improving Equity

Introduction

The 1990s are alive with the spirit of change in our system of education. The future of education will be affected by the recommendations of the various commissions, studies, and task forces cited throughout this book. To what extent *change* takes place - remains to be seen. It would appear that the tidal wave of reforms will produce basic changes in how teachers are educated, in how their career opportunities will be structured, and in how elementary and secondary schools will be organized. The future is bright and challenging as well.

It is easy to criticize America's educational system because; as we have seen throughout this text, discrepancies between the *ideals*, as embodied in the slogan of *quality-with-equity* and *reality*, as documented by our inequities that are plainly visible. The search for solutions to those problems has never been an easy one.

Over the past several years, extensive research and numerous studies have been conducted pertaining to schools and the issues of race, ethnicity, culture, language, laws, religion, sex, age, economic status, and the varying abilities of students. These past and present efforts have created inroads in establishing the meaning, value and virture of equity. However, like other educational doctrines - any evidence of a uniform acceptance and incorporation are the exception; rather than the rule. Where *quality-with-equity* is evident, the research indicates that the intended outcomes are learned by *all* students, regardless of the issues cited above.

There is a gap between the recommendations presented throughout the previous chapters and the specific information that schools and school districts need in order to begin an equity improvement process. Chapter 10 - **Stages and Strategies for Improving Equity** attempts to provide some direction in filling this void. This chapter is intended to assist school personnel and planning groups in identifying the various links and present the vast array of possibilities for improving equity. Those who administer or coordinate these changes will need to have information on questions such as: *What area(s) are involved in the equity improvement process? What factors need to be in identified at the beginning? What does the process of equity improvement look like?* This chapter is designed to address these questions and assist individuals involved in the school improvement process. The chapter is designed to further build upon the concept of quality-with-equity; with the notion that as educators we must take a personal role and responsibility. *We need to choose to be involved, to lend our efforts and to possess an eagerness to make a difference.*

As we have learned, equity is not a course, subject area, nor is it restricted to simply infusing one's own curriculum. Equity (a multi-dimensional concept) does have a link to every facet of the educational system. This multi-faceted concept will require a detailed process and plan, but is essentially based on four simple statements. Approaching equity from; an individual educator; as a department; or as a total school staff - these four statements are the foundation for improving equity.

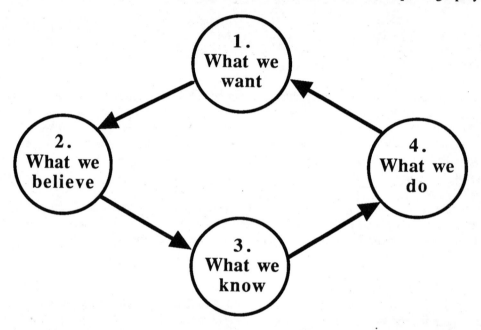

What do we want from our students? Do we have a common understanding of the goals, objectives and outcomes that we expect our students to achieve? Do we have a common mission in our school? What is it? And, more importantly, what does it mean?

What do we believe? Do we believe that all students can be successful learners? Do we believe that we can teach ALL children? Do we believe our schools must be accountable to the public? Do we believe that our schools must continually strive to improve?

What do we know? What is the evidence to support equity? What does the research literature suggest about teaching and learning? What evidence is there to suggest that things aren't as well off as one may suspect? What do we know that works? What do we know that doesn't work?

What do we do? How do we plan? Who makes the decisions? How do we know if we make a difference? Are we willing to take a risk? Do we allow for flexibility (trial & error)? How do we evaluate our progress?

These four statements can be the foundation for the total school improvement process. Although the statements are simple, the process to answer each is more complex.

Stages and Strategies for Improving Equity is organized to provide a designed process with specific examples on how to approach the improvement process - from three different levels:

I. Equity Action Plan
(Individual Lesson Plans or Activities)

II. Classroom Applications
(Analysis of Policies and Practices)

III. School-Wide Applications
(Analysis of Policies and Practices)

First, at the individual level, *Equity Action Plans* are outlined to assist and guide you in the development of specific plans, lessons or activities that can be incorporated within your teaching area(s). Second, is an extension of the individual lesson plan or activity to a process which analyzes your *Classroom Applications*; for example, this may involve examining your policies with grouping students, instructional materials, teaching styles, learning styles, classroom climate or an evaluation of the curriculum. The third link is the *School-Wide Applications*; which may examine: administrative support, school mission, on-going assessment of school programs, course scope and sequence, enrollment patterns in courses (upper and lower division courses), support services, dropouts, suspensions, and remedial programs.

This linkage from the individual classroom teacher to the school-wide applications are necessary stages that will address the four fundamental statements of: *what we want, what we believe, what we know and what we do.*

The Concept of Change

The first stage toward equity improvement is that of assessing current beliefs, attitudes, policies and practices that are prevalent in the school. The second stage is the design and implementation of a plan that will ensure the concept of equity within the total school improvement process.

Research studies (Clayton, 1985) that focus on the school improvement process do so because they believe the way a *change* is instituted determines how effective and long lasting the change will be. Several studies, in fact, suggest that *the most important improvement a school can make is to develop a permanent capacity for change*, a capacity that would allow the school to continually improve itself and to respond to the changing needs of both its students and the outside world. This capacity consists of the development of a planning group on an agreed-upon process for articulating needs, designing and implementing changes to meet them.

The following describes a common expression when discussing change at any level - how many times have we heard the comment "I will believe it when I see it." I suspect that this is a fairly common reaction; which supports my claim that if we don't *believe* in what it is that we want changed; any *real change* will not occur.

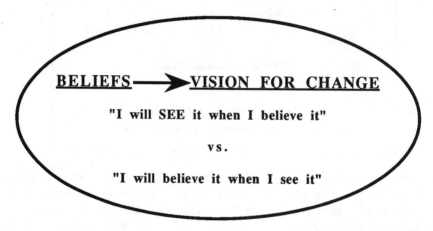

General assumptions for accomplishing change in our schools are based on the following:

* *Planning for equity improvement is a process; not a prescription.*

* *Planners should start with a long-term view based on their vision of quality-with-equity, not with a single problem.*

* *There is no one vision of quality-with-equity. Each school must develop an individual vision.*

* *Basic to the equity improvement planning process is the establishment of a planning group that represents all who will be involved in making the improvements.*

* *The plan of action developed by the group should specify clear objectives for equity improvement activities, anticipated costs of the activities, personnel responsible for carrying out each activity, evaluation, and how and when each action will be evaluated.*

* *Equity improvement plans should be flexible enough to change as obstacles arise.*

I. An Individual Equity Action Plan

As the previous chapters suggested, one can become overwhelmed with the vast amount of information that should be considered with the equity concept. With this acknowledgment comes a sense of not knowing where to begin. It may indeed require a period of time to organize, plan, develop the necessary strategies for an individual action plan.

The first step is to identify one area, issue, group or topic under the large umbrella of equity to incorporate within your instructional area. *One very important decision that should be made at the beginning is to limit yourself to one specific area, issue, group or topic*. This strategy will force you to focus more specifically; which will produce a greater likelihood of success. Certainly, the ideal is first to understand the process of designing an action plan and becoming comfortable with it, and then, to begin the process of adding and modifying other areas, issues, groups or topics to your overall instruction - *a total integration is the ultimate goal*. This process is not intended to give the impression that teachers need only to integrate and diversify their curricular offerings to be equitable, but rather it provides a strategy for evaluating and improving our own classroom(s) or subject area(s).

Levels of Equity Understanding.

The analysis of one's curriculum or teaching area should also examine the *levels of equity understanding* that teachers and students need to move through to gain the desired competence and outcomes. Working definitions of these levels are:

* *Awareness - Consciousness Level*. What should students feel or believe? For teacher trainers - research clearly shows that teachers can make a difference; regardless of the background of the student(s).

* *Knowledge - Content Level*. What should students know? Example: For teacher trainers - examination and study of different learning styles and classroom arrangements could capitalize on students needs.

* *Skill - Implementation Level*. What should students be able to do? For teacher trainers - design a unit which allows students to utilize different learning styles to arrive at the unit objectives and outcomes.

What are the outcomes that you expect from your plan? Is it intended to provide your students with a level of awareness, specific content information, or teach a skill? Using these levels, a detailed and specific plan can be designed. To often, we design lesson plans or activities in our classrooms that are too general and the proposed outcomes are unclear. On the following pages a SAMPLE outlined organizational sequence is provided.

EQUITY ACTION PLAN FORM

Name: Jane Brown

Level: _____ Elementary _____ Middle __X__ Secondary

_____ Postsecondary _____ Special populations

Subject Area: SOCIAL STUDIES

Area of Concern: Sex-Role Stereotyping

Method for change I will use: Introduction of values-clarification materials to raise their awareness about sex-role stereotyping.

Level of plan: __X__ Awareness _____ Knowledge _____ Skill

Desired outcome of your plan: Having my students becoming more aware and sensitive to their bias and stereotyping with regard to males and females and apply this awareness to the social studies curriculum.

What do you want to happen as a result of your plan?

Objective 1: Students will be able to identify at least five characteristics of male-role stereotypes.

Objective 2: Students will be able to identify three problems and sacrifices that result from conforming to the male-role stereotype.

Objective 3: Students will be able to identify and analyze at least three of their present values and attitudes toward sex-role stereotyping.

Objective 4: Students will be able to identify at least five school practices that may encourage and reinforce sex-stereotyping (within the social studies curricula).

Curriculum and Instructional Materials (titles, type of material(s) that you will use with your plan):

Readings: Dick and Jane as Victims: Sex Stereotyping in Children's Books

A Consumer's Guide to Sex, Race, and Career Bias in Public School Textbooks

Biased Textbooks: Action Steps You Can Take.

Additional Resources (displays, hands-on materials, worksheets, activities, teacher-made materials, speakers, consultants):

Learning Center in the classroom (which will include posters, books, value clarification exercises (individualized) and selected readings.

Assessment Procedures:

How will you know if and when your objectives have been met?

Method: After activities and unit discussion, ask students to: (1) list five characteristics they could include in female/male stereotypes; (2) list three advantages and disadvantages of conforming to the stereotyped roles of each sex; (3) describe at least five practices the encourage stereotyping in social studies.

Stumbling Blocks:

What constraints might hinder the implementation of your plan?

Possible peer pressure from students to openly discuss their values and attitudes concerning sex-stereotyping. Possibly, some teachers and parents may object to such "nonsense" in a social studies course.

EQUITY ACTION PLAN FORM

Name: _____

Level: _____ Elementary _____ Middle _____ Secondary

_____ Postsecondary _____ Special populations

Subject Area: _____

Area of Concern: _____

Method for change I will use: _____

_____

Level of plan: _____Awareness _____ Knowledge _____ Skill

Desired outcome of your plan: _____

_____

_____

What are your objectives? (Write them in measureable terms)

Objective 1: _____

_____

_____

Objective 2: _____

_____

_____

Objective 3: _____

_____

_____

Objective 4: _____

_____

_____

Curriculum and Instructional Materials (titles, year of publication, type of material(s) that you will use with your plan):

_____

_____

_____

Additional Resources (displays, hands-on materials, worksheets, activities, teacher-made materials, speakers, consultants):

_____

_____

_____

_____

_____

Assessment Procedures: (Outcomes)

How will you know if and when your objectives have been met?

Method: _____

_____

_____

_____

_____

Stumbling Blocks:

What constraints might hinder the implementation of your plan?

_____

_____

_____

_____

_____

_____

II. Classroom Applications.

The second stage in the equity improvement process is to examine and analyze classrooms, specific subject areas or departments. This stage is designed to answer two questions: (1) what are we currently doing? and, (2) what area(s) could we improve upon? *Figure 26 - Classroom Applications*, is a sample of the levels of analysis that should be addressed: (a) **personal reflection** (beliefs on learning, expectations, management style, discipline policies, evaluation methods); (b) **instructional materials** (analysis of the curriculum for equity perspectives, criteria for evaluation, supplementary materials, teacher-made materials, and use of the informal curriculum as a teaching tool); and (c) **allowance for differences** (classroom climate, learning styles, teaching styles, analysis of classroom interaction patterns with students, and grouping of students).

Figure 26

CLASSROOM APPLICATIONS

Personal Reflection (Individual Analysis)	Instructional Materials	Allowing for Differences
* Mission of the School vs. Teaching Philosophy * Beliefs about Teaching & Learning * Expectations for Students * Management Style * Discipline Policies	* Analysis of Curriculum * Use of Supplementary Materials * Teacher-Made Materials * Use of Informal Curriculum * Scope and Sequence * Outcomes Based * Mastery Learning * Field-Based Experiences * Community Resources	* Classroom Climate * Learning Styles * Teaching Styles * Grouping Placement Policies * Interaction or Patterns with Students (Perceived highs & lows) * Assessment

Subject Area or Departmental Analysis

Figure 27- Analyzing Your Department outlines the process for improving specific subject areas or departments. This model can easily be adapted to fit any educational level(elementary, middle, secondary and postsecondary). As mentioned earlier, there is no blueprint that exists for equity improvement that will work for every school, nor should there be one. The differences among schools would preclude the *package deal* from working for everyone, but direction and guidance is essential.

Figure 27

ANALYZING YOUR DEPARTMENT

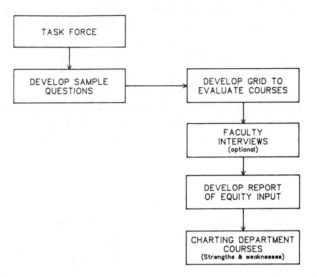

Establish a Steering Committee.

This steering committee should not be only representative of the classroom teachers involved, but should also include administrators and individuals outside the particular department or subject area. The steering commitee should: (1) have a working knowledge and understanding of the equity concept; (2) define a vision of equity for the department; and the school, and (3) collectively compile a list of criteria which will be used to analyze specific courses, texts, specific subject areas, or departments. A sample of questions are briefly outlined:

* *Disaggregate student data - what students are enrolled in these specific subject areas or departments? (race, sex, income levels, exceptional populations)*

* *Are course objectives reflective of equity?*

* *What are the policies and practices for sorting students into various classes?*

* *Are supplementary materials used? If so, are they equitable in their perspective?*

* *Are there gaps or overlapping of content within courses?*

* *Are textbooks and instructional materials evaluated for equity perspectives? How often? By whom?*

* *Are there prerequisites for course placement?*

* *Is equity content integrated throughout the course, in textbooks, and in subject areas?*

* *What method(s) are used for evaluation, promotion and placement of students?*

* *What students are successful? What students are not as successful? (Disaggregate the data according to sub-groups present in the school).*

Each faculty member should supply course descriptions (objectives, outlines, syllabi, activities and proposed outcomes) to the steering committee.

Visit with Each Faculty Member

Each classroom teacher should be visited to determine what equity concerns he/she considers most relevant for their particular area and in general; for the school The communication between the individual steering committee member and the faculty member will serve to sensitize faculty to the greater range of issues and reinforce the importance of their role and responsibility. Also, many times individual faculty members are hesitant to speak out in larger settings. Finally, this process allows the individual faculty member to clarify and amplify upon any information they provided.

A list of questions that are to be considered should be prepared before communicating with individual faculty members. (Disseminating the questions prior to the visit is recommended). Some sample questions are shown below:

* *What students are most likely to enroll in your classes (middle and secondary levels)?*

* *Are there any prerequisites that prohibit certain students from being able to be in your classroom?*

* *Does the equity concept relate to your course or subject area? If so, how? If not, why not?*

* *What is your policy or practice in sorting students within your classroom for certain activities or instructional methods?*

* *Do your textbooks and instructional materials reflect an equity perspective?*

* *With regard to equity, what strategies or methods do you believe your course or subject area is strong in?*

* *Do you believe quality-with-equity is evident in your department or subject area? In the school? Why or why not?*

* *Are there any special instructional skills or methods used to address the needs of low-achieving students? What are they?*

* *What method(s) are used for the evaluation, promotion and placement of students? Are they consistent between teachers and departments?*

* *Generally speaking, who are the students, who do well in your classroom? Generally, who are the students that don't do as well? Can you explain this?*

Develop A Report on the Level Equity Input.

Analysis to this point is based on the information that has been provided by the individual faculty members, subject areas, or departments. The goal of this stage is to: *determine what areas, issues, and outocmes are being achieved and in what depth.* An equity scale upon which to evaluate over-all input and integration is provided with <u>Figure 28 - Rating the Level of Equity Input</u> (which is the same scale used in evaluating instructional materials). A summary of the findings and the overall recommendations should be prepared and written.

A Workshop Model.

Based upon this analysis and evaluation of the department or subject area(s), the information obtained should be shared and discussed with all members of the teaching staff. The following is a workshop model that can be adapted for this purpose. *The goal of this stage is to share, discuss, prioritize, and plan for improvement.* The model is designed to address the following areas:

* *Participants to be involved;*

* *Discussion of the analysis and evaluation;*

* *Determination of the objectives, needs, and outcomes;*

* *Individual faculty goals, objectives, needs, and outcomes.*

This workshop design not only provides the opportunity to examine the above analysis process but allows the faculty to begin the process of establishing departmental or subject area equity goals, as well as individual goals. <u>Figure 29 - Workshop Model</u>, outlines the two phases of this particular process.

RATING THE LEVEL OF EQUITY INPUT

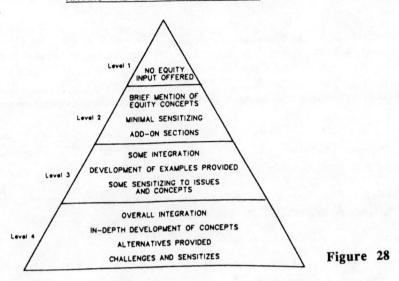

Figure 28

WORKSHOP MODEL

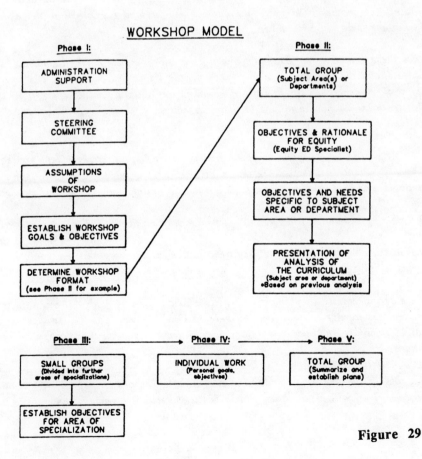

Figure 29

Planning for the Workshop - Phase I. A successful workshop involves detailed preparation with carefully chosen participants. It is vital that selected representatives from different constituencies be included, for example - administrators, special area faculty, consultants, equity specialists, classroom teachers, and teacher trainers. (If you plan to include students, parents and local community leaders, do so from the very beginning). Crucial steps during the workshop preparation:

* *It is essential that the faculty commit themselves to a study of equity and overall school improvement. The faculty must make a further commitment to developing and implementing plans related to equity in their departments or subject area(s).*

* *Ensure that the administration has given official approval and support for the workshop. Workshop participation by the administration must be strongly encouraged. It is clear that the workshop will not take place if this official support is lacking.*

* *It should be clear that the administration must attend the entire workshop without interruption. These individuals will often play a pivotal position at the departmental or subject area levels regarding any program changes. Without full support and participation of the administration, a workshop should not be planned.*

* *Once these commitments are made, the organizational phase comes into being. A steering committee should be formed, made up of key people - i.e., administration, the workshop leader(s), key staff, students, - with the task of planning and communicating the program to their peers. This team should handle all the local arrangements of invitations, dates, logistics and administration.*

* *A lengthy "lead time" (four to seven months) is an important ingredient for the success of the workshop. It takes time to work on arrangements, to announce and re- announce the workshop purposes, and to do the mailings, logistics and the initial analysis of the curriculum.*

* *The steering committee will have to determine the best format for the workshop sequence.*

* *The steering committee should prepare a statement of the workshop goals and send advance copies to all participants.*

* *The steering committee will also need to consider certain budget items. It is highly recommended that faculty be paid for their release time. Other costs for the workshop may be minimal. (Obviously, the budget will vary greatly depending upon logistics, speakers and accommodations, etc.)*

* *The role of the workshop leader involves diverse responsibilities, so two leaders are recommended. They will assist in all phases of the workshop; planning, running the actual workshop*

and directing the follow-up activities. They support and reinforce each other and provide a change of pace for the participants.

* *A paid clerical staff person from the department or subject area should be responsible to the steering committee for making the physical arrangements including preparing notices of the workshop, mailings, meals/snacks and other details.*

<u>Assumptions of the Workshop</u>. Those who are asked to implement a new concept must have a role in deciding if they want to become a part of that concept. *If people feel ownership for the concept then it has a good chance for success.* The staff members must decide if objectives are important for them. Designing the concept will vary from school to school, department to department and from faculty to faculty.

Reasons for a new concept must be clearly understood by all parties. Much discussion is needed to clarify each person's position and understand the position of others. It takes effort and study to understand how to continue to teach the existing curriculum and in addition, make a contribution to school improvement. Reasons for any change must make sense and be clearly defensible by everyone involved.

New concepts must build on the past. Change is part of the process of evolution from what was to what will be. To change does not mean that what happened in the past was inadequate or wrong. Rather, change is the result of learning and improving on what exists. New concepts must interface with existing programs. *Change is usually seen as a <u>threat</u> or an <u>opportunity</u>.*

New concepts should be designed for adaptation and continuous evolution. The workshop will assist the participants in looking at objectives which are flexible. The responses or the programs that result from the objectives can be revised and modified to reflect the current needs of the students and the staff.

New concepts must involve the total staff. The responsibility for equity and overall school improvement rests with all staff members in every discipline or position with students. A concept must not be imposed upon people; everyone affected should have the opportunity to help decide if the concept or the thrust is for them.

New concepts can best be implemented in schools at the individual department or subject area level. To succeed, an equity perspective requires total staff involvement. The best efforts of only a few individuals in the administration, or one department, or selected teachers, or active citizens are inadequate. Successful adoption and incorporation of new concepts in a school (at any level) is the result of an integrated commitment of the staff, students and the community within one physical building or department.

Agreement on essential matters should permit wide variation on other points. Administrators should capitalize on differences rather than attempt to get agreement on every aspect. What is important is that staff members feel they are properly treated even though they may have different views.

Points to Reinforce. The workshop has certain key characteristics. All participants should be made aware of them:

---

* It will not give any "pat" answers to complex equity issues

B U T

it will provide general background information to assist in drawing conclusions.

* It will not provide any formula for instant success in teaching from an equity perspective

B U T

it will provide the opportunity for consideration on how participants will jointly develop and design educational experiences.

* It will not impose what and how to teach

B U T

it will ask the school community to approve or disapprove the concept of equity .

* It will not make the participants "content" specialists

B U T

it will introduce them to a variety of issues and critical educational problems.

A Suggested Workshop Format - Phase II. In designing and planning a workshop format, the overall goals of the workshop must be kept in proper priority. For example, some of the following could be chosen to be your workshop goals. The staff will:

*   *Become better acquainted with each other and will develop a greater respect for one another.*

* *Establish open lines of communication and be willing to listen to other points of view and to consider alternative value systems.*

* *Become more sensitized to others and be better prepared to help students and teachers know and accept differences of other students and teachers.*

* *Experience specific skills in small group dynamics including complex processes of coming to a consensus.*

* *Examine and clarify one's own value structure in various areas connected with equity and excellence.*

* *Understand the value structure of other participants*

* *Increase the awareness level about equity issues in the school and community so its members will better under- stand the complexity of a pluralistic society.*

* *Seek to understand the various academic approaches to complex equity concepts.*

* *Develop an awareness that equity issues do affect the community and do affect people's lives.*

* *Approve or reject the objectives to serve as guidelines for responses that the faculty might want to make in the area of equity.*

* *Identify the steps involved in translating the objectives into the life of the school.*

* *Establish a timeline and plan for continued study and improvement.*

The following workshop format is designed to provide an example of a workshop experience that allows for the sharing of information to a larger group. The format also allows for specific departmental or subject areas to address and analyze equity improvement, as well as to provide for individual attention.

TOTAL GROUP

Discuss objectives and rationale for the equity improvement process.

* Presentation(s) by an equity consultant (be selective)

* Question and answer session

<u>Discuss equity objectives, outcomes and the needs specific to a department or subject area.</u>

*   Historical background

*   Present "state of the art"

*   Question and answer session

<u>Present the analysis of the departments or subject areas.</u>

*   Share results of the analysis (Dissagregate the data).

*   Provide opportunity for reaction and suggestions for modifications and elaborations.

*   Determine what further information is needed on current programs.

*   Decide what should be done and what approaches need to be addressed, based on the analysis.

SMALL GROUP

<u>Identify equity objectives and outcomes for department or subject area.</u>

*   Arrive at general objectives and outcomes for the total department or subject area.

*   Come to a consensus.

*   Prepare report for larger group.

<u>Identify equity objectives and expected outcomes for area of specialization.</u>

*   Faculty should divide into their areas of specialization.

*   Develop specific objectives and outcomes for each discipline.

*   Record objectives and outcomes.

*   Report to larger group.

* Record all group responses to examine continuity, gaps or overlap that appear as a result of the group reports.

INDIVIDUAL WORK

Determine personal objectives to the equity improvement process.

* Record specific objectives and outcomes for the equity improvement process - on an individual basis.

* Record and present objectives.

* Determine what is needed to accomplish these objectives and outcomes.

TOTAL GROUP

Determine future plans for equity improvement.

* Summarize the presentations.

* Summarize the activities.

* Set specific time frame(s) and responsibilities (establish timelines)

* Set priority of next steps to be taken.

* Provide specific direction for follow-up activities (steering committee).

III. A School-Wide Model

It is important to avoid presenting the equity concept in airtight compartments; it should instead be integrated into all content areas and policies and practices of the school - the multi-dimensional linkage. The areas, issues, questions, problems, knowledge level(s) and skill level(s) which are a part of any concept can be most effectively understood when all faculty are involved. Too many times, schools attempt to incorporate or improve concepts and often they fail - primarily because a designed plan and purpose was not organized well enough. The following model that is proposed will hopefully allow you and your colleagues to have at the very least a direction, a guide and a focus to the equity improvement process. (See Figure 30 - School-Wide Model).

Figure 30

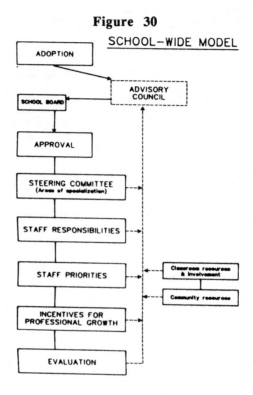

SCHOOL—WIDE MODEL

In order for any concept to succeed, the administration and the faculty must express enthusiasm and support for it; the equity improvement process is no different. The concept should be initiated by the school or department before support can be generated from school policymakers. If the objectives are understood and supported by the school policymakers, support from the board of the school is likely to follow, enhancing the probability of greater support.

There are many critical issues and decision points in the improvement process - decision points such as adopting a vision, identifying goals, determining priorities, establishing timelines, etc. In each instance, commitment and consensus should be attained.

The faculty is the backbone of the improvement process. The faculty, the students, and the community must function well together. Failure to have a high percentage of faculty support will likely result in less than satisfactory results.

The school or department must have the flexibility to move as slowly or as rapidly as the conditions warrant. To try and force a new concept on everyone at the same time is not in the best interest of the faculty, students, or the basic tenets upon which the equity improvement process is built.

Individuals must not only be allowed to be different, but differences must be appreciated, supported and encouraged. Assuming common goals, individuals can make unique contributions by utilizing their own expertise, personality and content.

If the faculty members are informed about and involved with the concept and improvement process, it becomes a part of them and they begin to own it. Ownership immediately makes them concerned about the success of the improvement process.

If school-wide equity improvement is to be successful, the diverse perspectives of the school community must be incorporated. While it would be impossible to reach consensus on each and every item, faculty and staff rapport may assist the council in drafting and implementing a well-rounded, meaningful set of goals. The diversity of opinions also serves as an example of what equity is all about - different people working together for a common purpose. The faculty and staff is rich in resource and the basis upon which equity for school improvement is built on. Failure to make significant use of the faculty and staff will result in a much less effective school improvement plan. Even the smallest schools are diverse and complex and from them meaningful learning can emerge if planning is careful and thoughtful. However, a word of caution is outlined below:

Focus on the BEST interest for all

vs.

The SPECIAL interest of some

The issues, questions, problems, knowledge and skills which are all a link to equity, can be most effectively understood when all faculty and disciplines are utilized. Thus, inter-disciplinary teaching and learning gives all teachers the opportunity to contribute uniquely to the equity improvement process.

The professional growth needs of faculty members are diverse. Personalized programs can avoid wasteful "over teaching" and still guarantee higher levels of staff competence. The limited budget allocations for in-service should be directed toward faculty members whose needs and interest are greatest.

The greatest gains can be made when the faculty is involved in the establishment, monitoring and evaluation of the equity improvement process. Since the concept is not curricular in the sense that instructional materials are provided, the success of the plan depends heavily upon the staff's under-standing of the equity vision, goals and objectives and the willingness to develop and improve all students' learning experiences. Faculty and staff members must be willing to define their own professional growth needs. While external evaluation may be used to assist the staff in evaluating school improvement effectiveness, some of the monitoring of the plan should be a staff responsi-bility. *Figure 31 - School-Wide Application* is a global examination of the areas that should be addressed in the process of equity improvement.

Figure 31

SCHOOL-WIDE APPLICATIONS

Administrative (District and Building Level)	Assessment	Faculty and Staff

* Level of Support
* Priority Level
* On-going Process
* Contact Person
* On-going Evaluation
	* Disaggregation of
	   Student Data
	* Course offerings
	* Enrollment trends
	* Grouping Patterns or Policies
	* Retentions, Suspensions,
	   Referrals, Dropouts.
	* Special Populations
	* Support Services
	* Scope and Sequence
	* Assessment Practices
	* Grading Policies
		* Needs & Priorities
		* Staff Development
		* Teacher Assessment
		* Teaching Loads
		* Teaching Rotations
		* Diversity of Staff
		* Master Teachers

Figures 32 through 40 detail specific steps in addressing the overall school-wide equity improve-ment process. These figures provide a step-by-step process from initial *adoption and approval of an equity improvement plan to evaluation.*

Figure 32

ADOPTION	NOT APPLICABLE	INCOMPLETE	IN PROGRESS	DATE COMPLETED
Designate one person to be in charge of initiating and planning for the development of the equity concept.				
Assign one or more persons from the "administrative group" office to be responsible for providing assistance to those planning and implementing the equity concept.				
Establish an advisory council for equity education (membership should be voluntary). Representation of administration, faculty, students and the community is strongly encouraged.				
Provide an in-service session(s) for the advisory council on the equity education concept. [Note: It is usually best to use someone outside the school; use extreme caution in the selection of the consultant].				
Have the advisory council begin to develop a rationale and policy statement for the school.				
Disseminate a draft of the rationale and policy statement to the administration, faculty, students and community representatives for input.				
Establish an advisory network to support the concept; for example, state department personnel, social service agencies, community groups, school districts, higher education personnel, consultants.				
Present the rationale and policy statement (after first draft modification/deletions) to the administration or governing board for approval.				

* The school should issue a statement(s) indicating that equity education concepts are individually designed at the school level. Therefore, there should be no expectation of standardization.

* At all stages the staff members must be encouraged to use their own creativity and initiative.

APPROVAL	NOT APPLICABLE	INCOMPLETE	IN PROGRESS	DATE COMPLETED
The school should disseminate the rationale and policy statement to the faculty, students and advisory network.				
The advisory council should design the objectives for the school year (that is, inservice sessions, goals, individual department or subject area goals, meetings, etc.) Have realistic expectations.				
The staff should combine its goals, position statement, course content, and resources to devise a general plan that will provide direction for the concept.				
Staff participation must be directed and continuous. Scheduled regular meetings during the school year with stated objectives and a clear understanding for each meeting is strongly advised.				
Allow release time for planning. Don't expect great enthusiasm for the concept if all the work is being done on top of a regular teaching load. (If you believe the concept is important, it should be reflected in the scheduling of work sessions and inservice meetings.)				
If possible, keep in-service for faculty separated by "area of specialization," that is, History, English, Special Ed., Music, Psychology, etc. AVOID providing an inservice session for your entire faculty at once.				
Each faculty member should begin research on equity education perspectives as they relate to his/her subject matter. (This information will be carefully incorporated into an individual plan of action.)				
Staff progress should be monitored by and reported in the faculty bulletin or newspaper (or memos) in an effort to keep everyone enthusiastic and informed.				

Figure 33

STEERING COMMITTEE

	NOT APPLICABLE	INCOMPLETE	IN PROGRESS	DATE COMPLETED
A steering committee should be formed to develop and assist in implementing the concept of equity education in particular areas of specialization, and to set goals and objectives. The steering committee should be representative of the area of specialization involved. A member of the advisory council on equity education should be a member of the steering committee. (This may help to ensure that the steering committee is on "target" with equity issues and objectives.)				
Release time needs to be provided for meetings and planning sessions.				
The advisory council on equity education should outline and designate the authority and responsibility to the steering comittee.				
The steering committee should establish its own objectives, goals, and plans for its particular area of specialization.				
The steering committee presents it objectives, goals, and plans to the equity advisory council. Specific activities, dates, objectives, workshops, etc., should be included.				
The steering committee must report regularly to the whole staff in its grade level(s) or area of specialization.				

Figure 34

STAFF RESPONSIBILITIES

	NOT APPLICABLE	INCOMPLETE	IN PROGRESS	DATE COMPLETED
Each staff member needs to be actively involved in departmental or subject area goals, area of specialization goals, and his/her own individual goals. Each staff member's goals, objectives, and plans for incorporating equity education into his/her teaching area should be provided to the steering committee. Sharing goals can also be accomplished with the "workshop model," that was provided earlier.				
Staff members from different areas should be actively involved in working together to coordinate lessons and develop inter-disciplinary activities.				
The advisory council on equity education and the steering committee should compile the needs and concerns expressed by their faculty members. (Positive and negative comments)				
The two committees (advisory council and steering committee), should prioritize those needs to assist in giving direction to the action or plan that will be taken. An example of the priorities that could be expressed are listed on the chart on the following page. (See: Possible Staff Priorities)				

Figure 35

Figure 36

STAFF PRIORITIES (SAMPLE)	NEED TO ADDRESS THIS NEED	LACK OF RESOURCES	HAVE TO BE ACCOMPLISHED	ONGOING	COMPLETED
In-service on rationale for equity education.					
In-service on awareness of diversity in education.					
Evaluation of curriculum materials for bias and stereotyping.					
Simulations, activities, or games for classroom use.					
Developing classroom materials.					
Individualizing instruction for diversity.					
Interdisciplinary approach to teaching.					
Resources for classroom use.					
In-service on a "specific" group that may be posing special problems for the school.					

Figure 37

CLASSROOM RESOURCES AND INVOLVEMENT	NOT APPLICABLE	INCOMPLETE	IN PROGRESS	DATE COMPLETED
Each faculty member should begin to maintain a card file of equity education ideas, strategies, or resources to be interwoven into lesson content.				
Each area of specialization could compile a "master file" that would serve as an idea bank for the faculty.				
Periodic news releases and newsletters should be generated.				
An information bank should be set up in the library to provide faculty quick and easy access to a variety of support material and to serve as a distribution center for innovations and suggestions from faculty and consultants. A list of what might be included in the information bank is provided below.				
Books on equity education activities. Accompanying these should be annotated listing of the activities with evaluations of each and suggestions for adapting them to the needs of the students.				
An annotated listing of articles and readings addressing the needs of diverse student populations.				
Books providing information on different cultural groups, equity education, learning styles, etc.				
Models and methods of other schools that have incorporated the equity education concepts into their curriculums.				
A yellow pages of resources for equity education. This might include a list of speakers, resource persons, agencies, organizations, and places for good out-of-class learning experiences within the community.				

Figure 38

COMMUNITY RESOURCES

	NOT APPLICABLE	INCOMPLETE	IN PROGRESS	DATE COMPLETED
School policies should encourage use of the community as a learning laboratory.				
A systematic plan should be developed to make the best use of available resources and to coordinate their uses at the school-wide level.				
There must be an ongoing effort to discover the many possibilities for using the community as a laboratory.				
Students and staff need to be involved in actual experiences in the community.				

Figure 39

INCENTIVES FOR PROFESSIONAL GROWTH

	NOT APPLICABLE	INCOMPLETE	IN PROGRESS	DATE COMPLETED
Provide incentives to encourage professional growth in the form of a policy statement to the faculty.				
Provide a variety of inservice activities for individuals, small groups, and occasionally for larger groups.				
Award professional growth credit for successful completion of inservice programs in equity education.				
Give recognition to teachers who develop materials for instruction in equity education.				
Provide funds for summer curriculum development to encourage faculty, with the assistance of students, to evaluate course content for its effectiveness in stimulating equity awareness.				
Give faculty opportunities for long-term observations of classrooms, both at the university level and at K-12 levels, in which an equity focus is being implemented.				
Give faculty release time to investigate important current issues related to equity education.				

Figure 40

EVALUATION

The steering committee may appoint a task force to develop assessment methods to determine if: objectives are being met, indicators of achievement are present, areas that need improvement can be identified ideas and alternatives are provided, and overall evaluation of progress is evident.			
Periodic evaluation procedures need to be established. Following evaluation, discrepancies between goals and achievements should be recognized and plans for improvement be made.			
The media, mode, materials, level of difficulty, and assessment methods for learning activities must be made available to all members of the teaching staff and community.			
The results of assessments and plans for improvement should be made available to all members of the faculty and community.			

Summary

During this century, perhaps no concept has given educators more difficulty than that of equality. As teachers and administrators, we have gradually come to realize the inequities that have existed in our educational systems for so long. Segregated schools invariably penalized Asians, Blacks, Native Americans and Hispanics. Although boys and girls attend school together, too frequently we educate them by traditional images of male and female roles. We are still far from genuine educational equity. Our human responses have seemed to function much like a pendulum. Where once we educated only the few and ignored many, we now attempt to educate all, but from a single and traditional perspective. By doing so, we mistake uniformity for equality. Equity is a positive response in that it broadens perspectives and provides a more meaningful and effective education for all.

Implementation of a concept to accommodate the necessary competencies for an equity perspective will require significant changes in policies, practices and academic content that are currently provided. These changes will affect all facets of the educational program and will require the cooperation of a large segment of the academic community.   Internally, the faculty of each school must become aware, sensitive, and committed to the concept of equity school improvement. Anything less than a concentrated, committed and cooperative effort will result in mere tinkering with the existing program(s).

When changes are small or when only a few people are involved, our procedures for monitoring, evaluating and revising plans can be informal. Implementing changes at a classroom, department, or school-wide level requires more systematic procedures. We need to be continually learning from our experiences and the experiences of others.

Improving schools has become a national goal. National commissions, governors, corporation executives and educators are determined that education must change. Some of us contend that schools are more successful than the public seems to think, but we also want them to be even better.

There is much less agreement, however, about the kinds of changes that are needed - and about how those changes should be made. Much has already been written about what schools should do: raise standards, ensure quality-with-equity, identify and better serve at- risk students, examine teacher training programs, teacher expectations and ensure purposeful outcomes for all students.

Some of those who advocate these changes have suggestions for how to implement them, but most have little to say on the subject. It is a matter of either convincing reluctant educators to try something new or having some authority outline the plan. This chapter has identified the necessary stages for evaluating and improving upon equity; and has offered specific strategies for the initial stages.

One of my beliefs is that it takes the energy of a lot of people, over a fairly long time, to improve a school. Primarily, this chapter is written for educators responsible for an improvement effort in their own community: for the principal engaged in school reform, for the classroom teacher, for the department head trying to change the emphasis on the department, and for the administrator responsible for the new staff evaluation process.

The contents of this chapter also has important implications for those who train teachers and administrators, for those who provide expertise and support to schools from the outside, and for those who make decisions that schools have to implement. Schooling and its improvement is everyone's business. It is critical that those who are involved both directly and indirectly know how to make things happen.

WORKSHEET 1

1.   What are the three levels of equity involvement?

_____

_____

_____

2.   What we want. What we believe. What we know. What we do. In your opinion, which of these four statements is most important? Why?

_____

_____

_____

_____

_____

_____

3.   Why is it essential to analyze and review the subject area(s) and department(s) for equity?

_____

_____

_____

_____

4.   What is the difference between the awareness level, the knowledge level and the skill level?

_____

_____

_____

_____

_____

_____

5.   Identify specific areas or issues that classroom teachers should examine for equity.

_____

_____

_____

_____

_____

6.   Identify specific areas or issues that schools should examine for equity (school-wide).

_____

_____

_____

_____

_____

7.   What would you consider the top priority in addressing an equity improvement plan?

   a. Classroom application: _____

_____

_____

_____

b. School-wide application: _____

_____

_____

_____

8. What is meant by, "I will see it when I believe it." _____

_____

_____

_____

_____

REFERENCES

Clayton-Felt, Marilyn Improving Our Schools. Education Development Center, Inc., Washington, D.C., 1985.

SUGGESTED READINGS

Crandall, D. P. "The Teacher's Role in School Improvement." Educational Leadership 41, November, 1983.

Huberman, A. M. "School Improvement Strategies that Work." Educational Leadership 41, November, 1983.

Loucks-Horsley, S., & Cox, P. L. "It's All in the Doing: What Recent Research Says About Implementation." Paper presented at the annual meeting of the American Educational Research Association, New Orleans, 1984.

Louis, K. S., & Rosenblum, S. "Linking R & D with Schools: A Program and Its Implications for Dissemination and School Improvement Policy." Abt Associates, Cambridge, MA, 1983.

Peters, T. J., & Waterman, R. H., Jr. In Search of Excellence. Harper and Row, New York, NY, 1982.

INDEX

AACTE 5, 49, 52
Abington School District v. Shempp 189
Academic Performance 115
Academic Freedom 181
Accelerated School Model 85
Adler, Mortimer 26, 27, 87
Age Discrimination Act 184
Amalgamation 135
Analyzing Your Department for Equity 271
Anglo-Conformity Theory 137
Antolopolis, D. 77
Arnold v. Carpenter, 1972 193
Arreola v. Board of Education 158
Assimilation 135
Association of American Publishers 217, 224
At-Risk Students 103
Attitudes Toward School 116
Audio-Lingual Method 169
Awareness-Consciousness Equity Level 265

Baca, Leonard 168
Baker, Gwendolyn 9
Banks, James 3, 4, 9, 128, 133, 137
Bannister v. Paradis, 1970 192
Barriers to Excellence Report 61
Bennett, Christine 133
Bernstein, Harriet 220
Biased Materials 233
Bilingual Education 158, 161
Bilingual Education Act Title VII 157, 167
Bills, David 108
Blanco, G. 167
Bloom, Bill 77
Board of Education v. Pico 188
Boros, Michael 111
Bowler, Mike 220
Boyer, Ernest 26, 28, 41, 74, 81, 94
Brandt, Ron 55
Braly, K.W. 229
Brophy, J. 77
Brown v. Board of Education 25, 27, 186
Buckley Amendment 199

California State Board of Education 223
Carlos, J 170
Carpenter, Susan 110

Castellanos, Diego 155
Catterall, James 111
Cervantes, Hermes 168
Chapter I, Federal Program 111, 157
Child Abuse and Neglect 107, 196
Chinn, Philip 23, 131, 139
Civil Rights Act (1964) 157, 161
Civil Rights Division v. Amphitheater Unified
    School District, 1984 191
Classroom Applications for Equity 271
Cody, Caroline 217, 218
Cohen, A. 167
Colangelo, Nicholas 3
Coleman, James 29, 46, 70
College Board 26, 41
Collier, Virginia 170
Compensatory Education 110
Communications-Based ESL 169
Conant, James 83
Conklin, Nancy 153, 156
Connick v. Myers 187
Continuous Progress Programs 84
Continuum of Equitable Competence 57
Cooperative Learning 84
Corporal Punishment 195
Crawford, James 155, 164
Cronin v. Moody, 1979 192
Cross, Patricia 114
Cuban, Larry 109, 112
Cubberly, Ellwood 136
Cultural Pluralism 138

Dawson, Martha 3, 12, 22
Demographics of School Populations 132
Devos, G. 133
Dewey, John 27, 138
Diana v. State Board of Education 158
Discrimination (legal definition) 182
Doss, Harriet 108
Dougherty, U. 46
Doyle, Denis 30
Dress Codes (students) 192
Dropouts 104
Drug and Alcohol Abusers 106
Due Process 191, 198
Dustin, Dick 3

Edmonds, Ron 43
Educating Americans for the 21st Century 28
Education Commission of the States 28
Education Consolidation and Improvement Act (1981) 111
Education for All Handicapped Children Act of 1975 ....184, 197
Effective Schools 45
Effective Teaching 72
Eighth Amendment 196
Elementary and Secondary Education (1965) 111, 157
English as a Second Language 163, 169
English-Only Movement 165
English-Plus 166
Enrichment Bilingual Education Program 168
Equal Access 31
Equal Outcomes 31
Equal Pay Act 183, 186
Equal Treatment 31
Equity Action Plans 265
Equity Involvement (3 Levels) 263
Ethnic Studies 3, 128
Ethnic Minority Group 133
Ethnicity 133
Evolutionary Pattern of Language Treatment 154
Executive Order 11246 184
Exemption Syndrome 12

Faculty Interviews for Equity 273
Family Educational Rights and Privacy Act .199
Family Structure and Poverty 108
Farr, Roger 220, 227
Federal Law Summary Sheet 185
Federal Spending for Bilingual Education 164
FERPA 199
Finn, Chester 61
Fischer, Louis 187, 188, 191, 199
First Amendment 185
Fishman, Joshua 66
Forester, Leona 3
Formula for Discrimination 182
Fourteenth Amendment 185
Fowler v. Williamson, 1979 193
Foxley, Cecilia 3

Fragmentation and Isolation in Materials 232
Funding for Textbooks 223

Garcia Ricardo 7, 170
Gay, Geneva 7
Glazer, Nathan 112, 138
Gollnick, Donna 7, 126, 131, 139
Goldberg, Kirsten 232
Goldstein, P. 218
Gonzales, Josue 156, 167
Goodlad, John 26, 28, 30, 44, 70, 74, 81, 94
Gordon, Milton 137
Goss v. Lopez 191
Grammar-Based Instruction 169
Grammar Translation Method 169
Grant, Carl 7
Grouping and Tracking Practices 80
Guttmacher, Alan 111

Harvard Encyclopedia of American Ethnic Groups 132
Hayakawa, S.I. 166
Hazelwood School District v. Kuhlmeier, 1988 195
High School Graduation Rates by State 104
Higher Standards 114
Hodgekinson, Harold 1, 129, 140
Horace's Compromise 71
Humphrey, Hubert 111
Hunter, William 136

Identification Strategies for At-Risk Students 117
Increasing the Length of the School Day or Year 114
Individualized Education Program (IEP) 198
Ingraham v. Wright 195
Institute of Educational Leadership 1, 132
Invisibility in Curriculum Materials 228
Inventory Fact Sheet for At-Risk Students ...121
Involvement in School Activities for At-Risk Students 115
Involvement with Juvenile Justice System ...116

Katz, K. 229
Keyes v. School District 1 162
Knowledge-Content Level of Equity 265

Kolstad, Andrew 104
Korentz, Daniel 102

Language in Curriculum Materials 225, 232
Lau v. Nichols 160
Lemon Test... 190
Levin, Henry 85, 103, 112
Limited English Proficient 158
Limited English Speaking 158
Lippman, W. 229
Local Stratagies for Textbook Selection 226
Lourie, Margaret 153, 156
Love, Ruth... 26
Low-Performing Students 104
Lubbock Civil Liberties v. Lubbock Independent
    School District, 1984 190
Lum v. Rice, 1927 186
Lyke, Bob 104

Macroculture 134
Maintenance Bilingual Program 168
May 25th Memorandum 159
McCloud, Paul.. 219
McCune, Shirley 31
McDill, Edward 111
McNett, Ian 102
Melting Pot Theory 134
Meyers v. Nebraska 155
Microculture 134
Minority Enrollment by State......................... 130
Miranda v. Arizona 192
Moody, Charles 121
Moran, L.. 77
Moynihan, Patrick 44, 138
Mozert v. Hawkins County Public Schools .. 231
Multicultural Education 5, 7
Multiethnic Education 4

National Center for Educationl Statistics 102
National Child Abuse Prevention and Treatment
    Act 196
National Commission on Excellence
    .... 25, 47, 72, 98, 103
National Education Association 158, 218
National Science Board Commission.............. 28
National Science Foundation 26
Natural Approach (ESL) 169

Nativism 138
Nature of Family Support for At-Risk Students
    116
NCATE 47
Need for Employment of At-Risk Students .. 116
Neglected and Abused Children 107
New Jersey v. T.L.O. 194
No One Model American 5, 135
North Central Accreditation 49
Novak, Michael 138
Number of Persons with Non-English Mother
    Tongues 156

Oakes, Jeannie 25, 41, 80-83
Odden, A 46, 70
Outcomes Accreditation 50
Owings, Jeffrey 104

Palmer v. Board of Education, 1980 189
Passow, Henry 3
Physical Desegregation 31
Pickering v. Board of Education 187
Plessy v. Ferguson 57, 186
Pollas, Aaron 116
Pratte Richard 135
Pregnancy Disability Bill 191
Pregnancy Discrimination Act 184
Prevention Strategies for At-Risk Students .. 117
Publishers Respond 224
Purkey, S. 45

Quality Outcomes for Equity Levels 31

Race and Ethnicity with At-Risk Students 108
Rating the Level of Equity Input................... 274
Ravitch, Diane.. 138
Reagan Administration Budget for Bilingual
    Education 164
Regional Accreditation..................................... 50
Rehabilitation Act of 1973 183
Religion in Schools 189
Restoration of Bilingual Program 168
Rosenthal & Jacobsen 77
Run-Away Youth 106

Sadker, David 228, 232
Sadker, Myra 228, 232

Schmuck, P. 235
School Attendance 115
School Desegregation..................................186
School Records 199
School-Wide Application for Equity 284
Scott v. Board of Education, 1969 193
Selectivity and Imbalance in Curriculum
    Materials 230
Separatism 137
Serna v. Portales Municipal Schools 161
Sex Discrimination 190
Sizer, Theodore 71, 72
Skill-Implementation Level for Equity 265
Slavin, Robert.......................................84, 122
Smith v. School Commissioners of Mobile
    County, Alabama 231
Sorting and Classifying Students 83
State Involvement in Bilingual Education 165
State-Required Testing for Certification 53
State Textbook Adoption Policies.................218
State Textbook Adoption Process 221
States Using Minimum Competency Tests ...113
Stereotyping in Curriculum Materials...........228
Student Behavior 116
Student Searchers 194
Students Grooming......................................193
Students and Free Speech 188
Success for All 85
Swann v. Mecklenburg...........................162, 186

Task Force on Education for Economic Growth
   28
Teacher Education 47
Teacher Expectations 76
Teacher Testing and Certification 52
Teen-Age Parents 105
Teen Suicide 108
TESA 78
Toch, Thomas 112
Textbook Evaluation 227
The Natural Approach (ESL) 169
Tinker v. Des Moines Public Schools 188
Title VI of the Civil Rights Act.....................183
Title VII of the Civil Rights Act 183
Title VII (Bilingual Education Act) 157
Title IX (Sex Discrimination) 183, 190
Total Physical Response (ESL) 169

Tracking 80
Transitional Bilingual Program 168
Tulley, Mike 220, 227
Twentieth Century Fund 26
Tyack, David 109

United States Crime Statistics Report 105
Units Required for High School Graduation ...55
U.S. Department of Education 44, 103
Unreality in Curriculum Materials 230

Ventresca, Marc 102
Verdugo, Richard 116
Vocational Education Act (1963).................183

Washburn, David 8
Wilbur, Gretchen 31
Wirth, Louis 133
Wood v. Strickland......................................181
Workshop Model for Equity 274

Young Offenders 105
Youth Unemployment 106

Zangwill, Israel 134
Zorack v. Clausen, 1952 190